JOURNAL FOR THE STUDY OF THE OLD TESTAMENT
SUPPLEMENT SERIES
209

Sheffield Academic Press

Narrative Art,
Political Rhetoric

The Case of Athaliah and Joash

Patricia Dutcher-Walls

Journal for the Study of the Old Testament
Supplement Series 209

Copyright © 1996 Sheffield Academic Press

Published by
Sheffield Academic Press Ltd
Mansion House
19 Kingfield Road
Sheffield, S11 9AS
England

Typeset by Sheffield Academic Press
and
Printed on acid-free paper in Great Britain
by Bookcraft
Midsomer Norton, Somerset

British Library Cataloguing in Publication Data

A catalogue record for this book is available
from the British Library

ISBN 1-85075-577-9

CONTENTS

Preface   7
Abbreviations   9

Chapter 1
ISSUES AND METHODOLOGIES   11

Chapter 2
NARRATIVE ANALYSIS   23
    2 Kings 11   27
    2 Kings 12   49
    Summary   61

Chapter 3
RHETORICAL ANALYSIS   64
    2 Kings 11   69
    2 Kings 12   86
    Summary   98

Chapter 4
IDEOLOGICAL ANALYSIS   102
    Athaliah and the Omride Dynasty   110
    Temple and Priest   113
    Covenant   122
    King and Dynasty   127
    Regnal Summaries and the Kings' Reigns   135
    Summary   139

Chapter 5
SOCIOLOGICAL ANALYSIS   142
    Social Roles and Locations   148
    Factional Politics in Agrarian Monarchies   152

Religion and the State   158
International Politics   166
Propaganda in the Politics of Elites   168
Summary   176

Chapter 6
CONCLUSIONS   180

Bibliography   188
Index of Biblical References   194
Index of Authors   197

PREFACE

This book began its path to publication eight years ago as a proposal for a doctoral thesis. Warned by friends in the doctoral program to pick a topic that could not only contribute to the field but also be one I liked because I would be living with it for a long time, I had no idea just how long that would be. But my choices of family and professional responsibilities have meant that the dissertation and its revision for this book have had to blend in with several other commitments. Fortunately, I found that the thesis idea and my interest in it grew and developed with time so that its potential contribution is still current and, even in this last revision, I have still enjoyed the project.

Many people have helped and challenged me along the way and to them I express my appreciation. I am grateful to my doctoral advisors, Marvin Chaney, Bob Coote and John Endres, SJ, for their guidance on this project and throughout my program. As mentors and colleagues, they remained patient during my long doctoral career, marked as it was by delays and detours. Their continual encouragement and scholarly engagement with my work inspired my confidence and persistence.

I give thanks for my friends and colleagues both in the doctoral program and in various academic circles. Together, we have helped each other to inspire curiosity, share frustrations and fears, and celebrate success.

I am especially thankful for my family. They have given balance to my life and reminded me about the gentle gift of laughter. My children, Ruthie and Wesley, have taught me that a good story is worth reading again and again. Above all, to my husband Tim go my deepest love and appreciation for his unfailing encouragement. When it all seemed so long and hard, his confidence in me gave me the will to continue and his practical support gave me the time to get it all done.

Toronto, Ontario
January 1996

A Note on Translation

All translations from the Hebrew Bible are my own except where noted with (NRSV); the latter are taken from the New Oxford Annotated Bible, New Revised Standard Version (New York: Oxford University Press, 1991).

ABBREVIATIONS

AB	Anchor Bible
AnBib	Analecta biblica
AusBR	*Australian Biblical Review*
BA	*Biblical Archaeologist*
BDB	F. Brown, S.R. Driver, and C.A. Briggs, *Hebrew and English Lexicon of the Old Testament*
CBQ	*Catholic Biblical Quarterly*
CBQMS	*Catholic Biblical Quarterly* Monograph Series
FOTL	The Forms of the Old Testament Literature
GKC	*Gesenius' Hebrew Grammar,* ed. E. Kautzsch, trans. A.E. Cowley
HSM	Harvard Semitic Monographs
HTR	*Harvard Theological Review*
HUCA	*Hebrew Union College Annual*
ICC	International Critical Commentary
IEJ	*Israel Exploration Journal*
Int	*Interpretation*
JBL	*Journal of Biblical Literature*
JNES	*Journal of Near Eastern Studies*
JSOT	*Journal for the Study of the Old Testament*
JSOTSup	*Journal for the Study of the Old Testament* Supplement Series
JSS	*Journal of Semitic Studies*
NCB	New Century Bible
Or	*Orientalia* (Rome)
OTL	Old Testament Library
RB	*Revue biblique*
RelSRev	*Religious Studies Review*
SBLDS	SBL Dissertation Series
SBS	Stuttgarter Bibelstudien
TDOT	G.J. Botterweck and H. Ringgren (eds.), *Theological Dictionary of the Old Testament*
VT	*Vetus Testamentum*

Chapter 1

ISSUES AND METHODOLOGIES

A well-told story can both entertain and instruct. Whether written or oral, a tale can delight and move an audience while it communicates an idea or lesson beyond its entertainment value. A well-told story can both reflect its time and speak to all times. Unavoidably using the language, social conventions and assumptions of the age when it is 'fixed' in some form by an author or tradition, it still has the potential to speak as a text in a very different age or culture. A well-told story can appeal to both the most naive and the most sophisticated. Accessible on many levels, a tale can be heard by the child, pondered by the adult, and dissected by the scholar.

The range and depth of appeal of the well-told story were impressed upon me once when I was conducting a Bible study with a women's group. In the group were two developmentally disabled adult women. In order for them to participate as fully as possible, I helped them during the individual Bible study time, leading them through the questions of a 'self-guided Bible study'. The passage used was Mk 5.24-34, the story of the healing of the woman with the hemorrhage. They answered such simple and direct questions as 'How did each person in the story feel?' and 'What is the message of good news in this story?' I realized that although reading and even speaking were difficult for them, they 'got' the story. They understood the woman's fear and joy, were glad for her healing, and knew how such good news made sense in their own lives. At the same time, this is a story that can be and has been discussed and debated with both pleasure and passion by scholars far removed from such a naive reading.

The ability of a well-told story to speak on so many levels, to be read in so many ways over time by people of varied backgrounds, persuasions and approaches is a testimony to the universality of the storyteller's art. And it is a caution to those of us who, in our scholarly pursuits, would use only one method or find only one meaning, or get lost in debates that lose sight of the story's pleasure, all far removed from an often-disdained 'naive' reading.

With this said, of course I want to enter into that maelstrom of debates about methodology and meaning. For the intriguing and paradoxical situation seems to be that a story's multi-faceted functioning and accessibility provide grist for the mill of modern critical debates about stories. This is particularly true of the literature in the Bible. Here the traditional significance and continued meanings of Scripture for the faithful co-exist with centuries of interpretations, methodologies, criticisms and arguments.

Thus, I shall be entering into one of the current debates in the field of biblical studies—that of the relation between, and the advantages of, different methodologies for understanding a text. This is a discussion with as many debaters as there are methods and criticisms. In recent years, practitioners of each method have continued to use and defend their particular craft, a few insisting on the exclusive applicability or usefulness of their method. Others have, more helpfully I find, explored the interactions between methods, attempted to understand the impact of assumptions and methods on results, or tried to create a synthesis of methodologies.

The various issues surrounding the methodological debates are many and complex, particularly when interpreters attempt to use or blend several traditional disciplines of biblical study. How does the interpreter deal with the sources, layers, redaction of a text? Are there ways to find a 'common ground between historical and literary study?'[1] What methods—old, new, in dialogue with other fields—best help explain and interpret a text? Does the social role of language have an impact on a text and its interpretation? Can literary methods which focus on the 'formal principles' of a text also allow for how language can engage the world of the writer?[2] Can an interdisciplinary approach enrich interpretation?[3]

---

1. D. Damrosch, *The Narrative Covenant: Transformations of Genre in the Growth of Biblical Literature* (San Francisco: Harper & Row, 1987), p. 7.

2. R. Alter, *The World of Biblical Literature* (New York: Basic Books, 1991), pp. 72, 53.

3. M. Bal, *Murder and Difference: Gender, Genre and Scholarship on Sisera's Death* (trans. M. Gumpert; Bloomington, IN: Indiana University Press, 1992), p. 138.

I want to add another voice to the growing list of critics who have attempted a synthesis of methodologies toward the goal of textual interpretation. To do this, I want to read a story from the Old Testament, 2 Kings 11–12, the story of Athaliah and Joash. Even from a naive reading, it is a wonderful story—full of intrigue and drama. However, I want to 'read' it with an awareness of its multi-faceted life as a well-told tale and that will require some methodological reflection on the type of questions set out above. I propose that a conscious attempt to use literary and rhetorical methods in tandem with ideological and sociological methods can help interpret a multi-faceted story.

One of the insights of sociological and feminist interpretation is that a text cannot be considered in its own or any other context without considering the context of the interpreter. This is because interpreters always bring their own 'social world', their own assumptions and judgments to the act of interpretation. However, while it is necessary to be aware of the assumptions and stance of the interpreter, this does not connote an absolute relativity of interpretation. The responsible use of carefully explained methods, previous scholarship and constant dialogue with the text itself can act as a balance against idiosyncratic interpretations. And, of course, to say this is to be obligated to identify my assumptions and approaches as I am aware of them.

Further, my approach is built on a study and assimilation of the work of many scholars. In order to get to the subject at hand, I cannot re-evaluate or re-establish the complex scholarly history of many of the issues referred to. For example, to re-argue the major controversies of modern literary theory or Deuteronomistic redaction would be to write two other books. What I can and shall do is to identify the scholarly opinions or consensus on which I build my ideas and give some sources for further research or background. Such reliance on previous scholarly work is a necessary condition for multi-disciplinary studies in order to gain a wider perspective. My hope is that, again, when method, scholarship and text are handled responsibly, a useful and accessible study can result.

But there is another way to view the task at hand. This could be seen as a 'case study' in the application of a multi-disciplinary methodology. In a sense, I am proposing: 'If I assume these premises, and if I use these particular methodologies to study this particular story, the following conclusions can be made.' A different set of assumptions can produce a variation in methodology or results; likewise, a different 'take' on the combining or use of methods can produce different results. The dis-advantage of a case study method is that its results are potentially limited to the case at hand; it needs further testing as to its wider applicability. The advantage, however, is that it allows a wide range of premises, methods and data to be focused at one point in a useful way.

When I say my aim is to read the story of Athaliah and Joash, I intend to focus on the form of the story in a particular context. This intention assumes some 'common sense' premises about the story: that it is a literary composition written by someone at some particular time for some particular reasons(s) and that something can be said about the story itself as literature, and about its author, and its author's time and reasons. The quotation marks around 'common sense' acknowledge that seemingly self-evident propositions cannot be taken for granted in fields fraught with controversy. Indeed, such an intention lands me squarely in the middle of long and acrimonious debates on both the literary and historical sides of the aisle. So my assumptions about the context in which I place 2 Kings 11–12 should be spelled out.

In general, I assume that the broad context for the book of Kings is the Deuteronomistic History. As identified by Martin Noth in his landmark study,[4] originally published in 1943, the Deuteronomist was responsible for the writing and compilation of a history of Israel comprising the biblical books of Deuteronomy to 2 Kings—the Deuteronomistic History. Since Noth's work, the provenance, location and influence of the Deuteronomist(s) have been the subject of numer-ous and conflicting scholarly studies. But the general theory of a con-tinuous history exhibiting the thematic and theological interests of Deuteronomistic editing has stood the tests of time and scholarship.

This theory about the Deuteronomistic History functions as a back-drop for this study. Several of the methods used in my multi-disciplinary approach depend on some preliminary assumptions about the context in which the story was produced. For example, one part of the study examines the ideological worldview which is both inherent in the text of 2 Kings 11–12 and reflective of the story's context. For this, the assumption of basic Deuteronomistic shaping encourages parallels to be drawn to other passages in the History and allows general reference to

---

4.   M. Noth, *Überlieferungsgeschichtliche Studien* (Tübingen: Max Niemeyer Verlag, 2nd edn, 1957); ET *The Deuteronomistic History* (JSOTSup, 15; Sheffield: JSOT Press, 1981).

Deuteronomistic interests and theology that have been well established by scholarship.

However, a number of scholars have proposed a more specific context for the production of the Deuteronomistic History. This is the theory that the Deuteronomistic History underwent only two major editions. The primary one was a pre-exilic edition that created the history from various sources, both written and oral, during the reign of Josiah (639–609 BCE). A later, exilic edition made the changes necessary to update the history in drastically changed circumstances. The principal statement of this theory was made by Frank M. Cross,[5] and numerous critiques, proposals and counter-proposals have been made by scholars in response.[6] However, Cross's theory has been supported by a large number of critics. While their studies are not unanimous on textual details nor the strict division into two editions, scholars representative of this viewpoint include Richard Nelson, Moshe Weinfeld, Norbert Lohfink and Mark O'Brien.[7] These and others have generally supported the idea of a Deuteronomistic movement which produced the primary edition of the History in the Josianic era.

This proposal of a Josianic context provides an assumption particularly useful for another of the methods used in this study. The final section examines the sociological context of the story—the social structures and dynamics mentioned in and addressed by the narrative. While general Deuteronomistic shaping could allow broad comments on social location, preliminary adoption of the Josianic provenance theory allows a more specific and helpful sociological study to be done. That is, the story can be seen as a product of and communication for an elite social structure, the monarchy with its attendant institutions, in an agrarian society in a pre-exilic context. The use of the Josianic theory as a *working* assumption does not require a final commitment to the theory nor does it impose evidence on the story. Rather, in a case study format, it asks: 'If the story is placed in a sociological model in such a way, can insight be gained for the story's interpretation?' What will become clear as the study progresses is that the literary evidence accumulated by the

---

5.   F.M. Cross, 'The Themes of the Book of Kings and the Structure of the Deuteronomistic History', in *Canaanite Myth and Hebrew Epic* (Cambridge, MA: Harvard University Press, 1973), pp. 274-89.

6.   See G.E. Gerbrandt, *Kingship according to the Deuteronomistic History* (SBLDS, 87; Atlanta: Scholars Press, 1986), pp. 1-17 for a brief discussion.

7.   See the bibliography for relevant works by these authors.

multi-disciplinary approach actually provides support for the theory of Josianic provenance. Although this was not one of the intentions of the study as originally conceived, it will nonetheless turn out to be a noteworthy result.

Methods for this Study

A brief discussion of methods and types of evidence will be useful here. To interpret a story in its own context means to use two kinds of evidence and analysis or methods.[8] One kind is internal evidence, evidence garnered from the story itself about the story's structure, point of view and meanings. This type of evidence is amenable to synchronic, literary types of analysis in particular. External evidence, on the other hand, is gathered generally from outside the story—historical information about the time of composition, the culture in which the story was written, other sources or writings. Often this type of evidence is available through diachronic, historical-critical analysis or comparative studies. In seeking both types of evidence, it is clear that several kinds of methods must be used. It is exactly in reading the story in its own context that this study will be bridging 'gaps' by bringing a full range of methods and analyses to bear on interpretation.

To describe the focus of this study, the multi-dimensional life of a story, several different metaphors could be used. One could speak of the levels, aspects or perspectives, or, as Vernon Robbins does, the 'textures'[9] that are present in a text. Since the term used can have unwanted connotations (for example 'levels' could imply 'higher' or 'lower' and perhaps 'better' or 'worse'), I wish to use terms that imply the interconnectedness and varied reality of the story's life. Most simply, I find helpful the idea of the story's aspects, each of which represents one dimension of the story; so, the narrative aspect or dimension comprises the whole text as an artistically shaped narrative and the rhetorical aspect or dimension comprises the story's persuasiveness.

However, the dimensions of a story are connected; at a minimum, they overlap by each being intrinsic to the text. So a metaphor descriptive of these connections is needed. A useful image here is that of

---

8. P.R. Petersen, *Rediscovering Paul: Philemon and the Sociology of Paul's Narrative World* (Philadelphia: Fortress Press, 1985), p. 6.

9. V. Robbins, *Jesus the Teacher: A Socio-Rhetorical Interpretation of Mark* (Minneapolis: Fortress Press, 1992), p. xxix.

concentric circles that expand around the text. The 'inside circle' is the narrative itself; other dimensions that connect the text to its context are the larger circles in which it stands.[10] For example, a text may reflect ideological concerns of the period in which it was written, so the narrative is at the center of a larger ideological circle. The study of each aspect of the story, or correspondingly, each concentric circle, requires a method appropriate to that aspect. And the shift from one dimension to another will mean a shift in perspective as the study steps back to view a larger circle of concern about the story.

I want to start by reading the story itself; thus, its 'dimension' as a narrative in the 'center circle' is the first focus. In doing this, I view 2 Kings 11–12 as literature amenable to narrative analysis. The methods used here could vary widely, as a number of different literary approaches have been developed, particularly in the modern critical study of the novel and narrative.[11] And the method(s) used can influence how the story is analyzed, as Jerome Walsh has shown in an article applying three types of synchronic analysis to the same story.[12] He states that 'the choice of a critical method is not a neutral act; it is one of the moves by which a reader contributes to the production of meaning in a literary text'.[13] Acknowledging this, I choose an analysis using a close reading strategy that makes elements of narrative art as straightforward and accessible as possible. This strategy has been employed by a number of biblical literary critics—Alter, Berlin, Bar-Efrat and Sternberg.[14] Under the rubrics of biblical 'poetics' and 'narrative art', this type of literary analysis considers such things as narrative structure, point of view, narrative time and space, characterization, and narrative gaps and repetitions.

The aim of the chapter on narrative analysis will be to explore the literary dimensions of the text as a well-told story. What are the characteristics of the 'story world' created in the text? Using evidence internal to the story itself, what is the reality contained within the narrative that

10. This image of interpenetrating circles is used by Petersen, *Rediscovering Paul*, p. 17.

11. See W. Martin, *Recent Theories of Narrative* (Ithaca, NY: Cornell University Press, 1986) for a survey.

12. J.T. Walsh, 'Methods and Meanings: Multiple Studies of I Kings 21', *JBL* 111.2 (Summer 1992), pp. 193-211.

13. Walsh, 'Methods and Meanings', p. 194.

14. See the bibliography for relevant works by these authors.

is created and maintained by the artistry of the story-teller?

However, even from an initial reading, one can see that there is more to the story of Athaliah and Joash than the entertainment value of a good story or art for art's sake. The characters are important people—a queen, kings, priests. Significant events are related—assassinations, a coronation, a temple reform. The highest institutions of the nation are involved—kingship, court, priesthood and temple. It seems that there are 'good guys' and one very bad 'gal'. Such intimations of significance prompt the questions, 'What type of story is this?' and 'What is the point of the story?' And these questions lead to the consideration of the next dimension of the story, its rhetorical aspect. In the case of any text that has a function beyond entertainment, I understand rhetoric to be a persuasive element. The author 'makes a case', with some amount of conscious intention, for certain ways of looking at things. In moving on to the dimension of rhetoric in the text, the circle examined expands now to include the audience for whom an author writes.

The field of rhetoric serves to analyze the way an author communicates persuasively to an audience. No longer concentrating on just stylistic flourishes in speaking and writing, the 'new' rhetoric 'covers the whole range of discourse that aims at persuasion and conviction, whatever the audience addressed and whatever the subject matter'.[15] Such discourse is not strictly logical but must be reasonable in order to make it effective in attracting and persuading an audience,[16] as the aim of the argumentation is to win over an audience to a point of view or course of action. An entire set of rules and guidelines can be identified that help a speaker or writer in the making of influential arguments or aid an interpreter in the analysis of arguments.[17]

However, more than just portraying the story in a persuasive way, rhetorical arguments point to yet another aspect of a story. It appears that certain meanings are given to events in the narrative for specific reasons and that these reasons may be related to an ideological or apologetic intent. So the dimension of ideology and the larger circle of ideological reflection are the next concerns for my study. The connection between rhetoric and ideology is conceptually grounded in the idea

15. C. Perelman, *The Realm of Rhetoric* (Notre Dame, IN: University of Notre Dame Press, 1982), p. 5.

16. Perelman, *The Realm of Rhetoric*, p. 21.

17. See, for example, G.A. Hauser, *Introduction to Rhetorical Theory* (Prospect Heights, IL: Waveland Press, 1991).

that any representation of life, whether in literature, art, politics, religion, or even in one's own self-consciousness, is a part of a social construction of reality, to use the title of Berger and Luckmann's influential book.[18] To interpret experience, even to 'experience' experience, people create or inherit, with varying degrees of awareness of the process, a symbolic universe that is their 'world'. A socially constructed reality is the means by which people represent to themselves and others the values, qualities, structures, forms and language of their common life. Any particular formulation of these elements is an 'ideology' by which people seek to express or shape their reality.

As I intend to focus on the primary Deuteronomistic redaction of 2 Kings 11–12, the ideological world to be explored is the Deuteronomistic worldview. This worldview has been the focus of intense study by scholars over a number of years. In my study of the text itself, as well as where I extend beyond the text into intertextual work in the Deuteronomistic History, I shall be able to use the insights and conclusions of many notable critics. Under the rubric of the 'theology' of the Deuteronomist, such scholars have studied the thematic interest surrounding kingship, prophecy, court and temple, centralization of worship, and similar topics. I shall not try to re-establish the results of such studies, nor provide a comprehensive statement of the Deuteronomist's worldview. I shall concentrate on those aspects of ideology that emerge from the text of 2 Kings 11–12 itself.

In moving from the narrative to the rhetorical and ideological aspects, I move into a larger compass, or larger concentric circles around the text. One way to see this move is to note that in the narrative study, one is concentrating on the relationship between the narrator, the text and the reader; in the rhetorical and ideological studies, one focuses on the communication between author and audience through the text. Another way to characterize the shift is that one moves from internal evidence to external evidence as the circle enlarges from text to context. It is important for the connectedness of a multi-disciplinary approach to say, however, that I am not just leaping from the text to the context, or from internal to external evidence, as if they were two separate things to be examined. Both the rhetoric and the ideology are intrinsic to the story, expressed in and through the words of the text.

All through my discussion of the concepts and methodologies that

---

18. P.L. Berger and T. Luckmann, *The Social Construction of Reality* (repr.; Garden City, NY: Doubleday, 1966; Anchor Books, 1989).

enable an interpretation of the rhetorical and ideological aspects of the
story, I have referred to the context in which the text exists. The understanding of this context is the final necessary step in explicating the
coherent dimensions in and around a text. Thus, the study of the 'social
world' is the fourth and last analysis that I shall bring to bear upon the
interpretation of the story. Without an examination of the social world, I
would be slighting the largest concentric circle, the actual social forms
and structures which the text expresses and which reflect the context of
the Deuteronomist.

My aim in explicating the social world is to understand the sociology,
the social structures and arrangements of ancient Israel well enough to
place both the story and its Deuteronomistic author within this world.
The methods used to explicate a social world are those of sociological
analysis, which proceeds on the basis of building a model from extensive
cross-cultural data about societies. Basic texts in the field, such as
Human Societies by Lenski and Lenski, analyze society as a system by
which humans communicate, meet needs, provide protection, socialize
and control behavior.[19] By dividing societies into types based on the
level of technological advance, and by studying many societies at a
similar level, sociologists such as the Lenskis are able to make detailed
studies of the social arrangements, class structure, use of technology,
production of goods and services, and cultural endowments of a
'typical' societal type.

For ancient Israel, the type applicable is the agrarian society, marked
by relatively advanced agricultural technology but no industrialization.
This typology indicates that agrarian societies are highly stratified, with a
very high percentage of wealth and power held by a tiny percentage of
the population. The study of this agrarian, aristocratic type of economic
and political power structure can suggest useful answers to questions
about the social location, power and concerns of the Deuteronomistic
worldview.

A further discussion of the interplay of evidence and method is
needed as I move to this last dimension. Up to this point, either internal
evidence or a combination of internal and external evidence has been
garnered by the methods used in analysis of the narrative, rhetorical and
ideological aspects. One way of describing the shift in perspective from
the first three analyses to this last sociological analysis is to say that

19. G. Lenski, P. Nolan and J. Lenski, *Human Societies: An Introduction to
Macro-Sociology* (New York: McGraw–Hill, 7th edn, 1995), pp. 23-51.

evidence external to the text is more extensively used at this point. Data intrinsic to the text do give some indication of the social world with which it is concerned, that is, the most powerful persons and institutions of the age, royalty and priesthood, court and temple in the capital city. As will be seen, that is indeed an excellent brief description of the social location of the author. But a sociological method will principally bring evidence from sources outside the text to the explication and interpretation of the story.

By the end of this study, the narrative, rhetorical, ideological and sociological aspects of the Athaliah/Joash narrative as a well-told story should appear. The study of these dimensions should give a multi-faceted awareness of the text as an artful story and as communicative discourse. But these dimensions of the text are not disparate, unattached items of study. My argument is built on two proposals. The first is that these four aspects are inherent in the text, intrinsic to it as a story that entertains and communicates. The aspects cohere in and through the text as the concentric circles around the text expand. The narrative art helps create emphasis in the story and the narrative form itself creates persuasiveness by giving structure to arguments. The rhetoric gets its power and shape from the ideology on which it is based. Both the rhetoric and ideology reflect the social location of the author. Permeating throughout all four dimensions and relating each to the other are the meaning patterns of the context in which both the author and audience stand.

The second proposal is that since the text itself is a multi-dimensional reality, its interpretation demands a multi-dimensional methodology. The study builds on the basic historical-critical work that has been done on the books of Kings. But it ranges far afield from a narrow conception of historical-critical work in calling on a number of other methods in a necessarily coordinated fashion. Leaving any one aspect unexamined would neglect an intrinsic dimension of the story and its context. Narrative criticism reveals, through close reading of the text, the narrative strategies that create an interesting story. Rhetorical analysis examines the persuasive strategies of the narrative that structure the argumentation. Ideological analysis combined with thematic study of the Deuteronomistic worldview sets the passage within its ideological framework. Sociological study of societal systems places the Deuteronomist within a culture and class whose interests are represented and served by the telling of the story.

It is clear that my multi-disciplinary method is indebted to the work of many scholars. Conceptually and methodologically, I am mining the riches of numerous scholars in a variety of fields. A number of them have presented similarly multi-dimensional methods. Their works stand as models, at some points quite direct, for the study I undertake. By no means, however, would all of the scholars I use agree with my conclusions or even this undertaking; some might protest the use of their insights for my ends. I have used what is helpful to my conceptual and methodological program and have tried to make it clear when I am expressing views of my own that extend beyond those of any other author.

The chapters ahead will each deal with one of the 'aspects' I have identified in the text of 2 Kings 11–12, using the methodologies I have proposed. While each chapter will deal with just one analysis—narrative, rhetorical, ideological, sociological—overlap between them is inevitable, which is not surprising given my proposal that all four dimensions are intrinsic to the very telling of the account portrayed by the Deuteronomist. For the sake of clarity and focus in these four middle chapters, I have separated various comments into one or another chapter. In some cases a particular aspect of the story, such as the covenant in ch. 11 or the temple repair in ch. 12, can be seen from all four perspectives. This type of item will then be discussed in an appropriate way in each chapter. Sometimes, to avoid unnecessary repetition, I decide that a certain aspect, while functioning narratively, might best be covered only once in the particular chapter where its main emphasis seems to be. The demarcating lines between the topics in each chapter are fluid and somewhat artificial, for the story does not separate out its narrative from its rhetorical, ideological, or sociological import.

I have tried to explicate the conceptual and methodological approaches that give shape to this study; more detailed methodological explication will be found in each chapter as the study progresses. When all is said and done, and the detailed and lengthy analysis is over, I hope the many words written will illuminate the multi-dimensional fascination of this well-told story.

Chapter 2

NARRATIVE ANALYSIS

To begin to read the story of Athaliah and Joash in 2 Kings 11–12 as a story is immediately to confront the issue of '*which story?*' Given the background of Old Testament studies that divide texts up into pieces through textual, source and redaction criticisms, the issue of what words, phrases and verses will be included and read as the story is significant. Several principles and assumptions have guided my decisions in textual and narrative matters.

My overall aim is to do a narrative analysis of the story as it might have been crystallized by the Deuteronomistic author. This aim focuses my study on an intermediate stage in the assumed evolution of the story. Because my interest is the shaping of the story by the Deuteronomist, and because I assume that any earlier version[1] or sources[2] have been recast to suit the aims and purposes of the Deuteronomist, the possibility of pre-Deuteronomistic layers is bracketed from my purview. At the same time, I do not seek the 'final version', the assumed end of the text's evolutionary process. My aim to read the Deuteronomistic story thus determines the issues I need to grapple with, particularly the possibility of later editing or additions by post-exilic/priestly redactors.

In the heyday of historical-critical scholarship, commentators often divided ch. 11 into two sources, a 'priestly source' in vv. 4-12 and 18b-20 and a 'popular source' in vv. 13-18a.[3] In so doing, these scholars

1. As, for example, Lloyd Barré attempts in *The Rhetoric of Political Persuasion: The Narrative Artistry and Political Intentions of 2 Kings 9–11* (CBQMS, 20; Washington, DC: Catholic Biblical Association, 1988).

2. As classical literary criticism has done with this story; see, for one example among many, J. Gray, *I and II Kings* (OTL; Philadelphia: Westminster Press, 1970).

3. Gray, *I and II Kings*, p. 566. Many other scholars take a similar tack; cf. J.A. Montgomery, *A Critical and Exegetical Commentary on the Books of Kings* (ICC; New York: Charles Scribner's Sons, 1951); C.F. Burney, *Notes on the Hebrew Text of the Books of Kings* (New York: Ktav, 1970); and G.H. Jones,

often did not focus on the meaning of the whole narrative other than to note what the popular source added by way of emphasis to the priestly one.[4] Among scholars emphasizing source divisions in a different vein are Barré and Levin. Barré finds within chs. 9–11 of 2 Kings an early narrative source written shortly after the events of ch. 11 which functioned as a justification for Joash.[5] Levin traces the literary history of ch. 11 from an early annalistic source through three later redactions.[6] 2 Kings 12 is treated by historical critics as largely from a priestly hand because of its emphasis on the temple. Various conjectures of state archives or a separate temple history are given as the source behind the priestly redaction.[7] Both because I have not sought earlier sources and because such source-plus-redaction criticisms tend to ignore or destroy any unified narrative reading, I neither evaluate such theories nor report at length on them in my analysis.

However, the possibility of reading a posited Deuteronomistically shaped story is, in turn, well supported by the critics. Regardless of their various theories on sources, and irrespective of when they date the Deuteronomistic redaction, virtually all scholars since Noth posit a major, if not final, shaping of both chs. 11 and 12 by the Deuteronomist. Gray, here representative of the 'classical' historical critics, holds that the priestly and popular sources of ch. 11 were combined by the Deuteronomic reformation under Josiah.[8] For several of the more recent studies, focusing on the major Deuteronomistic story allows scholars to overcome the atomistic tendencies of the source-plus-redaction approach. So Cogan and Tadmor in the Anchor Bible consider the historian-author of Kings to be an adherent of the Deuteronomic school and treat ch. 11 as a single source.[9] Long finds the source theories to be unconvincing, accepts Deuteronomistic authorship of 1–2 Kings as a unified work and reads ch. 11 as a 'formal and thematic unity'.[10]

---

1 and 2 Kings (NCB; 2 vols.; Grand Rapids, MI: Eerdmans, 1984).

4. For example, Jones, *1 and 2 Kings*, II, p. 477.

5. Barré, *Rhetoric*, p. 56.

6. C. Levin, *Der Sturz der Königin Atalja: Ein Kapitel zur Geschichte Judas im 9. Jn. v. Chr* (SBS, 105; Stuttgart: Katholisches Bibelwerk, 1982), p. 95.

7. See, for example, Gray, *I and II Kings*, p. 582.

8. Gray, *I and II Kings*, p. 568.

9. M. Cogan and H. Tadmor, *II Kings* (AB, 11; Garden City, NY: Doubleday, 1988), p. 132.

10. B.O. Long, *2 Kings* (FOTL, 10; Grand Rapids, MI: Eerdmans, 1991), p. 147.

Hoffmann, in delineating what he sees as the Deuteronomistic history of cult reform throughout Kings, reads chs. 11–12 as a thematically unified, Deuteronomistic account of a religious reform.[11]

Few scholars see any major redactional work after the Deuteronomistic hand except Levin who posits a priestly-Chronicler redaction.[12] For the classical historical critics, possible minor editing from a priestly hand or influenced by the Chronicler's account is discernible in the interest of both chapters in the temple.[13] With few exceptions I have found such supposed later changes to be suspect. The Deuteronomist by all accounts was interested in the temple so it is not necessary *a priori* to edit out 'priestly-type' references. Overall, I have found that positing and reading a narratively unified, Deuteronomistically shaped story in 2 Kings 11–12 is defensible. Using the results either of the historical-critical, source-plus-redaction methodology or of a method that focuses on the chapters as a single source, a Deuteronomistic story, comprehensive and comprehensible, is evident in these chapters.

My goal of reading the version that I judge had been written by the Deuteronomist also means that I have not grappled with questions of historical accuracy. The questions of 'what really happened' to Athaliah and Joash are significant questions for those who seek to understand the history of ancient Israel. These questions about the historical accuracy of the story have been many. Was a covenant really renewed? Was there really a Baal temple in Jerusalem? What was the attitude of the priests in ch. 12 towards King Joash? Several scholars have focused on the central issue of the legitimacy of Joash. Miller and Hayes question both whether Joash was an imposter set up by Jehoiada and why Athaliah would kill her own grandchildren.[14] Lowell Handy raises similar questions and decides that the story is untenable as history but was used to legitimate a pretender to the throne.[15] The best that any attempt to reconstruct actual historical events can do may be to say that the events recorded

---

11. H.-D. Hoffmann, *Reform und Reformen: Untersuchungen zu einem Grund-thema der deuteronomistischen Geschichtsschreibung* (Zürich: Theologischer Verlag, 1980), p. 111.

12. Levin, *Der Sturtz*, p. 95.

13. Gray, *I and II Kings*, p. 569.

14. J.M. Miller and J.H. Hayes, *A History of Ancient Israel and Judah* (Philadelphia: Westminster Press, 1986), p. 304.

15. L.K. Handy, 'Speaking of Babies in the Temple', Eastern Great Lakes and Midwest Biblical Societies, *Proceedings* 8 (1988), p. 163.

are believable but must be separated from both ancient and modern tendentious misconceptions.[16] My interest in how the history recounted in chs. 11 and 12 is portrayed by the Deuteronomist does not necessarily require historical judgments about Athaliah and Joash.

With my goal delimited as just described, my initial survey of 2 Kings 11–12 involves a comprehensive and simultaneous use of textual, literary, redaction and narrative criticisms. No priority is given to any single type of criticism beyond the important assumption that a cohesive and unified, if multi-faceted, narrative has been created by the Deuteronomist and can be 'read' by a modern reader. At the level of text-critical study, I start with the Massoretic text and use inter-biblical parallels, particularly other Deuteronomistic texts, as well as the Septuagint. I consider other readings as suggested by the versions and the conjectures and reconstructions of various scholars. Traditional literary-, form-, source- and redaction-critical insights are gleaned from a review of many of the major commentaries and monographs on Kings. Narrative sensitivity is gained from the reading of four significant scholars on biblical narrative—Alter, Berlin, Sternberg and Bar-Efrat—although none of them deals with the story of Athaliah and Joash at length.[17] Throughout, the results of traditional criticisms are subjected to narrative criteria, so, for example, the two versions of Athaliah's death (11.16 and 11.20) are not automatically attributed to two sources before the narrative implications of such repetition are considered.

Thus a practical give-and-take evolves whereby I evaluate the text with the dual purpose of deciding 'which story' to read and what that story says narratively. Because I want to get beyond debates about textual matters that sometimes have little bearing on the final narrative analysis, I often make working assumptions where two or more readings of a word are equally defensible (or indefensible when clear evidence is lacking). Always, I am aware that making such assumptions can be questioned on several valid, critical grounds. Likewise, a different reading of the nature and extent of the Deuteronomistic story, that is, with

16. L. Schearing, 'Models, Monarchs and Misconceptions: Athaliah and Joash of Judah' (PhD dissertation: Emory University, 1992).

17. R. Alter, *The Art of Biblical Narrative* (New York: Basic Books, 1981); A. Berlin, *Poetics and Interpretation of Biblical Narrative* (Sheffield: Almond Press, 1983); M. Sternberg, *The Poetics of Biblical Narrative: Ideological Literature and the Drama of Reading* (Bloomington, IN: Indiana University, 1987); S. Bar-Efrat, *Narrative Art in the Bible* (trans. D. Shefer-Vanson; Sheffield: Almond Press, 1989).

different judgments as to any post-Deuteronomistic editing, could be defended. It would be an interesting study, although one I have not done here, to run some of the alternate readings through the multi-disciplinary methodology I use to see what alternative insights are raised.

Because in this chapter on narrative analysis I am reading a story, I have organized my work by the scenes as I see them. This often corresponds to paragraph divisions in the Hebrew or English text, but not necessarily. As I cover each scene I give my own translation of the verses. In doing this, I often choose language that delineates the points I wish to make about the narrative more than capturing a smooth flow of English usage.

2 Kings 11

Scene 1: 2 Kings 11.1-3

> (1) Now when Athaliah, mother of Ahaziah, saw that her son was dead, she arose and destroyed all the heirs of the kingdom. (2) And Jehosheba, daughter of King Joram, sister of Ahaziah, took Joash, the son of Ahaziah, from the midst of the sons of the king who were being killed, him and his wet-nurse, in a bedroom. And they hid him from Athaliah and he was not killed. (3) So he was with her in the House of Yahweh hiding six years while Athaliah was ruling over the land.

The story of Athaliah and Joash starts with a brief flashback and continues with precipitous action. Opening with a circumstantial clause, 'Now when Athaliah saw that her son was dead',[18] the narrative moves on to the violent action of the queen, 'she arose and destroyed all the heirs of the kingdom'. Athaliah's characterization is thus begun in her abrupt introduction as a major force in Judahite royal politics, a characterization that will be enhanced both by her own actions and the plot.

The opening clause stops the reader and forces a flashback. Who Athaliah is and how she comes to this turn of events are related in the chapters which precede, particularly the story of Jehu's prophetically motivated overthrow of the Omride dynasty in Israel (2 Kgs 9–10). Athaliah was introduced indirectly in 2 Kgs 8.18 as the wife of King Jehoram of Judah and a 'daughter of Ahab' of Israel. In 2 Kgs 8.26, King Ahaziah's regnal formula, she is directly identified as the mother of King Ahaziah and a 'daughter of Omri, king of Israel'.

---

18. With the *qere*, I drop the *waw* from the perfect verb, 'she saw'.

The epithets applied to Athaliah in these passages are brief and author-itative in tone. This alerts the reader to the role of the narrator as an authoritative reporter of plot, character and evaluation. Following such scholars as Alter and Sternberg, I understand the narrator to be reliable and omniscient, whose word is to be taken as truth (if not always the complete truth and always a truth from a particular ideological stance).[19] How this affects the story will be seen not only in the narrative analysis but also in the other types of analysis in the following chapters. On a narrative level, these brief epithets serve to identify Athaliah as an Omride princess and queen of Judah by marriage, thus beginning to build her character.

Beyond the brief epithets in these two passages, the narrator has also given evaluations of Jehoram and Ahaziah which serve to build the characterization of Athaliah at the same time. In the regnal formulas for both kings it is said that they walked in the ways of the kings of Israel/House of Ahab, doing what was evil in the sight of the Lord. Both times the explanatory clause (כי) attributes the source of their evil to the marriage alliance with the Omride dynasty accomplished through Athaliah's marriage to Jehoram. The direct moral evaluation of the 'evil' of the northern kings includes Athaliah through her origin in the House of Ahab.

The textual problem between these two passages, whether Athaliah was Omri's or Ahab's daughter, is one of historical veracity which need not detain this analysis. Various coordinations are proposed by the translations; one commentator sets out to prove by chronological reck-oning that Omri was her father but that she grew up in Ahab's court under Jezebel's influence.[20] However this is resolved, her origin as an Omride princess who thus participates in and carries the evil of that dynasty is clearly presented by the narrator.

Not only are Athaliah's identity and character foretold in the chapters preceding 11.1, but also the events that bring her to see the death of her son are related there. Starting in 2 Kgs 8.28, the story of the alliance between Judah and Israel against Aram and of Jehu's revolution against the House of Ahab is told. Narratively, this story tells how Jehu was anointed king of Israel by the order of the prophet Elisha. The story goes on to report his murder and overthrow of King Joram of Israel and

19. Alter, *Art*, p. 184 and Sternberg, *Poetics*, p. 51.
20. H.J. Katzenstein, 'Who Were the Parents of Athaliah?', *IEJ* 5 (1955), p. 197.

subsequent murder of Ahaziah who had been visiting Joram after their campaign against Aram. Jehu's rebellion proceeds by violence as he arranges the murder of the whole House of Ahab (10.11 and 10.17), kills the relatives of Ahaziah (10.14), and carries out a thorough purge of Baalistic worship in Israel (10.18-28).

Besides the narrative connections of plot events in chs. 9 and 10 which lead up to Athaliah's entrance in 11.1, these two preceding chapters also contain parallels to the story in ch. 11. A number of commentators have detailed these parallels.[21] Narratively, the reader is prepared for the story in ch. 11 by having read in chs. 9–10 about: the overthrow of a monarch prompted by a prophetic word; the usurpation of the throne by an upstart king anointed in secret and acclaimed by the military; the violent consolidation of power by the new king; and his leadership in a reform of the cult issuing in the destruction of the temple of Baal and the murder of its priests.[22] The atmosphere of violent and abrupt political change and religious reform sets the stage for Athaliah. By the story's telling, she is the only surviving member of the House of Ahab and her son, the legitimate king of Judah, has just been killed in the coup that overthrew her family's power in Israel.

The narrative turns to action and sequential verbal clauses in v. 11.1b, signaling that narrative time has left its backward-looking mode and begun a forward movement. Athaliah acts: 'she arose and destroyed all the heirs of the kingdom'. The use of the consecutive imperfect of the verb קום as an auxiliary to another consecutive imperfect may be translated as incipient action, 'she began to destroy',[23] or as rapid action, 'she quickly destroyed'. To begin, the narrator seems to make use of analogical structuring: the murderous violence of the north continues in the south where again a royal house is destroyed. The use of rapid action and analogy creates an expectation that the plot must meet—will events unfold in Judah as in Israel?

Further, Athaliah's characterization is developed by the narration in this brief half-verse. As Sternberg indicates, action can develop the deep

---

21. R.D. Nelson, *First and Second Kings* (Interpretation; Louisville, KY: John Knox, 1987), p. 214; Hoffmann, *Reform*, pp. 104-105; and Barré, *Rhetoric*, p. 36-55.

22. This particular enumeration largely follows Nelson, *First and Second Kings*, p. 214.

23. Long, *2 Kings*, p. 148.

structure of a character whose surface was described by an epithet.[24]
The Omride princess, already guilty by association with the evil kings of
Israel and House of Ahab, acts decisively and directly to kill all the legitimate heirs to the throne of Judah, which is the import of the phrase
זרע הממלכה. As Alter points out, characterization through reported
actions leaves the reader in 'the realm of inference' about the character
revealed.[25] In this instance we have only an external point of view from
which to see Athaliah's action;[26] no inner life or motivation is ascribed
to her. By these actions, she is portrayed as having the political power
and the violent will to wipe out the royal family, including, one assumes,
her own children and grandchildren. She uses these attributes of power
and violence to her own advantage—when all heirs of the kingdom are
dead, she claims the throne.

The primary narrative complication of the plot arises in v. 2. Here we
are told that one of King Ahaziah's sons, Joash, is saved from death by
the action of Ahaziah's sister, Jehosheba. Against the murderous actions
of one woman, the queen mother, soon to be as ruling queen, another
woman of the royal court acts. The series of sequential imperfects in the
verse carries narrative time forward with some sense of urgency, but
there is enough descriptive material about the characters and actions
involved that the narrative depicts a full scene. Again an analogy on the
level of plot occurs with chs. 9–10; against the narrator's assured statements there that all the House of Ahab was wiped out, here the narrator
authoritatively describes the survival of one Judahite prince.

The characters in the scene are described by social epithets which
function narratively to identify their relation to the royal line. Jehosheba
is the daughter of King Joram and the sister of the just-deceased King
Ahaziah. Further direct characterization is lacking, but she is portrayed
by her actions: 'she took Joash', 'she stole him away from the sons of
the king who were being killed', 'they hid him from Athaliah'. The
plural on the final verb in this series, ויסתרו, has been subject to emendation because the first two verbs are singular when Jehosheba acts alone.
I find it unnecessary to change the text as the form may be an imper-
sonal or indefinite plural.[27] And narratively it may be proleptic for the

24. Sternberg, *Poetics*, p. 344.
25. Alter, *Art*, p. 117.
26. See Berlin, *Poetics*, pp. 43-81 for a helpful description of point of view.
27. Montgomery, *Books of Kings*, p. 424; and Gray, *I and II Kings*, p. 569.

wider conspiratorial circle to come.[28] The actions described speak of Jehosheba's clear resolve, knowledge of the palace and its inner workings, and direct and successful, if secret, challenge to Athaliah's actions.

The other named character is Joash. The narrator calls him 'the son of Ahaziah'; thus his status in the direct line to inherit the throne of Judah is irrefutably stated by the narrative. The threat to him from Athaliah is also narratively clear—he is 'among the sons of the king who were being killed'.[29] Also, the text signals that he is a baby by the phrase 'him and his wet-nurse'. The ellipsis in this phrase has been emended by critics adding ותתן, 'and she put him and his wet-nurse in a bedroom', which is what 2 Chron. 22.11 has.[30] However, the text could stand without emendation by taking the phrase 'him and his nurse' as an apposition to the object and, with Cogan and Tadmor, the phrase 'in the bedroom' as the location where the princes are being murdered.[31]

At any rate, Joash is a passive, almost flat character in the scene (and throughout almost the whole of ch. 11). His status as the king's son is critical to the story line; his characterization is not important to the plot and the narrator characteristically omits any direct elaboration.[32] The verse ends with a final, definitive statement that this son of the king survived the massacre: 'he was not killed'.

The scene closes with a summary statement from the narrator: 'And he was with her in the House of Yahweh hiding six years while Athaliah was ruling over the land'. The summarizing mode of the sentence is caught by the amount of narrated time covered—six years—and by the use of participles describing the ongoing state of affairs during this time period. The plot has reached a holding point, with the narrative complication represented by the surviving royal heir safely hidden away from the reigning queen.

The location of Joash's safe place is the temple, the House of Yahweh. This designation not only provides a location for hiding the prince but it signals an emerging important theme in the narrative. Joash has been taken from the bedroom in the palace, the house of the king, and is

---

28. Nelson, *First and Second Kings*, p. 207.

29. Reading the *hophal* with the *qere*.

30. So Montgomery, *Books of Kings*, p. 418; and Gray, *I and II Kings*, p. 570, among others.

31. Cogan and Tadmor, *II Kings*, p. 126.

32. Bar-Efrat, *Narrative Art*, p. 89.

hidden in the House of Yahweh. Burke Long describes how these two locations function here and in the rest of the story in ch. 11:

> Implicit are two value-laden images of space that will be mapped against each other as the narration progresses. Within the temple's bounds the scion of David survives; outside these protective courts, in the palace, Athaliah presides over Judah.[33]

The two locations also delineate a double point of view that will continue until the climax of the story. One view is from the palace and Athaliah's perspective; the other is from the temple and the perspective of Joash's supporters.

Athaliah herself again enters as a character; here she is 'ruling over the land'. Her characterization continues in the same vein as earlier. The story shows her power by stating that she has consolidated her position well enough through the murder of the royal family to rule for six years. However, while she is portrayed as having the power to rule, she is a flawed character as well. Although she saw that her son was dead (v. 1) she does not see that her grandson is alive. She does rule 'over the land' as the verse ends. However, the true extent of her rule over the land and its people is still to be seen.

This first scene thus begins and ends with Athaliah, a princess from the evil Omride dynasty who has seized the throne in Judah. She is powerful, decisive, violent. Her action to eliminate all the royal heirs is challenged secretly and successfully by a woman of that same royal family who saves the king's son and finds refuge in the House of Yahweh. The scene has introduced the basic conflict between ruling queen and royal heir, between the house of the king and the House of Yahweh, and between an Omride survivor and a Davidide survivor.

Scene 2: 2 Kings 11.4-8

> (4) But in the seventh year, Jehoiada sent and took the officers of the hundreds for the Carians and the runners and he brought them to him in the House of Yahweh. And he made with them a covenant and he made them take an oath in the House of Yahweh and he showed them the son of the king. (5) And he commanded them, saying, 'This is the thing that you will do: the third of you going in on the Sabbath and keeping watch at the House of the King; (6) now, a third at the Gate of Sur and a third at the gate behind the runners; [and] you will keep watch at the House instead.

33. Long, *2 Kings*, p. 148.

(7) And the other two of your parts, all those going out on the Sabbath, [and] they will keep watch at the House of the Lord on behalf of the king. (8) And you will surround the king all around, each with his weapons in his hand. And anyone coming toward the ranks will be killed. Be with the king in his going out and his coming in.'

Scene 2 opens with a temporal phrase that alerts the reader to the passage of narrative time: 'But in the seventh year'. An entirely new scene arises in this new time with a series of consecutive verbs carrying the story line. The principal action of the scene concerns the instigation of a conspiracy against Athaliah and in support of Joash.

The principal actor in the scene is quickly named, 'Jehoiada sent'. However, unlike the previous scene, no identifying epithet is offered for him. A narrative gap is created for the reader by this lack of identification—'Who is this guy?' Commentators have tried to close the gap by adding, as the Greek does, 'the priest'[34] or by noting that when the story was originally composed Jehoiada was well known.[35] I propose that the gap can stand as a narrative tool; it increases suspense and forces the reader to depend more on the narrator for information.[36]

We do learn, however, about Jehoiada's character as the story unfolds through his words and actions. He is associated with the House of Yahweh in that he brings the officers to himself there. He has the power to 'send for' and 'take' and 'bring' these officers and they obey wordlessly. He has knowledge of the movements and assignments of the officers and their men. He has the power to command them in detail about what they will do. He has the authority to make the officers swear an oath and make a covenant. He has control over the movement of the son of the king. By the series of active verbs, a number of them in the causative, describing Jehoiada's actions in this scene, he is depicted as a powerful, knowledgeable and authoritative person at the temple. A contrast with Athaliah has been set up deliberately by the narrator. Athaliah, too, was powerful in her seizing of the throne, but was never granted by the narrator any extended description of the use of her power as Jehoiada is. By the end of v. 4 we know that we have met a worthy opponent to Athaliah.

This opposition between the two strong characters mirrors several

---

34. Burney, *Hebrew Text*, p. 309.
35. Barré, *Rhetoric*, p. 88.
36. See Sternberg, *Poetics*, chs. 6 and 7 for a useful discussion of gaps and ambiguity.

other analogous oppositions. Jehoiada's power base is in the House of
Yahweh against Athaliah's at the house of the king. Burke Long again
describes how the metaphor of space—sacred versus profane space—
works in the narrative by showing how Jehoiada's actions seek to
reclaim the profaned royal palace 'for Davidide Yahwism as priest and
Temple come to dominate events and kingdom'.[37] Jehoiada stands on
the side of the Davidide survivor, who is identified by the narrator, again
authoritatively, in v. 4 as the son of the king. In v. 8, Jehoiada echoes the
narrator's stance, calling Joash 'the king'. Through the point of view
taken in this scene, the narrator casts his lot and the reader's on one side
of these oppositions, that of Jehoiada, House of Yahweh, and surviving
Davidide. We as readers thus become co-conspirators in that we know
what Jehoiada knows and what Athaliah does not know.[38]

The identity of the officers whom Jehoiada brings to the temple has
been open to various proposals in that the referent of the first term is
not clear. The word כרי, which I translate 'Carians', seems to have two
parallel attestations. In passages about David's rise to power and administrative lists the Carites, הכרתי, are mentioned as among the fighting
forces supporting David and later Solomon (2 Sam. 8.18, for example).
In 2 Sam. 20.23, in another list of David's officers, one group of
fighting men is called the 'Carians', הכרי. In both forms, they appear to
be bodyguards or palace guards directly associated with the king and
they remain loyal to him during Absalom's revolt (2 Sam. 15.18).[39]
Commentators generally consider both forms as types of foreign merce-
naries attached to the king as a royal bodyguard,[40] and I take that as a
sufficient identification for the use of the term here. The term translated
as 'runners' means literally that—these are elite royal guards set to run
before the king's chariot (cf. 2 Sam. 15.1; 1 Kgs 1.5). They are always
associated directly with the king and appear to be under his direct command and authority (1 Kgs 14.27-28). A parallel with the Jehu coup is
also echoed in the use of this term—Jehu, the new king, commands his

37. Long, *2 Kings*, p. 147.

38. Barré, *Rhetoric*, p. 91.

39. J. Prignaud sees the Keretim as David's personal guard of foreign mer-
cenaries and discusses the origin of the people; however, he also distinguishes the
Carians from the Keretim without further identification of the former; 'Caftorim et
Kerétim', *RB* 71 (1962), p. 227.

40. See the standard commentaries for further detail on these forms and their
origins; for example, Montgomery, *Books of Kings*, p. 86.

runners to kill the worshippers and priests of Baal and they do so (2 Kgs 10.25).

There is an importance to these terms which is significant narratively. These officers and their men, the Carians and runners, are the guards and private forces of the ruling monarch. They are thus associated with Athaliah and the house of the king. Jehoiada is, in this scene, usurping Athaliah's own royal guard, bringing them to him in the temple. In obeying Jehoiada, they thus 'switch sides' from Athaliah, the ruling queen, to Joash, the challenging king.

Other important elements in v. 4 are the covenant and oath Jehoiada makes with the palace guards. This covenant and oath commit the guards to the cause of the ruler's opponent. Cogan and Tadmor point out that the making of a covenant ל, 'with' (as here) is different than making a covenant עם, 'between'. The former implies the granting of a treaty or a coming to terms, lacking the mutuality between partners of equal status implied in the latter.[41] Clearly Jehoiada is in charge and is assembling an alliance against Athaliah.

With v. 5, the first direct speech of the story occurs. As Alter (as well as other scholars) delineates, direct speech carries a good deal of the narrative burden in biblical story-telling.[42] Especially as in this case, the first speech by a character can relay information about that character as well as convey important plot development. Also, as will prove true in this case, repetition of direct speech in some other form, a speech by another character or the narrator's comments, creates relationships between parts of a narrative and between characters.

The text conveying Jehoiada's instructions presents a problem for understanding both the divisions of the royal guards and the movements they are commanded to make. Many scholarly solutions involve leaving out various parts of the verses, often all of v. 6, in order to attain some clarity. Often arguments are made for the guards being 'off' or 'on' duty at some location and for the division of the guards into some number of units at these locations.[43]

I cannot solve the dilemmas definitively, and my translation offers only a possible reading. My attempted reconstruction is based on several

41. Cogan and Tadmor, *II Kings*, p. 127.
42. Alter, *Art*, p. 182.
43. See the commentaries for various discussions of the problems and solutions; for example, Montgomery, *Books of Kings*, pp. 419-20; Gray, *I and II Kings*, p. 572; and Cogan and Tadmor, *II Kings*, p. 127.

principles: (1) to preserve if possible the text as a narrative whole without recourse to secondary sources or later additions; (2) to keep the overall sense of the passage that is recognized by all scholars no matter how they solve individual textual matters; (3) to make elements of characterization and theme more visible than other solutions that delete parts of the verses; (4) to preserve a clear connection with v. 9 where Jehoiada's command is fulfilled; and (5) to highlight the commanded movement of the officers and guards without concern for whether they were 'on' or 'off' duty. In large part I follow suggestions for reconstruction proposed by Long who sees the section as a narrative whole.[44]

By translating as I do, keeping v. 6 in the passage, the first half of v. 6 functions as an aside or clarification. I think this is possible syntactically because a non-verbal clause can act in an explanatory or parenthetical way. I understand it as part of Jehoiada's direct speech, which adds to his characterization by portraying his detailed knowledge of the palace guard's assignments. (If the aside is taken as the narrator's intrusion, it breaks the time frame to add detail that lends an air of historical veracity and completeness to the narrative—a motivation quite possible for this narrator.)

The difficult word מסח at the end of v. 6, which some commentators label untranslatable, I take with a sense of 'instead'. This is a wild stab at a possible coherent meaning based on Montgomery and Gray who report favorably on Haupt's suggestion that sees a cognate נסח in Arabic, 'to replace'.[45] BDB notes that this Arabic cognate can mean 'supersede, change by substitution',[46] so perhaps a translation which indicates that Jehoiada commands this first division to keep guard at the House (of Yahweh, understood) *instead* of the house of the king is possible.

Two other minor textual matters can be covered briefly. Various commentators wish to delete אל־המלך at the end of v. 7.[47] I find retaining it, with a reading of 'on account of' or 'on behalf of' the king, acceptable, especially as the Greek preserves the phrase. It works narratively to focus Jehoiada's, and thus the guard's, concern on the king. In v. 8 the meaning of השדרות is unclear. It seems to be related to an Assyrian root

44. Long, *2 Kings*, pp. 149-50.
45. Montgomery, *Books of Kings*, p. 424 and Gray, *I and II Kings*, p. 571.
46. BDB, p. 650.
47. See, for example, Montgomery, *Books of Kings*, p. 425 and Gray, *I and II Kings*, p. 571.

meaning 'arrange in order'.[48] It has been explained either as an architectural term (as in 1 Kgs 6.9) or as a row or rank of soldiers, which could be the meaning here. I take the term 'ranks' to be able to refer either to a rank of pillars/beams or a rank of soldiers. At any rate, it is a 'line in the sand' past which any of Athaliah's adherents cannot go without peril.

Several elements in Jehoiada's speech refer to surrounding the king, the weapons the guards are to carry and the provision for killing anyone coming toward the ranks. These elements convey the thoroughness of Jehoiada's conspiratorial plans and thus his careful character. They also portray the situation of the conspiracy as a potentially violent one which reflects back, then, on Athaliah's character and her established use of violence to secure her ends.

Finally, in detailing the narrative strengths of this scene, the use of the verbs בוא and יצא must be noted. Jehoiada 'brings' the guards; the divisions 'come in' and 'go out' on the Sabbath; anyone 'coming toward' the ranks is to be killed and the guards are to be with the king in his 'going out' and 'coming in'. The frequent occurrence of these two verbs here and throughout the chapter establishes each of them as a *Leitwort* or key word, a basic element of repetitive structuring.[49] These words create a theme of movement in the story which complements and extends the theme of oppositional space between the House of Yahweh and the house of the king. The narrator takes care to choreograph a detailed 'dance' which reflects the characters, plot line and power relationships in the story.

By the end of scene 2 the oppositions laid out in scene 1 have been fleshed out with characters and a conspiracy. From the point of view of the House of Yahweh/surviving Davidide/Jehoiada, we see Athaliah's own royal guards usurped into an alliance and ready to be gathered at the temple to protect the king. Incipient action is contained in the command from a powerful, knowledgeable and authoritative Jehoiada.

Scene 3: 2 Kings 11.9-12

> (9) And the officers of the hundreds did according to everything Jehoiada the priest commanded. And they each took his men going in on the Sabbath with those going out on the Sabbath and they came to Jehoiada the priest. (10) And the priest gave to the officers of the hundreds the

48. BDB, p. 690.
49. Alter, *Art*, p. 95.

spear and the shields which were King David's which were in the House of Yahweh. (11) And the runners stood, each with his weapon in his hand, from the south side of the House to the north side of the House, at the altar and the House, about the king all around. (12) And he brought out the son of the king and he gave him the crown and the covenantal decree. And they made him king and they anointed him and clapped their hands and said, 'May the king live!'

Incipient action becomes fulfilled command in this scene and the point of Jehoiada's careful plans is revealed in the coronation and anointing of the king. Narrative time implicitly takes a jump of unspecified length—now it is the Sabbath and the detailed instructions to the guards about their movements on the Sabbath can be carried out. Further, the true identity of Athaliah's opponent and Joash's champion is revealed: Jehoiada is 'the priest'. This identification cements both his association with the House of Yahweh and his authority which was seen in the previous scene.

A key to this scene's plot structuring is repetition in the form of the performance by the guards of Jehoiada's command from the previous scene. Sternberg has explicated in detail the permutations of narrative repetition and his work is useful here.[50] Two of the constants of repetition are present: *forecast* in Jehoiada's command, cast as direct speech, and *enactment* in the guards' carrying out of the command, cast as the narrator's report.[51] With the narrator presenting the enactment, there is an authoritative witness that the command was fulfilled both by summary, they did 'everything which Jehoiada commanded', and in details reported. Such validation by the narrator enhances Jehoiada's authority.

Variants in the fulfillment of Jehoiada's command reveal nuances in plot, characterization and thematic development. The officers of the hundreds take those coming in and those going out on the Sabbath as explicitly instructed, but in fulfilling the direction to keep guard at the House of the Lord, they come to Jehoiada the priest who is at the temple. This minor variation serves to highlight Jehoiada's central role. When they arrive, a major addition from the commanded sequence occurs. Jehoiada hands to the officers the spear and shields that were King David's and are kept at the temple. Against critics that would delete this verse as interruptive and secondary,[52] I find that its added

50. Sternberg, *Poetics*, pp. 365-93.
51. Sternberg, *Poetics*, p. 376.
52. Barré, *Rhetoric*, p. 25.

details slow narrative time which increases suspense. It also adds to the characterization of Jehoiada as a careful planner concerned with both the effect and success of his effort.

The fulfillment sequence resumes in v. 11 where several phrases from v. 8 are repeated: עַל־הַמֶּלֶךְ סָבִיב, 'about the king all around', and אִישׁ וְכֵלָיו בְּיָדוֹ, 'each with his weapon in his hand'. That the king is not yet physically present to be surrounded has caused some commentators to drop the phrase 'about the king all around'.[53] But the close connection of the guard's actions to the emergence of the king makes the phrase anticipative.[54]

The additions in v. 11 which vary from v. 8 add significantly to the thematic idea of the space created by Jehoiada for the king in the temple. The encircling formation of the guards extends from the south to the north side of the temple. Robert Haak has helpfully explained the probable referent of כָּתֵף, 'shoulder', as the facade of a gate extending on either side of the entrance.[55] Thus the guards encircle the main entrance to the temple building itself, standing, as the text is careful to note, 'at the altar and the House'.[56] Long describes the theme of sacred space here: '[Jehoiada] provides a protective barrier between king and potential assailant (v. 8) or between holy and profane...[He] thereby converts the secret refuge (v. 3) into a public, royal and sacralized sanctuary'.[57]

Verse 12 has been rightly called the narrative climax.[58] Since the narrator conveys the actions, they stand as authoritative—the 'son of the king' is transformed into 'the king' within the scope of the verse. The transformation requires five actions, linked tightly as consecutive verbs giving a sense of urgency and accomplished purpose.

First Jehoiada gives to (or puts upon) Joash the נֵזֶר and the עֵדוּת. Both terms have caused scholarly debates as to their meanings, which may have to remain unclear in detail although they are significant in import. The term נֵזֶר has been translated 'crown', or 'diadem', some sort of royal symbol.[59] The term עֵדוּת has caused wider controversy. All the

---

53. Gray, *I and II Kings*, p. 571.
54. Montgomery, *Books of Kings*, p. 420.
55. R.D. Haak, 'The "Shoulder" of the Temple', *VT* 33.3 (1983), p. 277.
56. Nelson, *First and Second Kings*, p. 209.
57. Long, *2 Kings*, p. 150.
58. Nelson, *First and Second Kings*, p. 209.
59. BDB, p. 634; and Cogan and Tadmor, *II Kings*, p. 128.

versions support the form as given here and thus a translation implying a covenantal document which is handed to the king is accepted by some scholars.[60] Other scholars insist that no such document was ever given to kings at their anointing and that the term must be either emended in form or at least in meaning to royal 'bracelets' or 'jewels' or an ornamental head cover.[61]

The translation of the term as 'testimony' in the Septuagint and Targumim suggests its derivation from עוד, 'to bear witness', but 'in the Bible it is never used literally in this sense [and]...no satisfactory alternative has been posited'.[62] However, the extensive use of עדות in parallel to other terms signifying covenant and law (משפם, מצוה, חק, ברית, תורה) both in Deuteronomistic and other literature[63] justifies a translation here reflecting its covenantal character. The term also carries significant rhetorical weight which will be explored later.

After Jehoiada has given the son of the king the crown and covenantal decree, there is a perplexing change in subject in the next two verbs. Not only Jehoiada but 'they' make him king and anoint him. The plurals here have caused scholarly consternation because these actions are seemingly reserved for the priest alone. The Greek reads the singular and a number of scholars follow that reading.[64] However, Nelson points out, and I agree, that the plurals could reflect the narrative concern of the chapter to present Joash's restoration as a popular effort.[65] Finally, 'they' clap their hands and acclaim the king with 'May the king live!', or a more familiar version for the modern ear, 'Long live the king!' The 'they' in all these phrases is an unspecified subject which causes a sort of mini-gap in the narrative. The only characters besides Jehoiada and Joash who have been identified so far are the officers with their men. It is quite possible that these only make and acclaim the new king, but the narrator holds back further designation of who 'they' are until the

---

60. Gray, *I and II Kings*, p. 574; Jones, *1 and 2 Kings*, p. 481; and Nelson, *First and Second Kings*, p. 209.

61. Suggestions respectively from Montgomery, *Books of Kings*, p. 425; Cogan and Tadmor, *II Kings*, p. 128; and S. Yeivin, "'Eduth', *IEJ* 24.1 (1974), p. 20.

62. M. Weinfeld, *Deuteronomy 1–11* (AB, 5; Garden City, NY: Doubleday, 1991), p. 235.

63. See, for example, Deut. 4.45, 6.17, 20; 1 Kgs 2.3; 2 Kgs 17.15; Jer. 44.23; Pss. 19.8; 25.10; 78.5; 81.6; 99.7; 119.2; 132.12; Neh. 9.34; 1 Chron. 29.19.

64. Gray, *I and II Kings*, p. 571; and Jones, *1 and 2 Kings*, II, p. 481.

65. Nelson, *First and Second Kings*, p. 207.

narrative requires it. Sternberg has noted the artistic use of such a gap by the narrator.[66]

The characterization in this scene builds on that developed in scene 2. Jehoiada is still clearly in charge of events, the only one who has spoken, a careful and thorough king-maker. Joash continues as a passive character only; things happen to him but he does nothing. The officers and their men have become a more active, if still collective character, fulfilling and extending the command to surround the king. Significantly, Athaliah has not been mentioned in either scene 2 or 3. Her narrative absence from these scenes well represents her ignorance of the opposition arising to her rule.

This scene further builds the theme of choreographic imagery in the 'comings' and 'goings' of the characters. The officers take their 'coming in' and 'going out' men and 'come' to Jehoiada, so that they can set up the encirclement for the protection of the king. Then Jehoiada 'brings out' the son of the king in the climactic movement that makes what had been a private conspiracy a public action.[67]

By the end of scene 3, secret opposition has become public challenge. There are, for the time being, two monarchs in Judah—the Omride queen who is powerful but ignorant, and the true son of the king who has been anointed and acclaimed as new king. The House of Yahweh has become not only the protectorate of the Davidide but the location of his restoration, a sacred space toward which and in which all movement has been shaped by the priest.

Scene 4: 2 Kings 11.13-16

> (13) When Athaliah heard the noise of the runners (and) the people, she came to the people in the House of Yahweh. (14) And she saw, there! the king standing by the pillar according to the custom and the officers and the trumpets beside the king and all the people of the land rejoicing and blowing the trumpets. And Athaliah tore her clothes and cried, 'Conspiracy! Conspiracy!' (15) And Jehoiada the priest commanded the officers of the hundreds, those appointed over the army, and said to them, 'Bring her out between the ranks and anyone coming after her, kill with the sword.' For the priest said, 'Let her not be killed in the House of Yahweh'. (16) And they set their force against her and she came in by way of the horses' entrance to the house of the king and she was killed there.

66. Sternberg, *Poetics*, pp. 235-37.
67. Long, *2 Kings*, p. 150.

In a dramatic confrontation, the oppositions of the first three scenes meet and force a series of events that brings the chapter to a close. Suddenly Athaliah appears again, but only just has time to recognize the plot against her before she is killed. While she has been 'ruling over the land', an alliance has been designed that ultimately deprives her of her rule and her life.

Narrated time moves swiftly. The bridge between the last scene and this one is the noise made by acclaiming the king. The narrator in v. 13 describes Athaliah's hearing the noise and her entrance into the temple area. At the same time as Athaliah perceives, the reader perceives that more characters are involved than had been already portrayed. Suddenly, 'the people' are on the scene. What had been a small affair run by the priest and palace guards is now seen as a more popular movement.

The asyndetic juxtaposition of the words הרצין העם, 'the runners, the people' is one of the defects that provoked earlier commentators to see the start of a second, popular source in this verse with the 'runners' suspect as an addition creating the seam between the two accounts.[68] Because I am not convinced of the need to speculate about divisions into sources, I find acceptable either an apposition of 'runners—people' or the emendation made by adding a *waw*: 'the runners and the people', following Cogan and Tadmor.[69] Further, the two terms may not connote a contrast between military and popular groups; in Deuteronomistic contexts the term can imply a military force.[70]

As Athaliah enters the temple, the scene spreads before her (v. 14). The almost untranslatable והנה signals the abrupt change of perspective to Athaliah's point of view.[71] The verse follows this 'exclamation point' by giving evidence which, from Athaliah's point of view, shows that a coup d'état is in progress. 'The king': this designation had been the narrator's and Jehoiada's in the previous scenes; now it quickly becomes Athaliah's perception, too. 'Standing by the pillar': here the participle catches the virtual simultaneity of these events. 'As was the custom': this functions as a frame-breaking phrase from the narrator alerting the reader directly that anyone, including Athaliah, can immediately perceive the royal meaning of where the king was standing. The concomitants of

68. Gray, *I and II Kings*, p. 575.
69. Cogan and Tadmor, *II Kings*, p. 129.
70. See, for example, 1 Sam. 11.11; 2 Sam. 18.1-5 and 1 Kgs 20.15, 27.
71. Berlin, *Poetics*, p. 62.

a coronation are visible: 'officers and trumpets' are beside the king and
'all the people' are rejoicing and blowing the trumpets.

In a wonderful piece of alliteration hard to render into English,
Athaliah's reaction to the coup is recorded. She tears (תקרע) her clothes
and cries (תקרא), 'Conspiracy!' In the only direct speech given to her,
Athaliah correctly names the action taken against her. In this scene
devoted to Athaliah's perception of and reaction to her dethronement,
narrated time has almost out sped narrative time—it seems that it takes
longer to describe her perception of the coup than the portrayed events.
As the scene is depicted, all are against Athaliah as the opposition of
ruling queen and new king comes to a head.

Jehoiada's continuing authority over events is underlined by his
command in v. 15, which returns the narrative's point of view to 'his
side' and initiates a second command-enactment sequence. He addresses
what may be a new group of officers, פקדי החיל, 'those set over the
army'. This may distinguish these officers from those mentioned earlier
who are officers for the Carians and runners, but whether a separate
force is invoked here remains a question.[72] I tend to think that a separate
force is meant so that the narrator portrays the original protective circle
as intact even when Athaliah is removed.

The command given to these officers enforces the separation of
defined sacral space in the House of Yahweh from the desecration
represented by Athaliah.[73] The queen is to be removed from the temple
and anyone following her is to be killed with the sword. I have not
attempted any original rendering of the difficult combination of pre-
positions אל־מבית לשדרת. I have accepted a standard translation which
sees her taken out between the ranks (of pillars/beams or soldiers, as
above). Again we see a provision made for a possible defense of
Athaliah in opposition to Jehoiada's coup. As the story is told, no such
defense arises. This creates another contrast with Jehu's coup in the
preceding chapters where a ruthless purge of the members and
supporters of the Omride dynasty is carried out. That Athaliah must be
killed is not commanded; however, it seems to be understood. The
narrator catches this unstated outcome by reflecting Jehoiada's intention
in an aside, כי אמר הכהן, 'for the priest said'. The ambiguity of אמר as
either 'said' or 'thought'[74] could also mean that we have here an

---

72. Long, *2 Kings*, p. 151.
73. Long, *2 Kings*, p. 151.
74. Sternberg, *Poetics*, p. 97.

interior point of view for Jehoiada, reflecting his concern for the sanctity of the temple.

Jehoiada's command is enacted in v. 16, although with some variation. The interpretation of the phrase וישׂמו לה ידים ranges from a non-violent 'they made room for her' to the confrontational 'they laid hands on her' or 'they took her away by force'.[75] The first suggestion takes יד in the sense of 'room or space' following the Targum and Syriac; this ignores the more common sense of the word as 'hand' or, figuratively, 'power'. The following two suggestions do not coordinate well with the verb immediately following, ותבוא, 'and she came in', where Athaliah is clearly still moving by her own power and volition—she is not brought or taken in.

I would suggest that there is a parallel use of the construction used here: שׂים plus ל plus a direct object which makes my translation preferable. In Josh. 8.2 the phrase is used: שׂים־לך ארב לעיר, 'set for yourself an ambush against the city', and in Judg. 9.25 there is וישׂימו לו...מארבים, 'they set ambushes against him'. In both cases a violent confrontation is set up by ambush using ל to mark the object of the hostility and the direct object the means used. So, the phrase in v. 16 could well be taken, 'they set their force (hands) against her', thus physically blocking any movement on Athaliah's part except that of going out of the temple. This preserves the confrontational scene but allows Athaliah to leave under her own power as the next verb indicates.

Confronted by an implacable enemy, Athaliah leaves the temple. She 'comes in' to the house of the king by way of the horses' entrance—a nice detail of movement even if the architectural layout of the temple and palace is not understood. Both plot and characterization are carried by this phrase. Although her power has been met and bested, Athaliah is still an active and even regal person; she moves on her own to the palace. Her death scene warrants no attention from the narrator, only the notice that she dies in the house of the king.

This scene continues and develops the themes of space and movement. Once again movement between the House of Yahweh and the house of the king is underscored. Athaliah heard the sounds from the temple and 'came in' to the House of Yahweh, a space sanctified and now under the control of her enemies. Within this sacred space, devoted to the re-establishment of the Davidic monarchy, it is not allowed that

75. Respectively: Gray, *I and II Kings*, p. 579; Montgomery, *Books of Kings*, p. 422; and Cogan and Tadmor, *II Kings*, p. 130.

she be killed. She must be 'brought out'. Still in command of herself if no one else, Athaliah 'comes into' the house of the king and is killed there, outside the temple's holy space.

The plot movements in this scene bring into confrontation and then resolve the opposition between the Omride queen and the Davidic king. Athaliah's own royal and violent power has ultimately done her no good, for she falls victim to the careful plans and greater power of Jehoiada the priest. Faced by the new king, the priest, her own royal guard, the army and all the people, Athaliah moves alone. All the trappings of royal investiture and legitimacy rise before her as she views the scene in the temple. She can cry out a word that bespeaks the truth of the situation—conspiracy—but she cannot prevent her downfall and death.

Scene 5: 2 Kings 11.17-20

(17) And Jehoiada made the covenant between Yahweh and the king and the people to be the people of Yahweh and between the king and the people. (18) And all the people of the land went into the House of Baal and demolished it; its altars and its images they smashed thoroughly; and Mattan, priest of Baal, they killed in front of the altars. And the priest put overseers over the House of Yahweh. (19) And he took the officers of the hundreds and the Carians and the runners and all the people of the land and they brought down the king from the House of Yahweh and they came in by way of the runner's gate to the house of the king. And he sat upon the throne of the kings. (20) And all the people of the land rejoiced and the city was quiet after they killed Athaliah by the sword in the house of the king.

Particulars of time, space and movement create narrative interest in this final scene, but the dominant force is still the devolution of plot elements. Joash is king and Athaliah is dead but more remains to be done before the city will be at peace. Narrative time moves fairly swiftly with only enough description to convey the necessary details. But narrated time seems fluid and even ambiguous—the king is left standing in the temple for however long it takes 'all the people' to destroy the House of Baal.

Seemingly with no pause after the death of Athaliah, Jehoiada proceeds with the next action in his re-establishment of institutional legitimacy for the new king. With no hesitation ויכרת את־הברית, 'he made the covenant'. The definite article on 'the covenant' indicates the narrator's communication that the reader is familiar with this covenant as a customary procedure.[76] Scholars are much divided over the history and extent of this covenant-making scene. Are there two covenants or three being made? Was a covenant made every time a king was crowned? What is the relation of this covenant to the Deuteronomic legislation? As interesting as these questions are, they reflect concerns for authenticity and historicity of the covenant in royal investitures which are not my focus.

Of interest is the attention the narrator pays to the covenant as a necessary step in the making of the king, carefully placed after his anointing and acclamation and before his enthronement. Also evident is the detail the narrative gives to the parties to the covenants with no attention given to any ceremony or procedure. In using the term 'covenant' the narrative repeats a key word from v. 4, where Jehoiada started the events off by making a pact with the main conspirators. Now the circle has widened to the farthest point. The language in the first part of v. 17 is deliberately inclusive in describing the parties—the priest makes the covenant between Yahweh, the king and the people. The intent of the covenant-making is likewise described in inclusive language that has little detail in content but much sweep in reference: להיות לעם ליהוה, 'to be a people for Yahweh'.

The repetitive phrase at the end of the verse ובין המלך ובין העם, 'and between the king and the people', has been deleted by some scholars as dittography. But most, and I agree, take it as a reference to a separate, politically based pact whereby the people formally accept the king's sovereignty over them.[77] Again the language used by the narrator is inclusive but not detailed as to content or procedure. It is as if, in this whole verse, the narrator wishes to evoke a larger reality that 'should' be familiar to the reader but does so only in summary form by invoking a key word, 'covenant', and carefully listing participants.

One heavily laden verse is quickly followed by another. Verse 18 portrays the destruction of the House of Baal by 'all the people of the land'. The verse starts with two consecutive imperfects and then switches to disjunctive phrases when the direct objects of the destructive acts are given first. These phrases mirror the violence of the scene while indicating the concurrent actions taken in the course of the destruction. The house is demolished, the altars (reading the *qere*) and images thoroughly smashed, the priest killed.

76. Gray, *I and II Kings*, p. 579.
77. See Cogan and Tadmor, *II Kings*, pp. 132-33 for discussion.

The time sequence of the story seems particularly disrupted by this verse.[78] Enough detail and narrative time are given to typify fully the destruction; but narrated time is much longer even if this is imagined as a precipitous mob action. All the while the king (and priest and guards, one assumes) is left at the temple. The narrative makes no apologies for or even recognition of this time disruption, reading as if a logical course of events has taken place.

Once again, 'the people' emerge as a collective and active character. Here, they 'go into' the House of Baal, taking responsibility for the instigation of the action as well as the carry-through. This scene picks up yet another contrast to the Jehu revolt in chs. 9–10, where Jehu wipes out Baal from Israel (10.28). There, however, a much more murderous scene is depicted where all the worshipers, prophets and priests of Baal are destroyed along with the pillar and building. In the scene in ch. 11, only one person is mentioned as being killed—Mattan, the priest of Baal.

Attention and action return to the House of Yahweh at the end of v. 18: 'the priest set overseers over the House of Yahweh'. The term פקדות could have the meaning also of 'guards' in a military sense; read in such a way it stands as an echo of the officers set over (פקדי) the army in v. 15. By juxtaposing this setting of overseers/guards immediately after the destruction of the Baal temple, the narrative may suggest that it was done as a precaution against retaliatory violence against the House of Yahweh.[79]

The time sequence returns to its logical flow in v. 19, picking up the actions directly related to setting up the new king. Jehoiada, continuing his role as 'master of ceremonies', 'takes' the full complement of other characters. Quickly, however, the collective 'they' are active again—'they brought down' the king from the House of Yahweh to the house of the king. Space and movement again dominate. The action moves from the House of Yahweh, safe place and scene of the coronation, to the house of the king, which had been outside the sphere of legitimating priestly power when it was still under Athaliah's control. Now the palace is reclaimed, 'altering its status from illegitimate to legitimate seat of royal authority'.[80]

At the end of the verse the consummation of the whole scene is portrayed in a deceptively simple phrase: Joash 'sat upon the throne of the

---

78. Cogan and Tadmor, *II Kings*, p. 133.
79. Jones, *1 and 2 Kings*, II, p. 487.
80. Long, *2 Kings*, p. 152.

kings'. The narrative complication begun by Jehosheba in saving the son of the king reaches its fulfillment in his taking the throne of his fathers. The final action restoring the Davidic dynasty after the interruption posed by Athaliah has been completed. And with this action, Joash the king becomes an active character—for the first time he is the subject of an active verb. Literally and figuratively he comes into his own.

The scene quickly resolves in v. 20 with a narrative summary of the final state of affairs. Again the people are an active, collective character. The phrase והעיר שקטה could express a coordinating state of affairs, 'and the city was quiet', or a circumstantial situation contemporary with the rejoicing: 'while the city was quiet'. Several interpreters read an adversative sense, 'but the city was quiet', which then marks a contrast between the people of the land and the city.[81] Without ruling out the latter interpretation, I find the summary character of the verse favors one of the former readings.

Athaliah has, as it were, the last word: 'after they killed Athaliah by the sword in the house of the king'. I see no reason to interpret this as a separate account of her death, as is done by critics supporting the two-source theory. As a narrative reprise, information is added—she dies by the sword, and the location of her death is confirmed. Narratively it helps to close out the sense of the story. Athaliah began and ended the narrative (v. 1 and v. 20); she begins by perpetrating violence (v. 1), she ends the victim of violence (v. 20). Her hidden nemesis, Joash, is not killed when she had tried to make it so (v. 2) but she is killed by the forces who support him (v. 16). Raised by violence and illegitimate power to rule the land, she dies by violence, powerless against the greater and legitimate power of Jehoiada and his co-conspirators.

As the chapter and story end, the sense is established that all is again 'right'. The protagonists, Athaliah and Jehoiada, have each manipulated events for their own ends. Jehoiada has proven the expert is planning and execution (pun intended). A king has developed from a baby hidden and in danger into a rightful heir of his ancestors' throne. A host of supporting characters—officers, royal guards, people of the land—have put their collective power on the side of the king, obeying the priest's commands but also taking initiative as actors in the developing drama.

By the end, all of the oppositions set up by the narrative are overcome. The ruling queen has been removed and the royal heir has taken the throne. The House of Yahweh and the house of the king are once

81. Gray, *I and II Kings*, p. 582; and Nelson, *First and Second Kings*, p. 210.

again both legitimated and unified. The last Omride survivor has been killed and the Davidide survivor lives as rightful king.

2 Kings 12

Scene 1: 2 Kings 12.1-4

> (1) Jehoash was seven years old when he became king. (2) In the seventh year of Jehu, Jehoash became king and he reigned 40 years in Jerusalem. And the name of his mother was Zibiah from Beer-Sheba. (3) And Jehoash did right in the eyes of Yahweh all his days because Jehoiada the priest had taught him. (4) Only the high places were not removed; still the people were sacrificing and burning offerings at the high places.

The high drama and intensity of ch. 11 are left behind as ch. 12 opens. The first four verses are a summary report by the narrator of the reign of Jehoash (an alternate or royal name for Joash). Entirely typical of the usual regnal formulas used in the Deuteronomistic History, these verses give annalistic-style particulars about the reign of the king. Narratively, their presence in the continuous story about Joash signals a return to normalcy after the interruption of Athaliah.

The verses also slow the pace of the story, reporting details and moral evaluation with no action or movement implied. Written from the narrator's point of view, they give a long temporal view as narrated time covers the 40 years of Joash's reign. Because there is no action or suspense built through plot development, the net effect is flat narratively. But because the narrator is more visible in such a summary statement,[82] the verses convey the authority and certitude of the narrator. They thus function as an anchor point of surety for the whole story of Joash. This grants him a favorable review in all matters except those relating to the 'high places'. The evaluation by the narrator thus develops the characterization of Joash, telling of his moral character in the most direct way possible.

Some critics, following the Lucianic version, put v. 1 after v. 2a, which restores the more normal order for a regnal formula.[83] However, I follow commentators who keep the MT order because the verse then functions narratively as a bridge between the story of the infant Joash and the king Joash, creating a link to 11.4.[84] The only other significant

---

82. Bar-Efrat, *Narrative Art*, p. 34.
83. Gray, *I and II Kings*, p. 583.
84. Montgomery, *Books of Kings*, p. 427.

textual and narrative issue comes in 12.3. Influenced by the parallel in
Chronicles, Lucian and the Vulgate, the phrase כל־ימיו אשר הורהו could be
rendered 'all the days wherein Jehoiada instructed him'. This would limit
Joash's 'right' behavior to the period influenced by the priest. No
modern commentator reviewed here accepts this interpretation nor the
influence from the Chronicles account it rests on. The relative אשר, can
mean 'because' and the phrase כל־ימיו means 'all his life long'.[85]

With this summary, Joash has been formally introduced. The story of
his investiture and enthronement from ch. 11 has been confirmed by a
regnal formula and the moral stage set for his reign.

Scene 2: 2 Kings 12.5-6

> (5) And Jehoash said to the priests, 'All the silver of the sacred offerings
> which is brought into the House of Yahweh, silver of the assessment of
> each [silver of persons] according to their assessment and all the silver
> which the heart of someone wishes to bring to the House of Yahweh, (6)
> let the priests procure for themselves, each from their accountant, and then
> they will repair the deterioration of the House according to everything
> which is found there deteriorated.'

This launches the first of two reports about particular aspects of Joash's
reign which the narrator chooses to include (vv. 5-17 and 18-19). The
story moves quickly from summary to action with narrative interest
caught by the introduction of characters and the use of direct speech.
While no indication of the passage of time is given, the speech reported
appears as an act early in the reign of the king by its juxtaposition to the
summary in vv. 1-4.

The king who did little and said nothing in ch. 11 becomes the main
character now that his reign is under way. Again characterization and
plot development are carried by direct speech. Joash takes charge
immediately in speaking to the priests. There is no question in the narrative about his authority or ability to talk to them in this manner, merely
a matter-of-fact tone relaying what he said.

The general content of his speech to the priests is clear but a textual
puzzle makes an exact interpretation of the reported words in v. 5 virtually impossible. What is clear is that Joash is giving an order to the
priests to the effect that certain money (silver) which comes into the
temple should be used for the repair of the temple (vv. 5a and 6).

85. Burney, *Hebrew Text*, p. 312.

A general description of the money is given at the beginning, כל כסף הקדשים, 'silver of the consecrated (or sacred) offerings' which is brought into the House of Yahweh. The specification of this money which follows is often taken by interpreters to involve at least two types of offerings: 'obligatory taxes and voluntary gifts'.[86] But the exact designation of these monies is textually difficult and may well involve influence or emendation from a hand later than the Deuteronomist's. I attempt a reading that follows a majority of scholars and makes no claim for originality or certitude.

With a number of scholars, I drop the words כסף נפשות as a later addition influenced by Lev. 27.2.[87] By reading more closely with the Greek as a number of translators do, I then read ערך for עובר and כערכו for ערכו, ending up with a translation: 'silver of the assessment of each according to their assessment'.[88] The possibility of this type of assessment existing in a pre-exilic context is strengthened by the reference in 2 Kgs 23.35 where Jehoiakim supports a tribute paid to Pharoah by a taxation of the land איש כערכו, 'each according to their assessment'. Cogan and Tadmor do a credible job accounting for the existing MT text as a conflation of two manuscript traditions.[89] This reconstructed phrase then refers to obligatory taxes. The following phrase, to which I have added a ו at the beginning (lost due to haplography[90]), refers to 'voluntary offerings' brought by worshipers.

Regardless of how the text is reconstructed, the narrative picture contributes to the characterization of the king as knowledgeable about the inner workings of the temple, creating a parallel to ch. 11. There, Jehoiada is portrayed as a priest who is authoritatively knowledgeable about the royal guards at the palace and their assignments. Here, Joash is portrayed as a king who is authoritatively knowledgeable about the temple and its finances. In both cases, the knowledge is used to issue an order that changes the assumed normal pattern of affairs. The cumulative effect is that Joash has succeeded Jehoiada as the main active character and a picture of close association of palace and temple, king and priest has emerged.

86. Jones, *1 and 2 Kings*, II, p. 490.
87. Montgomery, *Books of Kings*, p. 432.
88. Gray, *I and II Kings*, p. 584; similarly, Montgomery, *Books of Kings*, p. 428; and Jones, *1 and 2 Kings*, II, p. 490.
89. Cogan and Tadmor, *II Kings*, p. 137.
90. Cogan and Tadmor, *II Kings*, p. 135.

The priests are to procure the stated monies, each from their מכרו. The traditional translation of this term, 'acquaintance', reflects a root נכר, 'to regard or recognize'. But a number of scholars have found a more satisfactory cognate מכר in the Ras Shamra texts. These texts mention a class of temple functionaries, associated with the priests, the *mkrm*, who seem to be a type of merchant or accountant or trader.[91] Some financial role seems appropriate for the context here. The priests in this scene are passive recipients of an order by the king. They do not react or speak and their characterization is close to that of an 'agent', a functionary character necessary for the plot.[92]

The object of the king's concern for the use of the silver emerges in the second part of v. 6. The House of Yahweh is in a state of deterioration or disrepair. The cause of the damage is not stated and is left as a gap, which the narrator does not close. The word בדק has a cognate in Akkadian with verb forms meaning 'to cut' and a noun form meaning a 'breach or tear'.[93] This suggests that the reader is to understand some structural damage, perhaps from normal wear and tear or the ancient equivalent of 'delayed maintenance'.

In this scene, the king takes charge of a situation of disrepair at the temple. He instructs the priests to set up a financial system to fund the repair and charges them with at least the administrative overseeing of the repair, if not the repair itself. The situation seems to be adequately addressed by the king. The characteristic biblical narrative pattern of command–enactment is initiated here and the reader's expectation is that some report of follow-through will ensue.

Scene 3: 2 Kings 12.7-9

> (7) But in the twenty-third year of King Jehoash, the priests had not repaired the deterioration of the House. (8) And King Jehoash called Jehoiada the priest and the priests and he said to them, 'Why are you not repairing the deterioration of the House? So now do not take silver from your accountants, but for the deterioration of the House you will give it.' (9) And the priests agreed not to take silver from the people and not to repair the deterioration of the House.

---

91. J. Gray, *The Legacy of Canaan: The Ras Shamra Texts and their Relevance to the Old Testament* (Leiden: Brill, 1957), p. 157.

92. Berlin, *Poetics*, p. 27.

93. J.C. Greenfield, 'Lexicographical Notes I', *HUCA* 29 (1958), p. 221.

At the first point where the enactment of the king's command could logically come, a narrative complication arises. In marked contrast to expectation, the king's order is not carried out (v. 7). The almost verbatim repetition of the words of the phrase from v. 6 highlights the failure of the priests to carry out the king's instructions. The specification of the year denotes the passage of narrated time, taking this new scene well into Joash's reign.

Immediately after the summary statement of the failure, the narrator reports a question Joash asks directly to the priests about their inaction (v. 8). The epithets (king, priest) for both Joash and Jehoiada remind the reader both of their social status and of their familiarity from the story in ch. 11. A close repetition of the phrase from v. 7 occurs in the question, with the king switching to the participial form to indicate the ongoing responsibility the priests have had.

There is no answer to the king's question. However, the asking of the question is pointed. Using the same phraseology as the narrator's words, the king's question highlights the priests' inaction. But the non-answering of the question by the narrative opens a significant gap as to the priests' motivation and evaluation. The narrative, seemingly deliberately, leaves entirely ambiguous the reason(s) for the priests' inaction in response to the king's instructions.

Into this gap have stepped numerous interpreters quite ready to speculate about the failure. Is this a situation of royal ineptitude or powerlessness?[94] Or are the priests negligent or morally culpable for their inaction?[95] One scholar goes so far as to state that the repair project 'was obviously hindered by Jehoiada for 22 years' and that the priest's reluctance shows that the temple 'was not in a bad state of repair'.[96] Other interpreters see the role of the priests portrayed positively or see only a mild reprimand in the king's question.[97] They also tend to read into the narrative inner motivations and moral evaluations that the narrator does not report.

Because no direct evaluation of the priests' inaction is given, any conclusions must be based on inference from the narrative itself, without

94. As suggested by V. Hurowitz, 'Another Fiscal Practice in the Ancient Near East', *JNES* 45 (1986), p. 290.

95. Gray, *I and II Kings*, p. 586.

96. G.W. Ahlström, *Royal Administration and National Religion in Ancient Palestine* (Leiden: Brill, 1982), p. 64.

97. Respectively: Hoffmann, *Reform*, p. 119; and Long, *2 Kings*, p. 158.

any attempt to read in motivations. The only basis I see in the narrative for evaluation is in the repetition of the phrase that the priests did not repair the deterioration of the House. Sternberg makes a case that charged dramatization, where there is a lingering over plot elements or informational redundancy, where 'superfluity launches a search for coherence', can shape the reader's response to characters and events.[98] When the reader is told twice that the priests failed to follow instructions, perhaps a general evaluation of negligence, ineptitude, or resistance to the king can be posited. Beyond that, the narrative will not allow one to go, and in fact, shows no interest in going.

The king himself moves directly from the question to a solution without dwelling on the inaction (v. 8). The previous plan is to be replaced; what it will be replaced with is not yet specified, but will be when the plot requires it (v. 10). More important here is the acquiescence of the priests to the king's new plan which is clearly communicated in v. 9. The priests bow out of the process. The narrator reports their agreement in a way that summarizes the previous plan which they will no longer follow—they will neither take the silver from the people nor repair the deterioration of the House.

Characterization in this scene dwells on both the priests and the king. The priests are developed as a collective character from their passive reception of the king's instructions (vv. 5-6) to an active failure to follow his instructions. Jehoiada is mentioned by name and status but does not (yet) contribute to the action of the scene. His presence at the inception of the new plan is important, however, given his role in the next scene. The king remains the central active character. He 'calls' and 'speaks'. The priests 'agree' with him without any indication of further resistance. He is in charge of the new plan.

Without clarifying the ambiguity about why the priests did not follow the first plan, this scene moves quickly to the inception of a second plan. The king continues to dominate the plot development of the story, being the only character who is given direct speech and who initiates action. The focus on the maintenance of the House of Yahweh continues. The king has expressed ongoing concern for this in the narrative and the priests, by bowing out, concede to the king's view of the importance of the repair work.

98. Sternberg, *Poetics*, p. 477.

Scene 4: 2 Kings 12.10-17

> (10) And Jehoiada the priest took an ark and he bored a hole in its lid; and he put it near the altar on the right as one comes into the House of Yahweh. And the priests who keep the threshhold would put there all the silver which was brought into the House of Yahweh. (11) And whenever they saw that there was much silver in the chest, the king's secretary and the [high] priest went up and smelted and counted the silver that was found in the House of Yahweh. (12) And they would give the silver which was measured out into the hand of those doing the work who were overseers of the House of Yahweh, and they paid it out to the wood crafters and the builders who were working on the House of Yahweh, (13) and to the masons and the stone cutters and to buy wood and hewn stones to repair the deterioration of the House of Yahweh, and for everything which was spent upon the House for repair. (14) Only in the House of Yahweh were not made cups of silver, snuffers, basins, trumpets or any vessel of gold or vessel of silver from the silver which was brought into the House of Yahweh, (15) but to the ones doing the work they would give it and they would repair with it the House of Yahweh. (16) And they did not keep track of the men into whose hands they would give the silver to give to the ones doing the work for with faithfulness they were working. [(17) Silver of the guilt offering and silver of the sin offering were not brought into the House of Yahweh; they were for the priests.]

The new plan for financing and carrying out the repair of the temple is enacted and a long scene narrating its details is given. The amount of narrative time devoted to the plan, given the generally terse biblical style,[99] shows its importance for the narrator.

Jehoiada becomes the agent who sets up the means by which the plan is accomplished in the first part of v. 10. His actions, described with normal narrative-style consecutive imperfects, show that he bored a hole in the lid of an 'ark' (the construct form of אֲרוֹן is unusual[100] but makes little change of meaning). The location of the box near the altar has caused translators problems because it seems to say that a worshiper would have to come nearer the altar than ordinary people were allowed. Emendations of the chest's location to *massebah*, 'pillar' or *mezuzah*, 'doorpost' have been posited.[101] However, Cogan and Tadmor point out that the MT is attested by all the versions and interpret that the text

99. Bar-Efrat, *Narrative Art*, p. 199.
100. Cogan and Tadmor, *II Kings*, p. 138.
101. Respectively: Montgomery, *Books of Kings*, p. 429; and Burney, *Hebrew Text*, p. 315.

portrays the worshiper handing the donation to the doorkeeper priest who then places it in the ark near the altar.[102] Jehoiada takes the initiative here and while the action has shifted from the king to him, the narrative connotes that his setting up of the chest fulfills the king's new plan. Jehoiada thus shows himself ready to carry through on the king's reorganization.[103]

In the second part of v. 10 and throughout the rest of the scene, the time sense of the narrative changes to an iterative mode. Signaled by the consecutive perfect ונתנו, 'they would put', the narrator now portrays repeated or customary actions.[104] Thus the reader enters a scene where narrated time itself becomes repetitive, giving details of an ongoing procedure. The indication of customary or repeated actions continues in v. 11 with the temporal phrase ויהי כראותם, 'and whenever they saw'. When the chest would become full, 'the king's secretary and the priest' would take over the administration of the funds. The compound subject is of interest. Textually, the presence of הכהן הגדול, 'the high priest', is an anomaly in a Deuteronomistic text, this term being used only in the Second Temple period. Its use here and in 2 Kgs 22.4, 8 and 23.4 is suspect of a later hand and Cogan and Tadmor note the 'accepted view' that it is a later accretion.[105]

More significant narratively is the combination of royal and temple officials who handle the money under the new plan. No longer left solely in the hands of the priests, the executive force for carrying out the repair of the temple using the collected funds now rests with both the palace and the temple. Also significant here is that these officials are not named in this verse, nor throughout the remainder of the scene. As time has entered a customary mode, so too has characterization. The secretary and priest are agents lacking in any characterization beyond the new plan.[106]

What this secretary and priest do with the funds has been clarified by a group of scholars working with ancient Near Eastern texts mentioning the smelting of precious metals. The verb form ויצרו is now usually taken not as 'emptied' or 'bound up' but as 'smelted' or 'cast'.[107] The

---

102. Cogan and Tadmor, *II Kings*, p. 138.
103. Hoffmann, *Reform*, p. 159.
104. Long, *2 Kings*, p. 159.
105. Cogan and Tadmor, *II Kings*, p. 138.
106. Hoffmann, *Reform*, p. 120.
107. C.C. Torrey, 'The Foundry of the Second Temple at Jerusalem', *JBL* 55

smelting or casting of the silver would make it uniform in quality, ready to be 'counted' and put to use.

Verses 12 and 13 detail the uses to which the money was put, again using the iterative consecutive perfect ונתנו 'and they would give'. A two-tiered structure for using the funds seems to be envisioned. The money goes first על־יד עשׂי המלאכה המפקדים בית יהוה, 'into the hand of the ones doing the work who were overseers in the House of Yahweh'. (I read with the *qere* and the parallel in 2 Kgs 22.9 the *hophal* participle המפקדים.) These officials appear to be temple functionaries, 'masters of the works'.[108] The use of a participial form of פקד here may remind the reader of the 'overseers' Jehoiada set over the House of Yahweh (11.8). This would locate the structural organization of the temple staff in Jehoiada's coup, which was then available for use in the king's plan. These overseers then use the money for the skilled artisans and supplies needed for the work.

The characters in these verses are identified, again, only by function—overseers, wood crafters, builders, masons, stone cutters—as the customary mode continues. The narrative describes in considerable detail the kinds of workers and supplies employed in the maintenance of the temple. Narrative time is thus slowed quite a bit and attention focused on the care given to the temple as the king's plan is executed.

In vv. 14-15, there is a restrictive clause introduced by the word אך, 'only', indicating a limitation on the use of the funds brought into the House of Yahweh. Some commentators delete the first בית יהוה as an intentional gloss or as a duplication of the phrase at the end of the verse.[109] As in the previous verses we see here a propensity for detail in the narrator's explication of the plan. Burke Long aptly describes the effect: 'specifying with priestly thoroughness certain limits and qualifications to the system'.[110] The notation of the workers' honesty in v. 16 adds another explicating comment on the system. Here the ongoing sense of time is carried in the imperfect verbs and the participle. The narrative underscores that all the while the work is being done

---

(1936), pp. 247-60; *idem*, 'The Evolution of a Financier in the Ancient Near East', *JNES* 2 (1943), pp. 295-301; and A.L. Oppenheim, 'A Fiscal Practice of the Ancient Near East', *JNES* 6 (1947), pp. 116-20.

108. Gray, *I and II Kings*, p. 587.

109. Respectively: Montgomery, *Books of Kings*, p. 430; and Jones, *1 and 2 Kings*, II, p. 493.

110. Long, *2 Kings*, p. 159.

financial overseeing is unnecessary because of the honesty of the workers.

Verse 17 is cast as a disjunctive explanatory remark, which functions as a narratorial aside or parenthetical note. By evident intent, it shows that the livelihood of the priests was not endangered by the king's plan because money of the guilt and sin offerings was not part of the funds brought into the House but went directly to the priests. A Deuteronomistic context for the verse is in doubt, however, because the offerings mentioned are most often seen in post-exilic contexts (P, Leviticus, Numbers, Ezekiel) and have few reliable earlier citations.[111] I take the verse as a later, post-exilic gloss which offers reassurance that the priests' income had not been cut off by the plan.

This long, highly detailed scene has set forth the king's second plan in a temporal mode that spans the years from its inception into a timeless future. The plan is revealed to the reader not in the command–execution format, but as repeated or usual procedure (vv. 10b-13) complete with necessary limitations and explanations (vv. 14-16, or 17, if included). The details speak of the thoroughness of the plan. The focus on the temple and the variety of skilled crafts used in its upkeep denote the care the House of Yahweh receives 'always'. There are no true characters here except for Jehoiada who first makes and places the ark for the funds. Only 'agents' function to carry out the plan with exactitude and careful, honest attention. The king, Joash, stands in the background as creator and initiator of the plan but even he is represented by his agent, the king's secretary. The king remains a distant yet commanding power, not only in his own time but through the years implied for the plan's viability. The true focus of the scene is the House of Yahweh which is mentioned in every verse except v. 16. The repeated intoning of בית יהוה emerges most forcibly as a constant reminder of the center of the narrative's attention.

Scene 5: 2 Kings 12.18-19

> (18) Then Hazael, king of Aram, went up and fought against Gath and captured it; and he set his face to go up against Jerusalem. (19) And Jehoash, king of Judah, took all the consecrated objects which Jehoshaphat and Jehoram and Ahaziah his ancestors, kings of Judah, had consecrated, and all his consecrated objects and all the gold which was found in the treasuries of the House of Yahweh and the house of the king and he sent to Hazael, king of Aram; and he withdrew from Jerusalem.

111. Gray, *I and II Kings*, p. 588.

The second report about an aspect of Joash's reign is narrated briefly, in two verses. It tells of an invasion by Hazael, king of Aram, who captured Gath and threatened Jerusalem. Joash gathers together and sends a tribute and manages to deter action against his capital city. The date and description of Hazael's incursion into Palestine are of great interest to historians of the era;[112] I am more focused on the narrative aspects of the incident.

The incident is not located temporally during Joash's reign. The initial word אז, 'then', is usually interpreted as a temporal marker which, with an imperfect as here, expresses an action 'which continued throughout a longer or shorter period'.[113] However, one scholar has made an argument that in certain cases אז plus the imperfect indicates not a future or sequential event but one that takes place simultaneously with, or is linked to, events just narrated.[114] Here the marker would explain why Joash needed the new finance system—because the treasury of the temple had already been depleted to pay off Hazael.[115] However, I find this argument less convincing than the term's well-attested use as a general temporal marker, and see the incident narrated with an unspecified time frame within Joash's reign and with no specific link to the preceding narrative.[116]

Two narrative characteristics of this brief incident are noteworthy—characterization and style. By clearly and repeatedly giving the status of both Hazael and Joash (king of Aram, king of Judah), the story signals that we are in the realm of royal international politics. These kings are powerful people whose realm of action includes the control of land, the waging of wars, the control of national treasuries, and the power relations of nation-states. Secondly, the story is told in a direct, factual style. The verses give no direct evaluation of the incident and very little hint of narrative devices that could reflect an evaluation indirectly. The storytelling does, however, follow its already established style of detailed narration in the listing of the tribute items Joash gives away.

112. See, for example, Gray, *I and II Kings*, p. 589; and Cogan and Tadmor, *II Kings*, p. 141.
113. GKC, p. 314.
114. I. Rabinowitz, ''AZ Followed by Imperfect Verb-Form in Preterite Contexts: A Redactional Device in Biblical Hebrew', *VT* 34 (1984), p. 54.
115. Rabinowitz, ''AZ', p. 62.
116. Long, *2 Kings*, p. 159.

Scene 6: 2 Kings 12.20-22

> (20) And the rest of the matters of Joash and all that he did, are they not written in the book of the annals of the kings of Judah? (21) And his servants arose and conspired a conspiracy and they killed Joash at Beth-Millo on the way going down to Silla. (22) And Jozabad, son of Shimeath, and Jehozabad, son of Shomer, his servants, struck him and he died. And they buried him with his ancestors in the city of David. And Amaziah his son became king after him.

The final scene closes out Joash's reign by noting his other actions as king, giving his manner of death and burial, and stating the succession. Narrative summary here contains little plot or character development except for the tantalizingly brief note about Joash's assassination. And within a brief narrative time, narrated time is complex, covering both the whole of his reign, 'all that he did', as well as the specific incidents of his death.

Verse 20 summarizes Joash's reign by referring to other actions taken by him and alludes to a record of such actions, 'the book of the annals of the kings of Judah'. By design, such a phrase acts as a pointer to a much extended and more detailed reality which is not portrayed. The reference to an 'annals of the kings' anchors the whole account, told and untold, in a source outside of the narrator's own authority. But in so doing, the narrator becomes visible as a narrator, abandoning the usual unobtrusiveness in telling the tale.

The story of the conspiracy is narrated very briefly. An odd combination of detail and ambiguity marks the account. The emergence of a conspiracy by the king's servants is stated and the location of Joash's death is given. The difficult text at the end of v. 21, בית מלא היורד סלא, has had various reconstructions proposed for it. Without being able to solve the difficulties in what may ultimately be an unreadable phrase, I have followed a number of translators in reading: (1) Beth-Millo as a location, a filled (מלא) earthwork or fortification, perhaps the same as that associated with David and Solomon (2 Sam. 5.9 and 1 Kgs 9.15); and (2) a further specification of location in היורד סלא, 'on the way going down to Silla'.[117] Reading the entire phrase as a location is possible as the narrative has already shown an interest in the location of the deaths of various characters (11.2, 16, and 20).

The details continue in v. 22 where the names of the king's assassins

117. Jones, *1 and 2 Kings*, II, p. 496 has a summary of the proposed reconstructions.

are given. The similarities of the names may be due to textual error and some manuscripts read 'Jozacar' for the first name; I have followed the MT. Their presence in the royal court as the king's servants is signaled. The ambiguity in the account, despite the details of conspiracy, location and names, is that no motivation is imputed to the act. The assassins are not characterized beyond the giving of a family name. And the narrator gives no evaluation of the action either. The story is told in a brief, straightforward manner without any apparent narrative shaping that would give any implication of moral comment.

The account of Joash's reign ends with the notation of his burial 'with his ancestors in the city of David'. The succession appears also to be a simple notation: 'his son' reigns after him. Again, a brief telling of events from the narrator's omniscient, selective point of view carries the story line with no apparent development of character or evaluation.

Summary

A wealth of narrative detail has occupied this study of the story told in 2 Kgs 11–12. Using textual and historical-critical commentary as well as narrative sensitivity to establish a probable Deuteronomistic account, I have tried to 'read' the story with a focus on its narrative artistry. In particular, I highlighted such techniques as: narrated and narrative time; characterization; plot development; repetitions of sounds, words and phrases; the presence of gaps and ambiguity; the uses of dialogue, summaries and command–enactment sequences; and the narrator's omniscience, visibility and evaluative presence. Throughout, a verse-by-verse analysis has blended with a reading of the scenic structure. The overall narrative impact of the two chapters taken as a continuous story of Joash's reign can be seen now that the more detailed study is done.

The two chapters tell of two 'phases' of Joash's reign. In ch. 11, his rule is incipient as he is a rightful heir to the throne prevented from ruling by the actions of Athaliah. In ch. 12, he is the ruler in a full, active sense. Thus the principal overall movement of the narrative is one of thwarted rule and anticipation to realized rule. The narrative signals this change in 11.19 where for the first time Joash is the subject of an active verb: 'he sat upon the throne of the kings'. Before, the king-to-be was a passive object of others' concerns. After, the king is an active subject, initiating plans on his own and acting like a king.

The rise of the king is, of course, contrasted with the downfall of the queen. Athaliah has the momentum in the first scene, but has little plot development centralized through her after that. She re-emerges only to react to the actions of others. As Joash emerges as the rightful king, she is killed, her 'ruling over the land' replaced by Joash.

The rise of the king is correlated with the stepping aside of Jehoiada the priest. In ch. 11, Jehoiada is the main active character, planning and plotting, directing the movements of others, in charge of all aspects of the revolt against Athaliah. But in ch. 12, he steps into the background, or better, to the side of the king. He is instructor to the king, and leader among the priests, taking action to enact the king's plan for financing the temple repair. If in ch. 11 Jehoiada plays the lead, in ch. 12 he concedes center stage to the king and becomes best supporting actor.

The alteration of attention from one main character to another is accompanied throughout the story by a consistency in characters as well. In both chapters, royal powers and priestly powers are the focus of action. Minor characters are included—officers, Carians, guards, people of the land, overseers, carpenters, stone cutters—but in both chapters they react to or move by orders of the king or Jehoiada. The royal and priestly center of attention gives an overall coherence to the two phases of the story.

The coherence of royal and priestly characters is paralleled by a continuing focus on the House of Yahweh, with a secondary focus on the house of the king. These two physical locations are also the centers of power, action and wealth. By the repetition of these locations throughout the narrative, the story denotes its underlying interest in the meaning and fate of these buildings/centers of power. In addition to the focus on location, ch. 11 shows a consistent interest in movement around and in the temple. This is most marked with the repeated use of בוא and יצא as indicators of the movement of characters.

The narrative itself shows a kind of movement. Most broadly, the story of Joash starts with royal murder and actions done in secrecy (11.1-11), moves to affirmation of royal power and openness of action (11.12–12.19), and finally, briefly, ends in conspiracy and royal murder (12.20-22). Also, the pace of the narrative moves from fast-paced intense action and drama in ch. 11 to a slower pace in ch. 12. This more measured pace of the second phase is created by several different time senses: a summary format in 12.1-4, 20-22; an 'ordinary time' of specific incidents and actions in 12.5-10a, 18-19; and iterative time which takes a longer-range view that extends even beyond Joash's reign in 12.10b-17. It is as if the 'evil' represented and caused by Athaliah requires intense concerted action which is mirrored in the pace of ch. 11. By contrast, the 'good' represented and caused by Joash allows normal, durative time to re-emerge in ch. 12. Form and content narratively complement each other.

So a story has been told and read. My first focus has been on the narrative art used in the telling of the story. However, even within the narrative analysis, elements that make the story vivid, that appeal to certain traditions, that make a point with an insistent tone have been evident. These elements include such things as repetition, regnal evaluation, the invoking of terms like 'David' and 'covenant', the switch to an iterative mode, and the portrayal of characters and events with intense drama. These elements prompt questions about what is being communicated by and through the story. Is there a point behind the story, or a reason for its being told in this way? Without abandoning the narrative as a good story, its implications from a rhetorical perspective must be explored.

Chapter 3

RHETORICAL ANALYSIS

2 Kings 11–12 tells a story and a good one at that. However, the pro-posals this study is exploring posit that neither the telling nor the inter-preting of 2 Kings 11–12 is complete with the text as 'only' a story, 'only' subject to the analysis of its narrative art. Inherent in the text as a whole are dimensions or perspectives that represent interests beyond story-telling for the sake of a well-crafted or entertaining story. One dimension already evident includes the story's portrayal of certain events and characters and its apparent insistence on how these should be understood. In other words, the story argues for certain points.

Using the premise that the author had some motive or reason for telling the story in the particular way it is written, I next want to explore the dimension of the story known as 'rhetoric'. For now, I take 'rhetoric' generally as the argumentation used by a speaker or writer, how a discourse makes its point in addressing an audience (a longer definition will follow). The premise that biblical narrative has a point or points to make is not new—interpreters have long included such an idea under the rubrics of the 'author's intention' or the 'theological import' or the like. And the idea that an author of a biblical text (or one of its posited sources) addressed a particular audience or context has long been studied critically in the idea of *Sitz im Leben*.

So the idea of a text's having a point in addition to telling a story is not novel. However, the use of rhetorical analysis to explicate how a text makes its arguments is relatively new to biblical studies. Thoughtful rhetorical analysis, with roots in both classical and modern studies of rhetoric, has been used to good advantage by recent New Testament studies. Of all the New Testament books, the letters of Paul are perhaps most easily recognized as arguments, as Paul seems to be arguing and debating points of Christian theology and practice with his correspon-dents. That such a discourse is amenable to rhetorical analysis, the study of argument-making, does not need much defense. Anne Wire in *The Corinthian Women Prophets*[1] demonstrates how a modern conception of rhetorical study can be used to explicate the types of arguments Paul makes, which can then be extended to re-create the rhetorical situation of Paul's audience and rhetorical opponents.

But such an analysis of rhetoric can also be made for narrative, where the 'argumentative points' are blended in with the story. Vernon Robbins in *Jesus the Teacher* uses a 'socio-rhetorical' criticism to study the structure and meaning of the Gospel of Mark. He shows how the arguments made by the author of Mark can be illuminated by understanding rhetorical forms present in the narrative and how those forms reflect the wider social environment of the Jewish and Greco-Roman world in which the Gospel was written.

A general case for the use of rhetorical criticism in Old Testament studies is made by Dale Patrick and Allen Scult in *Rhetoric and Biblical Interpretation*.[2] They argue that rhetorical analysis can be used for the Bible even though its authors did not know classical (let alone modern!) rhetoric. By assuming that any author shapes language with 'artful deliberateness', they find that 'the shape and form of the discourse is an indication of how he or she means for us to take the message'.[3] They urge critics to analyze 'the whole range of linguistic instrumentalities by which a discourse constructs a particular relationship with an audience in order to communicate a message'.[4]

Patrick and Scult go on to show the appropriateness of rhetorical analysis for biblical narrative. They support this first by an argument that the narrators of biblical texts 'construed God's actions as having an essentially rhetorical signification'[5] in that God was seen as communicating a message to an audience through language. A second argument follows, that the biblical narrators 'intended their own words to function in a similar manner'.[6] Historical narrative as a form used in the Bible conveyed this rhetorical purpose because it could address its readers as a

---

1. A.C. Wire, *The Corinthian Women Prophets: A Reconstruction through Paul's Rhetoric* (Minneapolis: Fortress Press, 1990).

2. D. Patrick and A. Scult, *Rhetoric and Biblical Interpretation* (Sheffield: Almond Press, 1990).

3. Patrick and Scult, *Rhetoric*, p. 13.

4. Patrick and Scult, *Rhetoric*, p. 12.

5. Patrick and Scult, *Rhetoric*, p. 31.

6. Patrick and Scult, *Rhetoric*, p. 32.

group or community with 'their own' story and thus had the 'power to create and define a community's identity'.[7]

Building on the three studies just cited to define and defend the use of rhetorical analysis for biblical narrative, I turn in this chapter to the task of understanding the rhetorical shape of 2 Kings 11–12. The scholars cited in this chapter are those who focus on rhetorical art. One is a holdover from the last chapter—Meir Sternberg, because in *The Poetics of Biblical Narrative* he addresses specifically the topics of the art of persuasion and the use of rhetorical devices in Hebrew narrative. Patrick and Scult, cited above giving a general argument, are also useful in some details of rhetorical arguments. The book *Introduction to Rhetorical Theory* by Gerard Hauser provides general background as well as particular points about argumentation. The most detailed and fruitful for my analysis has been Chaim Perelman's *The Realm of Rhetoric*.

Using these authors, a more exact definition of rhetoric and rhetorical analysis can be laid out. Hauser gives a very broad definition which can cover the use of rhetoric in many situations: rhetoric 'is the management of symbols in order to coordinate social action'.[8] Through rhetorical language, a speaker or writer addresses a particular situation and attempts to influence the persons involved in the situation. Generally understood, language is symbolic; it shapes perceptions and the way people understand and share their experiences.[9] In a situation where rhetoric is involved, symbols as language are used in 'instrumental communication' which is 'oriented towards goals such as changing opinions and actions'.[10]

Perelman focuses the study of 'new' rhetoric on argumentation, how arguments are advanced to seek support or rejection from an audience for certain debatable theses, as opposed to ('old') rhetorical studies that looked at language as 'ornamentation' only. So Perelman holds that rhetoric 'covers the whole range of discourse that aims at persuasion and conviction, whatever the audience addressed and whatever the subject matter'.[11] A rhetorical argument moves from premises that can be generally accepted by an audience to win consent for theses that are presented and argued for through various types of argumentation.

7.   Patrick and Scult, *Rhetoric*, p. 51.
8.   Hauser, *Rhetorical Theory*, p. 3.
9.   Hauser, *Rhetorical Theory*, p. 146.
10. Hauser, *Rhetorical Theory*, p. 45.
11. Perelman, *Realm*, p. 5.

Broadly, Perelman sees two techniques of argumentation. First are those arguments that try to build a liaison or association between the premises and the argued theses, 'which allows for the transference to the conclusion of the adherence accorded to the premises'.[12] Second are those that argue by dissociation, separating elements previously tied together in the audience's mind.

Using these discussions as background, I will understand rhetoric as the techniques a rhetor uses to make an argument that addresses a particular situation and to persuade an audience about certain opinions or actions. When this general definition is applied to biblical narrative, a rhetorical analysis seeks to discover the methods of argumentation used in the narrative. This argumentation makes the narrative persuasive in some way(s) and the points or theses held up for consent can also be discovered.

Following upon the narrative analysis just undertaken, a rhetorical analysis involves a noticeable shift in perspective. In exploring narrative art, one reads a text as from a 'narrator' to a 'reader'. Nothing need necessarily be implied about the narrator as an 'author', the reader's situation, nor the context of telling the story. In the last chapter, historical-critical study was used in dialogue with narrative study to posit and read a story as it might have been written at a certain point in time. In doing this, I already forced the analysis to be more aware of a context in which the story could be situated.

When the move is made to rhetorical analysis, terms and awareness shift more significantly. The narrator is now fully an 'author', a person consciously constructing a story for certain purposes that include but could go beyond well-crafted story-telling. And an 'audience' is assumed, situated at a certain time and place with certain presuppositions and perceptions already in place that the story must also presume or it will fail to communicate. Further, a 'situation' beyond the telling of the story is assumed—some contingency wherein persuasive discourse can make sense and perhaps make a difference in the audience's opinions or actions.

Restating my thesis may be helpful in viewing this shift of perspective involved in switching to rhetorical analysis. Rhetorical analysis does not involve importing some matter 'foreign' to the story into its analysis. Rather, it uses a particular type of critical awareness to study an aspect of the story that is inherent in its existence as a story. Argument-making

12. Perelman, *Realm*, p. 49.

is intrinsic to the story as story, not added onto an already independently-existing entity. The reality of an author who has in mind a certain audience which he or she seeks to persuade about certain ideas presents a larger circle of interest in and around the story, but it is a circle based in the story itself.

Before a word of text is analyzed rhetorically, the form of the Athaliah and Joash story as a narrative can be examined for its rhetorical impact. Because this is a *story*, it establishes a persuasiveness through its creative and dramatic format. Hauser notes that creativity can function rhetorically:

> The socially shared aspect of creativity is capable of making commentary, of exerting influence, of changing attitudes, beliefs and opinions. Creativity can lead to insight and to action. It can function aesthetically and rhetorically.[13]

This modern analyst also notes that drama, whether on the stage or in some other symbolic, discursive form like the dramatic actions of a story's plot and characterization, engages the audience and helps to make the arguments work. 'Considered rhetorically, drama establishes a relationship with its audience. It asks us to think, feel and value in certain ways while we are in this relationship.'[14]

A similar point is made by Patrick and Scult in reference to biblical narrative itself in that a narrator uses 'the arts of the story teller to add force to his persuasive argument'.[15] This goes beyond mere window-dressing, because the art and the rhetoric are closely linked. '[W]e would argue that narrative art is not an adornment but an essential aspect of what is communicated.'[16]

In rhetorical interpretation, the form as narrative also highlights the author's role in creating all of the techniques and aspects in the story that make the arguments. In particular, the author's creation of a narrator who is a voice in the story carries an especially significant rhetorical impact in biblical narrative. Narrative critics have clearly identified the omniscient and reliable character of biblical narrators. This plays an important rhetorical role. Hauser discusses Aristotle's concept of *ethos*, or the character of the speaker, which has an impact on the audience

---

13. Hauser, *Rhetorical Theory*, p. 61.
14. Hauser, *Rhetorical Theory*, p. 189.
15. Patrick and Scult, *Rhetoric*, p. 66.
16. Patrick and Scult, *Rhetoric*, p. 67.

through both the personal impression the speaker creates and the impressiveness of the arguments used. He notes that 'rhetoriticians have largely endorsed Aristotle's belief that a positive assessment of a rhetor's character could well be the most potent of all the available means of persuasion'.[17] When a biblical author creates a narrator who is omniscient and reliable, the audience has little basis to question the narrator's knowledge or character or the essential truthfulness of the story that is told. Thus the narrator has an ethos of believability and trustworthiness which lends the narrative as a whole a persuasive impact.

2 Kings 11

Scene 1: 2 Kings 11.1-3

The argumentation in the story of Athaliah and Joash starts even before the story itself opens. The straightforward labeling of the House of Ahab as evil in 2 Kgs 8.18 and 8.27 is an example of one of the most obvious rhetorical moves on the author's part. This is the direct evaluation of a character or action by the narrator, which carries, as Sternberg notes, the reliability and authoritativeness of the narrator[18] or, as a rhetorician would put it, the narrator's believable ethos.

When Athaliah is named as an Omride princess, the text thus makes an argument by association. Perelman shows how this kind of argument by association is made by 'establishing a structure of reality'. He explains that these arguments 'are those which, starting from a known specific case, allow the establishment of a precedent, model, or general rule, such as enable reasoning by model or example'.[19] The author has previously established the evil of the Omrides, a part of the 'reality' evoked by the larger narrative. By clearly stating Athaliah's birth origin in that dynasty, the author argues that Athaliah participates in the evil attributed to the Omrides.

But there are more subtle arguments in this scene as well which serve to characterize Athaliah and her actions and so shape the audience's perceptions. A number of these arguments can be identified by placing 2 Kings 11–12 in its context of the larger Deuteronomistic History to see parallels and contrasts. This is a technique that will be useful throughout this rhetorical analysis.

17. Hauser, *Rhetorical Theory*, p. 94.
18. Sternberg, *Poetics*, p. 476.
19. Perelman, *Realm*, p. 51.

One such argument can be seen by noticing what is *not* present in these verses. Athaliah is 'ruling over the land' (v. 3) and thus has seized royal power. But nowhere is she introduced by the usual regnal formulas that mark the start of each king's reign throughout the Deuteronomistic History.[20] Historical critics have noted this absence and perceived its meaning: 'this shows that [Athaliah's seizure of power] was regarded as a usurpation'.[21] But how is this persuasive to the audience? The argument is made by a dissociation of ideas, a type of reasoning 'characterized from the start by the opposition of appearance and reality'.[22] Athaliah appears to be a legitimate ruler but in reality she is not. The 'syllogism' behind this dissociation goes as follows: Legitimate rulers (even if bad or evil) are introduced by regnal formulas. Athaliah is not introduced by a regnal formula. Therefore, Athaliah is not a legitimate ruler.

Another type of argument which is made by reference to the story's context in the Deuteronomistic History is an argument made by analogy. Sternberg identifies analogical patterning as a rhetorical device which functions by creating a sense of relationship between two or more terms on a scale of similarity.[23] Perelman explains analogic argumentation by stating that one item (the theme) is clarified and evaluated in terms of what is already known about another item (the *phoros*).[24] Ronald Katz, in surveying the development of ancient rhetoric, identifies 'the use of theme and *phoros*, the building blocks of the analogy' as the 'key to an advanced thinking which grapples with the condition of the non-physical or spiritual universe'.[25]

The characteristics that are established about Athaliah are that she is a woman from the House of Ahab, a foreigner and a queen mother; in ch. 11 she rules over Judah as queen. Each of these characterizations, when seen as a 'theme', has an analogy or 'phoros' within the Deuteronomistic History which clarifies its meaning. A noteworthy woman of the House of Ahab who is a foreigner and a queen is Jezebel.

---

20. See B.O. Long, *1 Kings* (FOTL, 9; Grand Rapids, MI: Eerdmans, 1984), pp. 159-65 for a brief discussion of the regnal formulas.

21. Gray, *I and II Kings*, p. 569.

22. Perelman, *Realm*, p. 134.

23. Sternberg, *Poetics*, p. 479.

24. Perelman, *Realm*, p. 115.

25. R.C. Katz, *The Structure of Ancient Arguments: Rhetoric and its Near Eastern Origin* (New York: Shapolsky/Steimatzky Publishers, 1986), p. 8.

She has been portrayed by narratorial evaluation, her own actions and Yahweh's prophetic word in the narratives about the northern kingdom as thoroughly and irretrievably evil. Her story has been told together with her husband Ahab's throughout the chapters preceding 2 Kings 11 (1 Kgs 16–2 Kgs 9). In fact, she has just met her well-deserved (in the narrator's opinion) and prophetically foretold death during Jehu's revolt in Israel.

Another woman in Judahite history who was a queen mother is Maacah, mother of King Asa. In 1 Kgs 15.9-15, the reader is told that the king put away Maacah from being queen mother 'because she made a disgraceful thing for Asherah' (1 Kgs 15.13). Yet another reference which picks up on one of Athaliah's characteristics, a foreigner as ruler, is in the law of the king in Deut. 17.14-20 where it is stated that the people may not put a foreigner over them as ruler (Deut. 17.15).

What these analogies do for the reader's perception of Athaliah is to associate her even more closely with the evil of the House of Ahab, the worship of foreign deities and false images, and illegitimacy in ruling. As the narrator shows her evil roots, she becomes a kind of anti-model[26] in that she represents the evil that can disturb the covenant relationship between Yahweh and the people.

The opening verse of ch. 11 shows Athaliah moving to destroy all the claimants to Judah's throne. As Sternberg points out, the reporting of a drastic act by a character can be a rhetorical device used by an author to shape characterization[27] and thus the reader's opinion. Both Athaliah's action of murdering all of the king's descendants and how its portrayal as a sudden but decisive act seem calculated to provoke a reaction of horrified reprehension.

A subtle use of terminology reinforces the reprehensibleness of the act. Athaliah destroys 'all the heirs of the kingdom'. These are not neutral, descriptive words but terms loaded with a superfluity of meaning. Ishida has identified both 'seed' (זרע) and 'kingdom' (ממלכה) as terms that indicate the existence of a royal dynasty and that denote royal authority.[28] Athaliah is not just murdering anyone, but the very people who can legitimately inherit the throne of David and thus continue the royal line.

---

26. Katz, *Structure*, p. 89.

27. Sternberg, *Poetics*, p. 476.

28. T. Ishida, *The Royal Dynasties in Ancient Israel* (Berlin: de Gruyter, 1977), pp. 100, 106.

The rhetoric creates an aura of evil and threat around Athaliah but it does not go unchallenged. Jehosheba's stealing away and hiding an infant son of the king contains its own rhetorical force. The very emergence of a plot development that stands in opposition to Athaliah begins to make an argument of dissociation from her character and actions. She is not, as it turns out, the only 'reality' in the situation.

What develops in vv. 2 and 3 (and then continues throughout ch. 11) is a play of perspectives. Sternberg has identified a play of perspectives as a type of rhetorical development that can shape the reader's knowledge and thus judgment.[29] The same devices that shape narrative interest here shape rhetorical interest. Athaliah is powerful but does not know of the moves against her. She seeks to destroy the heirs of the kingdom: another woman acts to save one son. The import of the second perspective, which seeks to save the dynasty, is only incipient in this scene but it sways the reader to see the weaknesses in Athaliah's position and thus dissociate from her.

Another device has significant rhetorical force. As Lowell Handy has pointed out, the story of Joash fits an established literary form which has been labeled a 'Tale of the Hero Who was Exposed at Birth'.[30] The elements of the form in Joash's case create a narrative in which: a child of noble birth is threatened, here because he is a threat to the queen, and his life needs saving; an agent saves the baby from certain death; the infant is raised by a human, here an aunt; the infant is adopted by a royal person, cleric or deity, here Joash is raised by a princess and a priest in the House of Yahweh; and a record of the child's eventual kingship and deeds is preserved.[31]

The form is developed in brief compass but a rhetorical point is made. The literary form can be taken as a 'reality' already established by social and literary convention about what could happen to a hero or noble child. That the story about Joash is made to fill the form then becomes an argument made by illustration. The conclusions such a narrative form encourage the audience to reach include Joash's true nobility, the real threat to him, the providence of his saving and his proper rearing and development into a royal figure.

This literary form works in tandem with another kind of argument in this scene. By placing the epithet 'the son of Ahaziah' (v. 2) in the voice

29. Sternberg, *Poetics*, p. 478.
30. Handy, 'Speaking of Babies', p. 161.
31. Handy, 'Speaking of Babies', p. 162.

of the narrator, the author has given it the most authoritative force available. This simple move actually constitutes an argument from definition—a kind of quasi-logical argument which draws an identity between two terms.[32] The definition is complemented by the literary form of the hero exposed at birth. The definition claims without further argument that Joash is the king's son and thus is legitimate. The tale reinforces this claim with an illustration known by convention of what could happen to an infant prince.

Within this short opening scene much has been accomplished rhetorically which sets out the basic theses for the rest of the story. A primary argument by dissociation rules the scene—the play of perspectives represented by Athaliah and Joash shows that they are in total opposition to each other. The author's reasoning concerning Athaliah uses several associational arguments to convince the reader, simply, that she is evil. Her origin in the House of Ahab shows her as an illustration of that condemnable dynasty, her characteristics are analogous to those of other foreign queens or queen mothers, her drastic action against the dynasty shows her true nature. One decisive argument by dissociation, her lack of regnal formulaic introduction, is the clinching argument in her illegitimacy as ruler.

For the other side, two basic powerful arguments by association establish Joash's legitimacy. By authoritative narratorial definition, he *is* the son of the king. By his illustrating the tale of the hero threatened at birth his legitimacy as well as his vulnerability are confirmed. In short order and by powerful argumentation, the author has established a case that Athaliah, queen and only Omride survivor, is evil and rules illegitimately. A threatened but legitimate son of the king, the only Davidide survivor, backed by agents representing both the royal house and the temple, stands in opposition to her.

Scene 2: 2 Kings 11.4-8
The rest of the story plays out rhetorically the consequences of the arguments made in the first scene about the opposition between Athaliah and Joash. Joash's case becomes stronger and stronger as Athaliah's reaches its only allowable conclusion. In vv. 4-8 the opposition is crystallized narratively but the verses also make arguments about the import of the story that shape the reader's opinions.

The introduction of Jehoiada without any identifying epithet poses a

32. Perelman, *Realm*, p. 60.

question for rhetorical analysis similar to that of narrative analysis. Rhetorically, this 'unknown' must be evaluated by what is attributed to him and said about him. Perelman has described a type of associational argument which is based on the structure of reality. In this type of persuasion, a connection between a person and his or her acts is an assumed part of 'reality' (in the same way that cause and effect are linked) so that an argument can appeal to this reality structure to make a case.[33] Jehoiada's leadership, knowledge and prestige are presented in his actions; later these are confirmed by his status as 'the priest' (v. 9). The story portrays Jehoiada as one whose authority on behalf of the king is unquestioned. This creates what Perelman terms an 'argument from authority'[34]—if this clearly authoritative person supports the son of the king, then that helps the audience's support to be forthcoming as well. Note that this argument based on Jehoiada's authority works in tandem with an argument by definition. Both the narrator and Jehoiada define Joash as a legitimate heir to the throne (vv. 4, 8). This argument by definition was initiated in the first scene and is now continued and supported by the authority argument using Jehoiada's power and prestige.

The setting of the scene is also important rhetorically. Hauser notes, 'Where we picture events occurring greatly influences what we perceive as the event and the nature of its concerns'.[35] When a setting has a particular symbolic value, that can add to the signification of the space.[36] Because this scene is set in the House of Yahweh, all of the priestly authority, the royal sanctuary's religious domination, and a predictable ordering of national life which are evoked by the temple are associated with Jehoiada and his plans. The setting in the House of Yahweh argues for the legitimacy and righteousness of the plans created within it.

Verse 4 contains a number of other terms that carry rhetorical evaluation. Such an accumulation of terms creates an argument by establishing relationships among them. Hauser defines this as an associational cluster: 'Wherever there is purposeful, situated use of language relevant to the question posed by its situation, we will find relationships among the rhetor's ideas'.[37] What are the other terms in this associational cluster?

33. Perelman, *Realm*, p. 90.
34. Perelman, *Realm*, p. 94.
35. Hauser, *Rhetorical Theory*, p. 193.
36. Perelman, *Realm*, p. 101.
37. Hauser, *Rhetorical Theory*, p. 169.

'The seventh year' could be merely a historical note. However, Widengren proposes that this could be a number symbolic of seven-year cycles that each mark a new era in national life.[38] An enthronement at such a time could be particularly auspicious.

As already seen, the Carians and the runners are probably to be taken as palace guards, the personal guards loyal to the king. These terms evoke a wider symbolism as well. Within the Deuteronomistic History, the Carites (a term possibly related to Carians, cf. 2 Sam. 20.23) are particularly associated with David, as his loyal bodyguards and in his lists of administrators (1 Sam. 30.14; 2 Sam. 8.18; 15.18; 20.7, 23). The term 'runners' does not have the concentrated association with the dynasty's founder, but likewise is a harbinger of royal power. Jehu had used his runners to do the killing of the Baal worshipers during his coup (2 Kgs 10.25). The use of both terms plays out an analogic argument here—as kings, especially David, have their royal guard, so will the new, true king in Jehoiada's coup. These guards take an 'oath' by Jehoiada's command; here the solemnity and secrecy of the proceedings are evoked.

The whole cluster—royal guards called by Jehoiada into the House of Yahweh in the seventh year, taking an oath, being shown the son of the king—is epitomized by the use of a term with extensive symbolic connotations, ברית, covenant. This term plays an ideological role in the Deuteronomistic History as a key positive concept for promise and mutual faithfulness. Here an argument by definition is set forth. What is happening in this scene is no sneaky, illegitimate, run-of-the-mill conspiracy. Rather, it is a covenant being made with the support of a whole cluster of terms associated with royal power and authority.

The details of the conspiracy follow in vv. 5-8. Such an accumulation of detail plays a rhetorical role because it is a technique for emphasis used by a rhetor.[39] Through the details of commanded troop movements, the audience's attention is drawn to the knowledge of the commander, the carefulness of the plans, the royal object of all this planning, and the evident importance of the goal to be accomplished by such precision and forethought.

The commanded guard assignments reveal the use of the terms בוא and יצא, 'go in' and 'come out', as a theme of movement. This unifying theme has rhetorical power appropriate to the argumentation of the

38. G. Widengren, 'King and Covenant', *JSS* 2 (1957), p. 7.
39. Perelman, *Realm*, p. 37.

story. 'Go out' often implies a point of departure while 'come in' focuses more on a goal.[40] Together they also function as military terminology—going out to and coming in from battle. For example, when Saul names David as a commander, David goes out and comes in, leading the army (1 Sam. 18.13). The combination can particularly signify the actions of a leader or ruler, who can ably direct his or her own and others' movements.[41] In Solomon's dream at Gibeon, he defines his youth with the statement that he does not know how to go out and come in (1 Kgs 3.7).

The connotations of leadership and military power in these terms evoke an aura of royalty. The scene itself confirms this in v. 8 where the king's presence and power are summarized by the phrase 'when he goes out and comes in'. This word pair is repeated throughout the narrative. Sternberg reports that such key words can function rhetorically, shaping the reader's attitudes.[42] The point of this scene, by direct statement and indirect evocation, is the planning necessary to re-establish legitimate royal power.

With so much rhetorical attention focused on one side of the basic opposition in the narrative—Joash—the other pole seems to fade in significance. This is one of the ways in which the story induces allegiance to a desired outcome. When the narrative center of gravity shifts toward Jehoiada and the temple on behalf of the king, an indirect dissociation takes place: Athaliah is left out. This dissociation is explicit in two elements in the scene: the usurping of Athaliah's guard and the warning about possible defense of her by her partisans (v. 8).

Thus, scene 2 develops the arguments begun in scene 1, giving them more power by augmentation. The status of the son of the king has been confirmed by definition, the authority of a commanding priest, the symbolic power of the temple and the presence of the royal guards. The details of a plan for his defense have given emphasis to the critical importance of his person and safety. All of these factors have been clustered together under the rubric of a covenant, evoking the positive associations of that term. Movement itself symbolizes the comings and goings of a king as it 'mirrors the comprehensive possibilities of privileged royal movement and rule'.[43] Athaliah's power and status fade by

40. H.D. Preuss, 'יצא', *TDOT*, p. 228.
41. BDB, pp. 97-99.
42. Sternberg, *Poetics*, p. 480.
43. Long, *2 Kings*, p. 150.

comparison as Joash's grow. Even as she is ruling over the land, her own guards, prestige and authority are being taken out from under her by the argumentation of the story.

Scene 3: 2 Kings 11.9-12

The rhetoric built into the story line moves to an initial resolution about Joash's side of the opposition in this scene. The 'son of the king' becomes 'the king' through a ceremony of coronation. Along the way the argument in favor of his legitimacy is cemented with further persuasive elements, some based on analogy and others symbolic and evocative. Perelman explains the method and power of a symbolic argument. This kind of argument by association posits connections or 'liaisons of coexistence'

> between the symbol and what it evokes and [these liaisons] are characterized by the relation of *participation*. They are set in a mythic or speculative vision of a whole in which symbol and thing symbolized are equally parts... The symbol is indispensable for arousing fervor, religious or patriotic, because emotions can rarely be attached to purely abstract ideas.[44]

Analogy and symbolism work separately and together in this scene to build a case for Joash's legitimacy and to depict his coronation.

The personnel involved in the scene echo at least one other scene of investiture which creates an analogic patterning. For Solomon's coronation, a priest, Zadok, a prophet, Nathan, and an officer of the royal bodyguard, Benaiah, are charged by David with making Solomon king (1 Kgs 1.32, 38). Both priest and officers of the bodyguards are present for Joash's investiture. (The implicit presence of the prophet will be developed in the chapter on ideological analysis.) It is also noteworthy that the only time when royal bodyguards, specifically the כרתי , are present as part of the anointing and acclaiming of the king is at Solomon's investiture (1 Kgs 1.38).

Verse 10 gives an example of how symbolism and analogy work together. The naming of David's spear and shields has symbolic value—they are weapons of war, now arming those who will defend the king. Moreover, they are David's weapons of war. By invoking the name of the founder of the nation and dynasty, the author evokes the symbolic associations with that name: power, monarchic rule, dynastic succession,

44. Perelman, *Realm*, p. 101.

identity as God's chosen king. Through the efficacy of a symbolic liaison, the actions of Jehoiada on behalf of Joash participate in the 'vision of the whole' which surrounds the Davidic kingship. But the mention of David's name also establishes an analogy. David, the better-known element, clarifies the meaning and significance of Joash, a hitherto unknown element. He is, like David, to be a king of David's line, a man of valor and power, with priest and guards at his side.

Even without a specifically rhetorical analysis, it is hard to miss the rhetorical impact of a verse such as this. Robinson notes, 'These weapons were ceremonial ones, carried in the presence of the king, and their use here was to demonstrate Joash's legitimacy and the guards' loyalty to him'.[45] Long, who is more cognizant of the author's deliberate shaping of the scene, describes the aura created around the guards: 'their duty is so charged with the emotions of sacrality and dynasty that upon reporting for duty to Jehoiada, [they] receive certain public symbols of David's Yahweh-blessed rule'.[46]

Arguments by symbolic associations continue in v. 11. The guards are all around the king, marking off a line of security that includes king, priest and temple. The mention of the altar and house as within the defined circle evokes the symbols of the center of sacral power. Again, Long is one critic who catches the rhetorical power of a dramatic scene:

> Bulking large over this narrative and conceptual landscape, the temple and its sanctified priest mark out the inviolate zone of energy from which politico-religious action will gain the authority and power of ultimacy. Joash's claim to the throne carries a priestly, God-sanctioned, temple-blessed authority with the added weight of Davidide tradition behind it.[47]

Joash's transition in the v. 12 from 'son of the king' to 'the king' is the central transformation in the scene. But several symbolic associations create an associational cluster. While the specific referents of 'crown' and 'covenantal decree' are debated, their role as royal and covenantal symbols is widely recognized, as seen in the previous chapter. The נזר or 'crown' was pointedly removed from the fallen King Saul (2 Sam. 1.10). The עדות , 'covenantal decree', is significantly found in David's speech to Solomon, as he lies dying and enjoins his son to keep Yahweh's statutes, commandments, ordinances and decrees (1 Kgs 2.3).

---

45. J. Robinson, *The Second Book of Kings* (Cambridge Bible Commentary; Cambridge: Cambridge University Press, 1976), p. 110.

46. Long, *2 Kings*, p. 150.

47. Long, *2 Kings*, p. 150.

The particular overtone of royal covenant-keeping is signaled in this scene.[48] Specific language for the making of a king continues in the next phrase where 'they made him king and anointed him'. Both verbs are used of king-making throughout the Deuteronomistic History and their royal connotations are clear.

The phrase of royal acclamation 'May the king live!' or 'Long live the king!' is especially associated with the investiture of a king.[49] Of the four uses of the phrase in the Deuteronomistic History before this passage, only in the investiture of Solomon is the combination of anointing and acclamation found. There, the combination is used twice—in David's command to his officers (1 Kgs 1.34) and in the specific fulfillment of that command (1 Kgs 1.39). So in addition to the symbolic liaisons used in the cluster in v. 12, there is also an analogic argument being made to the investiture of Solomon which, as the better-known case, adds weight and clarity to Joash's investiture.

Another way of viewing the persuasiveness of this scene can serve as a summary. The scene has specifically involved, by stated action or use of particular terminology, the investiture, coronation, anointing and acclamation of Joash as king. The setting of the scene, the people present, the symbols evoked, and the actions taken form an associational cluster which presents this king-making scene as an illustration of legitimate royal investiture. Thus an argument by illustration appeals to a customary or known structure of reality, royal investiture, and makes it present to the audience in the specific case given as an illustration,[50] here the king-making of Joash.

Beyond the illustration of a general royal investiture, this scene also contains elements which appear to be invoking an analogy to a particular investiture, that of Solomon. The specific presence of priest, officers and royal bodyguards, the invoking of the symbolic term 'covenantal decree' as in David's last speech to Solomon, the combination of anointing and acclamation, and the specific phrase of acclamation are all part of the scene of Solomon's coronation. Of course, all of these elements appear singly and in various combinations throughout the Deuteronomistic History, but the particular *associational cluster* in use at both Solomon's and Joash's becoming king can present an argument

---

48. Nelson, *First and Second Kings*, p. 209.

49. T.N.D. Mettinger, *King and Messiah: The Civil and Sacral Legitimation of the Israelite Kings* (Lund: Gleerup, 1976), p. 132.

50. Perelman, *Realm*, p. 108.

by analogy. The succession of David by Solomon is the better-known event, the phoros, which makes evident the meaning of dynastic legitimacy and continuity in Joash's case.

Scene 4: 2 Kings 11.13-16

Scene 4 reintroduces Athaliah and, with her, the oppositions present in the story come face to face. The argument by dissociation concerning Athaliah reaches its climax in her death. And the persuasive shaping of Joash's coronation scene continues even as his only true rival is killed.

One of the ways in which audiences are persuaded is by having points or descriptions made vividly present to them through various techniques for emphasis.[51] And one of the ways to do this in narrative is by charged dramatization which brings to the foreground 'the plot elements designed for judgment'.[52] When Athaliah suddenly sees the king, the dramatic change of perspective is marked by הנה (v. 14) and the audience just as suddenly participates in the head-on collision of two perspectives. As Athaliah tears her clothes and screams 'conspiracy!' the audience's attention is riveted to the enraged queen. By high drama and intense emotion the author creates a scene which underscores for the audience the importance of the story being told.

The play of perspectives developed since v. 2 reaches its inevitable confrontation. The argument by dissociation used to persuade the reader that Athaliah was both an evil and illegitimate ruler is augmented here and finalized. Athaliah stands alone as she enters the temple and sees the king. All the other mentioned characters are on the 'other side', celebrating their new king. The expected defense of Athaliah (vv. 8 and 15) never materializes. Even the report of her reaction plays a part. 'The narrator's portrayal of Athaliah's outrage is clearly intended to alienate the reader from her perspective.'[53] The dissociation from this infamous queen must be so complete that she cannot be killed in the temple; the sacrosanct space can have nothing to do with her death (v. 15).

As the reader's dissociation from Athaliah builds and finalizes, the associational arguments in favor of Joash's legitimacy continue. Here three particulars about the investiture scene which convince Athaliah that her rule has been challenged persuade the audience as well.

Athaliah's initial perception upon entering the temple is of 'the king

51. Perelman, *Realm*, p. 35.
52. Sternberg, *Poetics*, p. 477.
53. Barré, *Rhetoric*, p. 95.

standing by the pillar according to the custom'. Here is a direct allusion
to a symbolic object which evidently stood for some association of the
king, the temple and Yahweh. Perhaps a reference to the pillars set up
by Solomon at the vestibule to the temple (1 Kgs 7.15-22) is intended.
Josiah, in a scene equally shaped with symbolic content, stood 'by the
pillar,' when he made a covenant (2 Kgs 23.3). The exact symbolism of
the pillars is debated among scholars, but, as Clements notes, they 'must
certainly be connected with royal dynastic oracles, and their primary
symbolic purpose seems to have been related to the ideas of permanence
and durability'.[54] Meyers notes that such pillars in the architecture and
iconography of ancient cultures depict the access point to sacred space
and convey divine legitimacy for the regime that builds the sacred
temple or shrine containing the pillar.[55]

Two things are clear rhetorically, however. Athaliah knows at once
what the symbolism means—she sees 'the king' standing by the pillar.
And in the phrase 'according to the custom', the author reveals the type
of argument being made. An appeal to custom is an appeal to a
structure of reality which the rhetor claims the audience should
recognize.

Two other elements in the scene work to confirm the validity of the
investiture that has taken place. The trumpets present by the king and
being blown by the people are a signal of royalty and honor.
Symbolically, they may lend the scene religious or mythical connotations
as well. One critic notes one type of association that they may have: they
'may reflect in the accession of the king of Judah the ritual of trumpet-
blowing in the theophany of Yahweh as king in the New Year festival'.[56]
The rejoicing of the people portrays the festivity of the actions appropriate to the investiture of a king. The concrete and symbolic content of the
pillar, the trumpets and the rejoicing mark this verse as a continuation of
the argument by illustration—truly Joash's investiture is an illustration of
valid king-making in Judah.

The mention of the trumpets and the rejoicing also functions to aug-
ment the analogic argument analyzed above, that Joash's investiture can
be understood by comparing it to Solomon's. There a trumpet (שׁופָר) is
blown and the people rejoice (שׂמח) greatly (1 Kgs 1.39-40). The analogy

54. R.E. Clements, *God and Temple* (Philadelphia: Fortress Press, 1965), p. 66.
55. C. Meyers, 'Jachin and Boaz in Religious and Political Perspective', *CBQ* 45
(1983), p. 175.
56. Gray, *I and II Kings*, p. 577.

is not exact in that some elements in 1 Kgs 1.32-40 are not present in
2 Kgs 11.9-14. But each investiture contains an associational cluster that
as a whole creates an analogy between the two scenes. By the end of
v. 16, the author has provided the arguments necessary to persuade the
reader that Joash has been correctly installed as king of Judah. Symbolic
associations—temple, covenant, pillar and trumpet—have invoked the
deeper significance of the actions taken. The plans of Jehoiada, set in
secret, have come to a public and justified conclusion.

The scene has also shown the justified conclusion of the opposition to
Davidic rule represented by Athaliah. Dissociation from her and all that
she represents is accomplished so persuasively that when she dies, there
is no one to mourn her passing either in the narrative or in the audience.
The play of perspectives between the oppositions is encapsulated in her
one word of direct speech, 'Conspiracy!' What to Jehoiada is ברית,
covenant, is to Athaliah קשר, conspiracy. Bruggemann captures the contrast from the queen's perspective: 'An act of *fidelity* is here perceived
as an act of *treason*'.[57] But all of the persuasive power of the author has
been used to convince the reader that, indeed, faithfulness to the Davidic
dynasty has been expressed in and through the 'conspiracy' that
brought Athaliah's downfall.

Scene 5: 2 Kings 11.17-20
The rhetorical force of the story continues through this final scene to
confirm the import of the king-making and to include two significant
actions: covenant-making and Baal-smashing. The actions described in
the verses extend and reiterate the central Yahwistic and dynastic tone
of the chapter.

Verse 17 summarizes the covenant-making scene led by Jehoiada. The
lack of specificity about the actual process of the making of the
covenants and about their stipulations means that the force of the verse
is largely symbolic—it evokes rather than designates or describes. A
sense of all-encompassing righteousness is intoned; everyone present is
involved, all agree without dissent, all goes according to expectation. The
use of the term 'covenant' reminds the reader of v. 4 where Jehoiada's
plans start with a pact with the officers. Covenant terminology was
invoked again in the 'covenantal decree' handed to the king in the
coronation scene. This kind of repetition rhetorically calls to mind all of

57. W. Brueggemann, *2 Kings* (Knox Preaching Guides; Atlanta: John Knox,
1982), p. 39.

the positive evaluative connotations of 'covenant'. (These connotations will be discussed at more length in the chapter on ideology). The persuasive force created by the author in using the term 'covenant' surrounds the narrative scene with intimations of Yahwistic righteousness and legitimation.

Verse 18 functions to make an equally sweeping evaluative point, but here the argument is made by dissociation. The true Davidic king just installed by the authoritative representative of the House of Yahweh can have nothing to do with any non-Yahwistic symbolism or religious center. And the same political force that supports the installation of the Davidide understands this well enough to initiate the destruction of the rival House of Baal. Prompted seemingly by the investiture and covenant scene just witnessed in the temple, 'all the people of the land' destroy the temple of Baal, its altars, images and priest. The dissociation argument thus made is clear and complete—nothing is left of this most potent symbol of non-Yahwistic religion and political legitimation.

The combination of kingship, covenant and religious reform invoked by the narrative in vv. 9-18 is an extensive one, reaching far beyond a mere report of actions as the plot develops. But the combination also uses two other rhetorical techniques to create its force.

Sternberg notes that a particular order for presenting narrative events, particularly when the sequence involves displacement or dechronologization from conventional patterns, creates evaluative ordering.[58] Narratively, when the Baal-smashing verse follows immediately upon the covenant-making verse, the king is awkwardly left standing at the temple for an unspecified period of time. How such non-sequential ordering is rhetorically powerful is now apparent. Before Jehoiada and the forces of Davidic legitimacy can complete the installation of the king, all the forces opposed must be eliminated. The House of Yahweh must and does extend its power to 'cleanse' the city of all non-Yahwistic rivals before the king can move from the center of Yahwistic sacrality, the temple.

The combination of kingship, covenant and religious reform in these verses makes a second argument possible as well. An analogic patterning is created; or more specifically, two patterns are created, one based on analogy and one setting up a counter-analogy. The movement by a king from covenant-making to religious reform is certainly exemplified by Josiah in 2 Kings 23. There, in detail far greater than in ch. 11, a

---

58. Sternberg, *Poetics*, p. 479.

covenant-making scene is described (2 Kgs 23.1-3) which is followed by an exquisitely detailed purge of non-Yahwistic religious symbols, places and personnel from Jerusalem, Judah and into what was Israel (2 Kgs 23.4-20). Scholars have noted the similarities between the two scenes; Long notes that ch. 11 'anticipates a similar sequence of actions that will mark Josiah's reign'.[59] Of significance here is that the argumentative use of analogy borrows the import and specificity of Josiah's actions to support and explicate Jehoiada's.

Another newly installed king who carries out a religious reform is Jehu in the chapters immediately preceding this narrative. According to at least one scholar, Lloyd Barré, there is an extensive rhetorical contrast between the chapters.[60] What looks like analogic patterning, a new king installed by a coup who then directs a purge of Baal, actually functions as a counter-analogy. Jehu's purge, in fact, all of Jehu's coup, proceeds by extreme violence. He kills several large groups of people including all the prophets, worshipers and priests of Baal (10.18-27). By contrast Jehoiada's coup in favor of Joash kills only two people, Queen Athaliah and Baal's priest Mattan. Barré's point is that the Jehu and Joash narratives are deliberately contrasted to show Jehoiada's coup in a positive light.

From analogic patterning in v. 18, the rhetoric of the narrative returns to its symbolic associational pattern in v. 19. Jehoiada gathers everyone involved in the actions of making Joash king and together they bring the king from the House of Yahweh to the house of the king. The Davidic and covenantal faithfulness and sacral power so exemplified by the House of Yahweh are here extended to absorb and eliminate any vestige of Athaliah's profane power at the house of the king.

And the narrative signals the rhetorical point. For the first time the subject of an active verb, Joash takes his seat upon the throne of the kings. Once again a term important symbolically is used at a key juncture. The 'throne of the kings' in one of the phrases Ishida identifies as part of a complex of terms used to express aspects of royal, Davidic ideology.[61] 'The "throne" was the most important symbol of royal authority...[which] symbolized royal rule. Similarly the expression "to sit on the throne" signifies "to become king."'[62] The argument has

59. Long, *2 Kings*, p. 152.
60. Barré, *Rhetoric*, p. 56.
61. Ishida, *Royal Dynasties*, p. 100.
62. Ishida, *Royal Dynasties*, p. 104.

come to a full conclusion—Joash is the true king as he takes his rightful place upon the throne.

The broad analogy already highlighted to the events surrounding the founding of the dynasty may also be extended here. Long notes that the procession from the temple to the palace is 'an act reminiscent of triumphal procession',[63] listing David's bringing the ark into Jerusalem (2 Sam. 6.15), the procession at Solomon's coronation (1 Kgs 1.38) and the entry of the ark into Solomon's temple (1 Kgs 8.1-13). The seating of the king upon the throne also echoes Solomon's action; after his coronation, he 'sat upon the throne of the king' (1 Kgs 1.46). These details serve to remind the reader that Joash stands in the line of David and Solomon as well as to create a parallel to the actions associated with these better-known ancestors.

Verse 20 closes the account rhetorically by a reprise of the people's joy and final dissociation from Athaliah. She had set this course of events in motion but she was not, finally, in charge of events. The mention of the city being quiet could argue for the lack of support Athaliah found even in her capital city. It also serves to alert the reader, as a final resolution, that 'all is well'.

When viewed as an entire story the rhetorical elements traced here center on the main characters. First, the argument of the whole concerns Jehoiada's actions on behalf of Joash. This highlights the role of rhetoric in an apologetic, or even forensic, type of narration, defending the characters from any 'charges of wrongdoing'.[64] Jehoiada's actions are not only defensible but commendable and Jehoiada is thoroughly justified by the account. Barré focuses on this rhetorical point. He describes the writer of the story as a court scribe whose task was to justify the overthrow of Athaliah: 'The scribe portrayed characters and events to show that unlike Jehu and his coup, which involved treachery, deceit and the most extreme displays of violence, Jehoiada's removal of the queen was carried out as a sacred task'.[65]

Secondly, the rhetorical power of the whole narrative has also been used to convince the reader of a double assertion concerning the basic opposition developed in the chapter. Athaliah was an evil, Omride intruder who seized the throne of Judah by violence and ruled illegitimately. Joash is the true heir of his father, Ahaziah, and has been

---

63. Long, *2 Kings*, p. 147.
64. Patrick and Scult, *Rhetoric*, pp. 63 and 146 n. 15.
65. Barré, *Rhetoric*, p. 56.

returned to his rightful place upon the throne of David through a ceremony replete with proper dynastic protocol and powerful symbolic
meaning. Narrative and argumentative details work toward the same
purpose—to gain the reader's adherence to the thesis that the Davidic
dynasty has been authoritatively and legitimately restored after an interruption explicable only as the death throes of the powerfully evil Omride
line.

2 Kings 12

Scene 1: 2 Kings 12.1-4
As if to confirm the main thesis in ch. 11, that a true Davidide once
again sits on the throne of David, the first section of ch. 12 adds another
argument about Joash's legitimacy. These four verses go on to create a
persuasive picture of Joash's reign responding to the complex rhetorical
situation which seems to be envisioned by the author.

These verses contain the introduction to Joash's reign, a resumé of
significant elements about his kingship. This is not the place to make a
study of the regnal formulas in the books of Kings; what is important for
the rhetorical analysis of the chapter is that these verses do contain the
elements that comprise the standard introduction for a Judahite king.
Using a brief list provided by Burke Long,[66] these elements are: (1) an
accession date given by a synchronistic accession formula (12.2); (2) an
age of accession (12.1); (3) the length and place of reign (12.2); (4) the
name of the queen mother (12.2); and (5) a theological appraisal (12.3-
4). The repeated use of the regnal introduction, largely parallel in each
case, for all the kings of Judah represents an argument by repetition that
establishes a reality about Judahite kingship. While the regnal formulas
function rhetorically in other ways as well, the force of the repetition
alone makes the case that this is how kingship is recognized in Judah.
This repetition thus creates, as Perelman would analyze it, a 'structure of
reality', the establishment of a precedent or general rule by which other
things can be judged.[67]

When the regnal formula including the five necessary elements is
stated for Joash, an appeal to the structure of reality is made. This says
two things. First, it establishes the legitimacy of Joash's kingship. But
Athaliah's years of ruling Judah had not been introduced by the regnal

66. Long, *1 Kings*, p. 160.
67. Perelman, *Realm*, p. 51.

formula (as noted above) which means that the continuity of Judahite kingship had been interrupted by her. So the regnal introduction for Joash makes a second point—true, legitimate kingship has been re-established with Joash's accession after the interruption.

Within the regnal formula for Joash several other arguments are made which seek to influence how the reader will view his reign. Joash's accession as a child parallels that of Josiah, who also came to the throne as a young boy (2 Kgs 22.1) after the violent demise of his father (2 Kgs 21.23-24). In this a mini-analogy to a great king is set up for Joash. Further, the otherwise inconspicuous notice that Joash reigned 40 years in Jerusalem may only reflect a historical remembrance. But several critics have caught the rhetorical possibility of the round number as a 'symbolic figure'[68] that echoes the 40-year reigns of David and Solomon. These would then be two more examples of analogic patterning to the exemplars of the dynasty.

Perhaps the most direct argument is made in the verses that state the theological evaluation of Joash (vv. 3-4). Sternberg, in his list of rhetorical techniques used in biblical narrative, calls such narratorial evaluation the most explicit device which shapes response to character and event.[69] Here there is the statement that Joash 'did right in the eyes of the Lord all his days'. This evaluation of moral rectitude is cast as a summary of the king's reign and so shapes all of what follows by way of incident and detail.

Another aspect of the verses that shape the audience's perceptions is the statement that Jehoiada taught Joash. Jehoiada, who had played the role of the authoritative and knowledgeable priest and leader of the conspiracy which brought Joash to power, here supports the king through instruction. The verb also includes connotations useful to the developing picture of the good king. The verb 'teach', ירה, used in a number of biblical traditions, has particular associations within the Deuteronomistic literature. These include: the role of priests and judges to direct or teach the people (Deut. 17.10); the prophet/judge Samuel's instructing the people in the good and the right way (1 Sam. 12.23); and, in Solomon's temple dedication prayer, his plea for the Lord to teach the people the good way (1 Kgs 8.36). From the same root is the word 'Torah', תורה, which serves to evoke key passages such as the copy of the Torah the king should have according to Deuteronomy's 'law of the king'

68. Miller and Hayes, *History*, p. 295.
69. Sternberg, *Poetics*, pp. 475-76.

(Deut. 17.18) and the book of the Torah which motivated Josiah's reforms (2 Kgs 22.8). Jehoiada's teaching of Joash thus uses a key word; this, with its significant associations, persuades by creating what Sternberg calls miniature analogies[70] which are nonetheless potentially powerful. These analogies remind the audience about covenantal terms and actions, as well as major figures who fulfill covenant stipulations.

Verse 4 functions as a dissociation argument that Joash's actions did not include the removal of the high places, local sacrificial centers. By dissociating Joash from a particular standard of kingship, it limits his goodness with specific regard for the centralization of worship practices. But it also reminds the audience that no simplistic view of the situation in Judah during Joash's reign as the narrative tells it is warranted. Hauser has described a 'rhetorical situation' as a set of circumstances 'that present problems that can be resolved meaningfully through the use of speech and writing'.[71] In particular, a rhetorical situation is almost always a complex blend of factors—'people, objects, events, relations and thoughts'—and so contains 'multiple features'.[72] With the notice in v. 4, the author acknowledges the complexity of the situation involving Joash and the events and people of the story. Correspondingly, the moral evaluation is not based on a single, monolithic criterion. Joash was a legitimate king and did 'right', but people and events are complex and so judgments about them are also multi-faceted.

With these arguments about Joash's kingship—its legitimacy, its re-establishment of dynastic rule, its goodness within limitations—the author summarizes the reign of the king. This summary prepares the way for the reports that follow. Here a reference to the wider literary context of this chapter is helpful. Within the Deuteronomistic History the reports on the kings' reigns vary in length. One extreme is a brief passage which basically gives little more information than the standard regnal introduction and conclusion (for example, Jotham's reign in 2 Kgs 15.32-38). The other extreme would be represented by the long narratives about David or Solomon or Hezekiah. How much is reported and what is reported are part of the author's rhetorical techniques, the means which give an author's ideas presence and emphasis for an audience.[73]

70. Sternberg, *Poetics*, p. 480.
71. Hauser, *Rhetorical Theory*, p. 34.
72. Hauser, *Rhetorical Theory*, p. 33.
73. Perelman, *Realm*, p. 37.

For Joash, two reports follow the summary which add specification to his reign. A long and detailed report about financing for temple repair and a brief report regarding Hazael's invasion fill out the picture which the author gives for Joash. In that the author expands the picture of Joash beyond the standard regnal summaries, the reports give emphasis to the figure of Joash in the larger history. And the details of the reports become a part of the rhetoric about Joash, so that the audience's views are shaped by what is reported in ways that expand, confirm or comment on the arguments in the summaries.

Scene 2: 2 Kings 12.5-6
Scene 2 begins the persuasion about Joash's reign to which the author wants to seek the audience's adherence. The entire section on the financing of temple repair, covering three scenes, works together to create a series of arguments about the status of the temple, the king's concern for the temple, and the establishment of a system that survives the test of time. It will be evident that although these incidents are part of the narrative section in Joash's reign, they refer to realities and actions transcending the particulars of his time.

The first scene (vv. 5-6) begins the presentation of Joash and his focus of energy on the House of Yahweh. By selecting this concern for narration, the author shapes the reader's picture of Joash—here is a king who is concerned for the temple. Little else may be related about his reign, but the emphasis on the temple is clearly presented. Such a selection points to the importance the author gives to the topic.[74] Joash's knowledge about and authority over the temple, its personnel and its finances help to structure the rhetorical point that Joash is a king who is directly involved in the administration and care of the state sanctuary.

An emphasis on detail and specification occupies much of the first scene. Joash gives details about which monies are to be used from the funds available to the temple. The parameters of the king's concern for the repair of the deterioration of the House are wide—everything which is in a state of disrepair is to be attended to (v. 6b). Any accumulation of detail is a technique for emphasis used by a rhetor.[75] Amplification is a basic type of argument, used in even the most primitive rhetoric.[76] In

74. Perelman, *Realm*, p. 35.
75. Perelman, *Realm*, p. 37.
76. Katz, *Ancient Arguments*, p. 8.

this way, the narrative shows the solicitous concern of the king for the House of Yahweh.

That the temple is the focus of the concern is also a significant part of the arguments made. The temple stands as a powerful symbolic reality, invoking a realm of religious meaning far larger than its physical presence. The care for the temple that Joash shows presents an argument based on the structure of reality, in which a symbolic liaison evokes the connection between the symbol and all that it stands for in 'reality'.[77] Joash is thus the king who is a decisive and willing adherent and servant of that reality.

Scene 3: 2 Kings 12.7-9

The narrative complication that opens this scene, the failure by the priests to carry out the king's plan, introduces a rhetorical complication as well. The complication works to affect the presentation of both the priests and the king. But the overall effect of the scene continues and reinforces the arguments begun in scene 2 by refocusing attention on the king and the temple.

Sternberg has discussed the rhetorical impact of a technique in which expected patterns are broken. Manipulation of and discontinuity in conventional patterns shape response to events and characters.[78] When the conventional pattern of command–enactment is not fulfilled in vv. 7-8 of this scene, rhetorical interest is focused on the failure by the priests. However, there is no speculation narratively or rhetorically about the cause of the failure. The expected enactment of the king's instructions by the priests is simply met with their inaction. Within the gap caused by the broken command–enactment pattern an implication of priestly negligence, ineptitude or resistance emerges. But neither the narrative nor the rhetorical movement of the scene focuses on the cause or evaluation of the failure.

Sternberg's analysis of rhetorical techniques is again helpful here. One method of rhetorical shaping is found in the play of perspectives in a narrative, where different points of view are reported from the standpoint of different characters or the narrator.[79] If the play of perspectives is examined in these verses, a picture of their rhetorical impact emerges.

In the previous scene, the point of view was exclusively the king's—

---

77. Perelman, *Realm*, p. 101.
78. Sternberg, *Poetics*, p. 479.
79. Sternberg, *Poetics*, p. 477.

only his words are reported and so only his concern for the temple, with its detail and specification, is emphasized. In v. 7, the point of view shifts to the narrator who reports about the priests' failure. In v. 8, the perspective shifts back to the king, who again states the failure in the form of a question. Never is the point of view of the priests given; the reader is never granted an inside view or anything from their perspective. Such a denial of an inside view does three things: (1) creates a gap which only inference about the priests' motivations can fill; (2) creates a complexity in evaluation and judgment of the priests and their actions; and (3) forces the reader to pay attention to the only perspective that is given—the king's.

When the king immediately follows his unanswered question with directions initiating a new plan, the perspective of the narrative stays with him. He directs, initiates, commands. The portrayal of the king from the previous scene as authoritative over the care of the temple is again shown. And a contrast is drawn to the priests. What the priests did not do, the king can and will do. If the first plan was not put into effect, then a second plan is needed and he is ready to put it into action.

Only in v. 9 does the point of view shift to the priests. But even here the shift serves to focus back on the king. The priests agree with the king, acquiescing on two points—they will have no part in taking the money from the people and no part in the repair of the House. An argument by dissociation is made in that the priests will no longer have a part in the maintenance of the temple. The momentum is clearly with the king and, in essence, the reader is given only the king's perspective on events. In this way the 'play of perspectives' is reduced to a singular view as the narrative focuses on the king.

In this scene, complexity has been added to the argumentation of the chapter. How to evaluate the priests' inaction is left open. But none of the arguments begun in the previous scene are negated by the complexity. The king's concern for the temple, and the temple as a powerful symbolic reality continue. In spite of the priests' failure, the king will go ahead.

Scene 4: 2 Kings 12.10-17
The institution of the king's second plan is successfully carried out in this long and detailed passage. Several types of persuasive techniques work to gain the audience's adherence to the author's expressed views about Joash and the temple. These arguments build on what has emerged in

the last two scenes, creating a rhetorical unit of the whole.

The most prominent technique for emphasis which is used in this passage is the repetition of a key phrase, בית יהוה, 'House of Yahweh'. In fact it will be useful to look at the whole temple repair narrative (vv. 5-16) for this technique of emphasis. In addition to the House, or the House of Yahweh, a number of terms are repeatedly associated with it in this passage. The key word 'House' or 'House of Yahweh' is used 18 times in 12 verses, echoing like a constant refrain throughout. Such repetition has helped create persuasion since the most primitive forms of rhetoric.[80]

The central concern of the king for the House of Yahweh is contained in a repeated phrase built from the terms חזק (to strengthen/repair), בדק (a breach/deterioration) and בית (House). Within the 12 verses, the full phrase 'to repair the deterioration of the House of Yahweh' (with minor variations in the tense of the verb) occurs five times (vv. 6, 7, 8, 9 and 13). In addition, a combination indicating the deterioration of the House (בדק and בית) occurs twice (vv. 6 and 8). And twice a combination indicating the repair of the House (חזק and בית) is used (vv. 13 and 15). The funds to be used for the repair of the House and how they are to be collected and administered appear with the term 'House' six times in the passage (vv. 5 [twice], 10 [twice], 11, and 14). Finally, terms indicating the work done upon the House or those working on the House are used three times (vv. 12 [twice], and 14).

Behind all of this language centered on the House stands the king who by direct command and indirect presence (through Jehoiada in v. 10 and his secretary in v. 11) shows his abiding interest in the well-being of the temple. Such a constant repetition alone makes this passage's persuasive point present to the audience—the care and upkeep of the House of Yahweh is the narrative's and the king's primary focus.

If repetition is not enough to convince the reader, the technique of detail brings to the foreground the king's concern for the care of the temple. Sternberg delineates the rhetorical use of detail: 'In a highly selective and functional discourse, there is little room for excess; and therefore informational superfluity launches a search for coherence in other terms, evaluative for example'.[81] Perelman would make the point by saying that giving details through amplification or aggregation increases the 'presence' of the elements detailed in the consciousness of

---

80. Katz, *Ancient Arguments*, p. 11.

81. Sternberg, *Poetics*, p. 477.

the audience. 'Only by dwelling upon a subject does one create the desired emotions.'[82]

The details in this passage which underscore the importance of the care for the temple include the types of funds used and the system for collection and distribution of the funds (vv. 5-6, 10-13) and the types of work, workers and materials used upon the House (vv. 12-13). The description of the workers' honesty (v. 16) adds detail to the working out of the plan. It also serves as a direct evaluative statement by the narrator who thus authoritatively commends the trustworthiness of the participants.

Details can increase opportunity for analogical patterning on a small scale. Such a kind of mini-analogy is found in the word used for the collection box, ארון , with its echoes of the ark of the covenant. The details of the workers and materials contain some terms also used in the description of the work and materials Solomon used to build the temple (1 Kgs 5.29-32). Exact or close parallels between terms in that passage and this text are: the 'stone-cutters' (חצב) in 1 Kgs 5.29 and v. 13; the 'ones doing the work' (מלאכה and עשׂא) in 1 Kgs 5.30 and vv. 12, 15; the 'dressed' or 'hewn' stones (אבני גזית) in 1 Kgs 5.31 and (אבני מחצב) in v. 13; the 'builders' (בנים) in 1 Kgs 5.32 and v. 12; and the combination of 'wood' and 'stone' as supplies (עצים, אבנים) in 1 Kgs 5.32 and v. 13.

The force of the repetition and detail is such that most of what we are told about King Joash's reign has to do with his care for the House of Yahweh. By creating this picture of the king, the author develops an analogy to the king whose main achievement was the building of the temple itself: Solomon.[83] The analogical patterning is broad in scope—Joash's persistent and detailed concern for the repair of the temple broadly echoes Solomon's persistent and detailed concern for the construction of the temple.

Besides presenting a picture of Joash's immediate concern for the temple, the narrative makes a rhetorical point that his actions toward the temple stand the test of time. With the switch to the iterative mode, the king's plan for financing and carrying out the repair of the temple transcends his reign and extends into the future. The switch also marks a displacement of the conventional pattern of narrating a king's reign in the preterite mode. Such a displacement draws the audience's attention to the change—here is something that should be noted about Joash's

82. Perelman, *Realm*, p. 37.
83. Long, *2 Kings*, p. 158.

plan. And when the iterative mode is used, an argument is made, to use Perelman's phrase, that establishes a 'structure of reality'. Based on Joash's plan, the maintenance of the temple is established as an activity that transcends routine time and becomes a part of 'how things are always done'.

The longevity and establishment of the plan as a reality extending beyond Joash's reign are clearly realized when the extensive parallel to this passage in Josiah's reign is considered. In 2 Kgs 22.3-10, there is a narrative which opens Josiah's reign where he sends his secretary to the temple to oversee the collected repair funds. The larger narrative movement of the passage involves the finding of a book of the law which then launches Josiah's reforms. But interest here is centered on the verbatim parallels to the description of Joash's financing and repair plan.

The parallels cover major elements of Joash's plan. They include: the description of the king's secretary and the priest counting the money which had been brought into the House of Yahweh and collected by the ones keeping the threshold (12.10-11; 22.3-4); the giving of the money into the hand of the workers who oversee the House of Yahweh, who use it for the carpenters, builders and masons, and for the wood and stones (12.12-13; 22.5-6); and the lack of accounting for the money because the workers are working with faithfulness (12.16; 22.7).

Josiah's speech thus repeats with almost verbatim accuracy the particulars of Joash's plan. What happens rhetorically when this second narrative of the temple repair is considered is dramatic. In the ongoing narrative of the Deuteronomistic History, Josiah's speech echoes Joash's plan some 200 years after the initial institution of the system. This creates the impression that things had been done this way throughout two centuries. It evokes an image of Joash's farsightedness and administrative competence in setting up such a system. It ties Joash's reign directly into Josiah's. It reiterates the close connection between the king and the temple with the king as the temple's guardian and caretaker. It reinforces the narrator's evaluation of Joash as a 'good' king because his system is also used without question by the undeniably good king Josiah.

Rhetorically, Joash functions as a model for Josiah.[84] This kind of argument appeals to a structure of reality already established and invokes it in a new context. Perelman notes, 'But not just any action is

84. Katz, *Ancient Arguments*, p. 88.

worth imitating; people imitate only those they admire, who have authority or social prestige because of their competence, their functions and their place in society'.[85] The structure of reality appealed to is Joash's plan for the temple which the iterative mode establishes as timeless; Joash is still a model worth imitating 200 years later.

By the end of this section of narrative (vv. 5-17) covering three scenes, a definitive picture of a major concern of Joash's reign emerges. The king who does right in the eyes of the Lord (v. 3) cares for the House of Yahweh with unswerving devotion and administrative farsightedness. The symbolic power of the temple is aligned with Joash. His care for it, like Solomon's, merits attention and approval. However, the reality portrayed is complex, as is seen by the inaction of the priests that had derailed the first plan. Even good kings must deal with unexpected turns of events and forces seemingly beyond their control. But the powers clearly in their control allow them to confront the complexity of situations. The second, successful plan endures and becomes a model for a future king.

Scene 5: 2 Kings 12.18-19

The account of Hazael's conquering of Gath, the threat to Jerusalem, and Joash's response plays a secondary rhetorical role in the account of Joash's reign. But when considered from the overall ideological perspective of the Deuteronomistic History the account's importance is amplified. This dual, complementary impact will thus be covered in both this and the next chapter.

In terms of rhetorical technique, vv. 18-19 contain a very simple, straightforward telling of Hazael's invasion and Joash's buying off of the threat by giving Hazael the treasures of Judah. Its rhetorical status in the portrayal of Joash's reign is secondary to the temple report. It is far more brief, written in an annalistic style, with little overt shaping to indicate the author's evaluative comment. Its argumentative importance, however relative, is signaled by three aspects. First, its inclusion as one of only two elements in Joash's reign certainly puts it in the realm of the author's concern. Secondly, the accumulation of detail in the listing of the treasures given to Hazael (v. 19) shows a certain emphasis. Thirdly, as Sternberg notes, a drastic act can serve as an evaluative vehicle.[86] Here the loss of the state's wealth to placate an aggressor is in itself a

---

85. Perelman, *Realm*, p. 110.
86. Sternberg, *Poetics*, p. 476.

shocking turn of events. This is balanced by the result of the king's action: Jerusalem is saved from incursion.

While the account is significant enough to warrant inclusion and some emphasis, it is not shaped to add extensive persuasion about Joash. Its main rhetorical point in the Joash narrative as a whole is to signal the complexity of the rhetorical situation. A persuasive description of Joash and his kingship evidently could not only focus on the good king who cares for the temple. The realities of international power politics intrude into the portrayal of the king (which of course may reflect historical veracity, but that is not the focus here). The king saves Jerusalem from invasion, a commendable action, but at the expense of the kingdom's wealth. The rhetor's awareness and inclusion of complexity and ambiguity in the reporting of the king's reign signifies a willingness to let the audience draw equally nuanced conclusions about Joash.

The passage's rhetorical power is extended when it is considered within the larger Deuteronomistic History, however. Analogies are drawn between the actions of a number of Judean kings concerning the state treasuries of Judah. A kind of 'history of Judah's treasuries' is woven throughout the stories of the kings' reigns, establishing a pattern of building up or losing the wealth of the House of Yahweh and the house of the king.

The relevant passages include: Solomon puts David's dedicated objects into the treasuries of the temple (1 Kgs 7.51); Rehoboam loses the treasures to Shishak of Egypt (1 Kgs 14.26); Asa brings his fathers' and his own gifts into the temple but then uses them to buy Aram's help against Israel (1 Kgs 15.15, 18); the treasuries build up again under Jehoshaphat, Jehoram and Ahaziah but Joash uses them to placate Hazael (2 Kgs 12.19); Amaziah of Judah is defeated by Jehoash of Israel and loses the treasuries (2 Kgs 14.14); Ahaz uses the treasuries to buy Assyria's help against Damascus (2 Kgs 16.8); Hezekiah gives a tribute of the the treasures to Sennacherib of Assyria (2 Kgs 18.15); and finally Nebuchadnezzar carries off all the treasures of the temple and palace (2 Kgs 24.13). This consistent reporting on the treasuries draws Joash into an extended rhetorical argument covering a number of kings which is heavily dependent on the ideological perspective of the writer.

So Joash, like a whole series of other kings, is caught in the complexities of international politics which involve the wealth of the temple and palace as a bargaining chip or spoil of war. What appears to be a brief note about Joash's salvaging of a bad military situation by using the treasuries as a tribute contains the outlines of an extended rhetorical/ideological pattern. For the moment, however, Joash has averted a threat to Jerusalem at the expense of four generations' worth of state treasures.

Scene 6: 2 Kings 12.20-22
The final scene is rhetorically structured to confirm the arguments of both chs. 11 and 12. A negative note is sounded in the report of Joash's assassination, but the disapproval redounds more to the portrayal of the assassins than the king. Joash himself is given a final authoritative summary as a legitimate Davidide.

The report of the conspiracy is handled in a direct style. The details of the assassins' names and the place of death mark off the report for emphasis. But the rhetoric involved seems to cast the whole act in a negative light. Again a drastic act speaks for itself—this is regicide, and that alone, particularly the killing of one who sits upon the throne of David, invites condemnation.

But the account uses other techniques to shape response as well. The choice of loaded language, especially its repetition, 'they conspired a conspiracy', underscores the narrator's reliable negative evaluation of the act. Echoes from the Athaliah story support this evaluation. The servants arise (קום) and conspire just as Athaliah arises (קום) and destroys (11.1); both times a precipitous, violent act against the Davidic line is perpetrated. Athaliah cries 'conspiracy!' (11.14) although she herself is the one guilty of such and dies for it. These men conspire against the one who had been brought to the throne by covenant (ברית in 11.4 and 11.17). This killing of Joash the king of Judah merits no explanation as to motive. What in a narrative analysis can appear as a gap—the lack of stated motivation for the act—in a rhetorical analysis functions as a negative evaluative comment. This despicable action is not worthy of explanation, only a portrayal that persuades the reader to condemn the act. The negative judgment on the action is confirmed in the story of Joash's successor Amaziah, when he puts to death the servants who murdered his father (2 Kgs 14.5).

However, the reporting of the assassination in the narrative structure may also make a rhetorical point that affects the evaluation of Joash's reign. In a paratactic narrative style, even a 'normal' chronological ordering of events can shape response or at least raise questions that influence the audience.[87] The juxtaposition of the passage about the loss of the treasuries with the report of Joash's assassination raises possibilities of relatedness between the events. But the narrative does not endorse any one theory about why Joash was killed and so a gap is created that remains unfilled. The ambiguity has 'implications for theme and judgement',[88] which can be better understood only within the extended ideological pattern noted in the previous scene.

The rest of the scene conveys a message about Joash quite in line with the two chapters about his reign. Verses 20 and 22 contain the elements of the standard regnal closing used by the writer for the kings of Israel and Judah. Three typical elements are all included here: (1) a citation formula alluding to a source of information, 'the book of the annals of the kings of Judah'; (2) a notice of death and burial: Joash dies and is 'buried with his ancestors in the city of David'; and (3) a succession notice: Amaziah 'his son became king after him'.[89]

The presence of the full formula makes an argument by analogy. Like the other legitimate kings of Judah, Joash deserves the inclusion of the usual notice of the end of his reign. But details in the notice make arguments as well. The citation of the book of the annals of the kings presents an argument by authority. The full validity of royal annals stands behind this report by the writer and appeals to the reader to take the report as trustworthy. The notice that Joash is buried with his ancestors in the city of David makes a double case for Joash's legitimacy—his ancestors were Davidides and he, like them, deserves to be buried in David's royal city.

The arguments in the two chapters have come full circle; the story of the king whose reign began in violence and doubt ends with the solid confirmation of legitimacy given by the regnal closing formula. Joash dies by an act of despicable violence but the succession is assured and he is buried with his ancestors.

Summary

It is clear by the end of these two chapters that there has been a whole lot of arguing going on. What to narrative analysis is a well-told story is to rhetorical analysis a series of persuasive arguments that seek to shape

87. Sternberg, *Poetics*, p. 478.
88. Sternberg, *Poetics*, p. 248.
89. Long, *1 Kings*, p. 161.

the audience's perceptions of the events recounted. The same words that tell a story create impressions and make cases as to how the reader should view the story that is related.

Using a definition of rhetoric that recognized the symbolic and instrumental use of language, this analysis focused on the techniques that a writer uses to address a particular situation and persuade an audience about certain opinions or actions. The author thus presents 'theses' for the audience's adherence. In a story, these methods of argumentation are used in a narrative format that makes the story itself persuasive.

Broadly speaking, two types of argumentation have been traced in the detailed analysis of the text of 2 Kings 11–12. One set of techniques aims to establish associational arguments, in which the adherence an audience has to a set of premises is transferred to the theses or conclusions being argued. Another set of techniques creates dissociational arguments in which elements previously or possibly linked in the audience's traditions or perceptions are separated.[90]

Techniques used in the text studied here which create association between premises and the proposed theses are: arguments based on the structure of accepted reality in which authority or definition make a thesis defensible; arguments in which a structure of reality is established by the author and then used as an illustration or model; the use of symbolic liaisons which evoke powerful mythic or visionary realities; persuasion based on analogic patterning, on both extensive and detailed levels; the setting of a scene creating expectations and responses; and the use of associational clusters in which the juxtaposition and coordination of a number of terms indicates a desired conclusion. Techniques used which seek to produce a dissociation between ideas are: the pointed omission of expected forms; a play of perspectives that creates opposition; a lack of emphasis and attention which denotes the subject's lack of importance; the portrayal of a drastic, negative act which reduces support or sympathy; and the use of counter-analogy to induce negative evaluation.

Other rhetorical techniques were found that can be used to create either associational or dissociational arguments depending on the context and how they are used. Direct narratorial commentary, either with a positive or negative evaluation, is perhaps the most obvious form of rhetorical shaping. But other techniques include: the accumulation of detail, specification and repetition, which add emphasis to a point being

90. Perelman, *Realm*, p. 49.

made; the portrayal of a drastic act or the use of loaded terminology or charged dramatization which calls evaluative attention to an event or character; a play of perspectives or different points of view in the narrative which creates complexity, ambiguity or relative evaluation; the disruption of conventional patterns that draws attention to the change in a charged way; and the portrayal of the complexity of the rhetorical situation being addressed.

As we have seen, all of this argumentative persuasion in 2 Kings 11–12 seeks the audience's adherence to several interrelated theses concerning the reign of Joash. Athaliah represents an evil Omride intruder who interrupts the dynastic succession in Judah and can only be seen as a violent, illegitimate influence. Jehoiada's actions on behalf of the true king are not only commendable but thoroughly justified by Yahwistic and Davidic tradition and mores. Joash is the legitimate heir of the Davidic line, who has been authoritatively and correctly restored to the throne of his ancestors and invested with the concomitants of royal power. Further, Joash is a good king as seen by narratorial evaluation and by his solicitous care for the House of Yahweh. Even as a good king, however, he faces the complexities of evaluation in his failure to remove the high places and in the necessities of international politics.

In support of these theses or conclusions to which the narrator seeks adherence, a number of premises are used which help to construct the arguments. These premises are not argued for separately. Rather, they are used as 'givens' or 'assumptions' in the arguments in support of the theses. Thus, they stand as correlates to the main theses.

Such premises include a number of statements. The priest is a powerful, authoritative leader in Judah. The House of Yahweh stands as a central sacral location whose power extends to the far reaches of the nation. Both the priest and the House of Yahweh legitimately use their power in the service of the Davidic dynasty. The symbolism of temple and dynasty is potent and evocative. The House of Yahweh and true Davidic kingship leave no room for non-Yahwistic worship or power— Baal has no place in Jerusalem. Everyone supports the true Davidide and the restoration of the monarchy. The covenant is significant as a formative and politically potent expression of the bond between Yahweh, king and people. The founders of the dynasty, David and Solomon, still act as prime expressions of Yahweh-blessed dynastic power. Doing what is right in the eyes of the Lord merits positive evaluation. Solicitous concern for the well-being of the House of Yahweh is a central role for a good king. Competent administrative systems endure through time and make their founders models for others. Royal evaluations are based on multi-faceted realities which may make the evaluation complex. A good king rests with his ancestors.

Together, the main theses and the statements of the premises create a broad rhetorical structure in these two chapters. The rhetoric can be analyzed in itself as I have done here, but it also points beyond its rhetorical impact. The rhetorical structure has as its basis an appeal to an ideology centered on the concepts of temple, kingship, dynasty and covenant. And this ideology is rooted in and expressive of a social structure in which elites hold power and make decisions as representatives of the very religious and political structure they themselves inhabit. So, the rhetorical analysis of any text is incomplete without an equally thorough analysis of the larger circles that it is connected to—the ideological and social structures in which it stands and to which it appeals.

Chapter 4

IDEOLOGICAL ANALYSIS

The previous chapter has demonstrated the pervasive rhetorical impact of the Athaliah and Joash story, as evidenced in the various types of argumentation present in the narrative. The author has not only crafted a good story, but has also shaped it to make certain points in a persuasive way. Taking chs. 2 and 3 together, I have shown that both the narrative artistry and the rhetorical persuasion are intrinsic to the story and amenable to analysis with the aid of interpretive techniques appropriate to each.

But the rhetoric of the story points beyond the particular arguments made about such topics as the legitimacy of Joash or his care for the temple. As was clear at certain points in the last chapter, a rhetorical awareness leads directly to questions about the ideas the author works with. Since the story emphasizes particular opinions and viewpoints about topics such as kingship, temple, covenant and dynasty, a suspicion arises that these are not just included simply because the story happens to be about the king and the temple. A more deliberate shaping is evident and this raises questions about the role of these topics in the overall worldview expressed by the author. In other words, the story and its rhetoric are contained in a larger circle of ideas which are expressed in and through the narrative. How do dynasty, kingship, temple, covenant and so on fit in with the author's wider view of what is significant in recounting the stories presented in the Deuteronomistic History?

So a study of rhetoric opens up questions about what I will call 'ideology', the broader views and ideas on which the particular arguments of the author are based. In turning to an ideological analysis, the third perspective from which to view the story is brought to bear on 2 Kings 11–12. Such a study of ideology is necessary in order to understand the referents and context of the narrative's language and argumentation. A first step in the analysis should be to define what is meant by 'ideology' and 'worldview' and to explicate the particular assumptions I work from in approaching the story ideologically.

This approach of examining a text's main ideas is not by any means a novel way to deal with a biblical text. Biblical scholars have long discussed the ideas of the author(s) of various texts in detailing the theology of the texts. In some ways, a biblical theology, or at least a statement of a text's or book's religious ideas, was seen as the capstone of any analysis. Gerhard von Rad wrote his *Old Testament Theology* at the height of his illustrious scholarly career. In the preface to that work he spoke of the proper subject of an Old Testament theology from his perspective:

> The history of tradition... has shown how Israel was at all times occupied with the task of understanding her history from the point of view of certain interventions by God, and how what God had rooted in the history presented itself in different ways in every age.[1]

Von Rad was one among many to propose a view about Old Testament theology and theologies; the explication and description of ancient Israel's ideas about God, humanity, and their interactions have occupied many critics.

My use of 'ideology' rather than 'theology' signals a shift in perspective that is rooted in sociological disciplines. Ideological criticism of the Bible is itself a wide field often informed by Marxist analysis of social structures and dynamics.[2] However, I have found most useful an approach based in the sociology of knowledge and cultural anthropology. Basic to the perspective used here are the ideas expressed in Berger and Luckmann's work *The Social Construction of Reality*. In that book, they focus on the generation of 'knowledge' and thus 'reality' as constructs of the social interactions of human beings. They set out the basic concepts useful for understanding 'the processes by which *any* body of "knowledge" comes to be socially established *as* "reality"'.[3]

Berger and Luckmann describe the particular social order in which any person lives as a social product,[4] created by the ongoing processes of human beings externalizing and objectifying their shared social habits so that they stand over against them as institutions. The roles and

1. G. von Rad, *Old Testament Theology* (trans. D.M.G. Stalker; New York: Harper & Row, 1962), I, p. v.

2. See, for example, the various essays in D. Jobling and T. Pippin (eds.), *Ideological Criticism of Biblical Texts (Semeia* 59 [1992]).

3. Berger and Luckmann, *Social Construction of Reality*, p. 3.

4. Berger and Luckmann, *Social Construction of Reality*, p. 52.

expectations of these institutions are then internalized by the society's members through socialization as the 'knowledge' they need to inhabit the social order thus created.[5] A dialectical relationship is inherent in the process in which human beings produce a social world which in turn produces what the human beings involved understand as reality. Language is a significant force in this process in that it facilitates the objectification of social habits by constructing symbolic representations that transcend 'here and now' realities.[6] Berger and Luckmann summarize this:

> What is taken for granted as knowledge in the society comes to be coextensive with the knowable... Knowledge, in this sense, is at the heart of the fundamental dialectic of society. It 'programs' the channels in which externalization produces an objective world. It objectifies this world through language and the cognitive apparatus based on language, that is, it orders it into objects to be apprehended as reality. It is internalized again as objectively valid truth in the course of socialization.[7]

Before going on, I should indicate how this broad understanding of the social construction of reality informs my analysis. This idea stands as an assumption for me, a basic orientation with which I begin but which I neither attempt to prove nor debate. That is, I take for granted that the biblical author(s) dwelled in a socially constructed ideational 'world', created over time through the influence of the ancient Near Eastern contexts in which they lived and the particular events their communities experienced. This world of ideas was shaped by their communities and in turn shaped what they saw and knew as 'real'. This world formed their economic, social and political institutions, interpreted to them their day-to-day lives, informed their decisions, guided their actions, and engendered their language, literature and art. Religious ideas or 'theology' are certainly a part of this world but only one part integrated with a comprehensive view of life.

Berger and Luckmann go on to describe aspects of the social construction of reality that are useful for my analysis. One idea is that of the 'roles' given by institutions for various individuals to play in the society. The authors single out certain roles as especially important because they not only maintain a single institution, but also represent the larger reality and its integration as a whole. A monarch in particular plays such a

5. Berger and Luckmann, *Social Construction of Reality*, p. 61.
6. Berger and Luckmann, *Social Construction of Reality*, p. 39.
7. Berger and Luckmann, *Social Construction of Reality*, p. 66.

strategic role, representing 'the integration of all institutions in a meaningful world'.[8] Another significant aspect of reality in some societies is reification, by which institutions have bestowed on them 'an ontological status independent of human activity and signification'.[9] That a particular world is understood as created by a god is a reification of that reality.

The working out of social realities in human communities also involves the maintenance and passing on of the reality to new generations and possibly 'outsiders' or 'non-believers'. Thus legitimation is a key process whereby a reality is explained, justified and maintained.[10] Particular institutions, theories and roles may be developed to aid the legitimation which eventually may involve the creation of 'symbolic universes', 'bodies of theoretical tradition that integrate different provinces of meaning and encompass the institutional order in a symbolic totality'.[11] Symbolic universes overall provide order and completeness; anything that threatens the social order must be absorbed, explained away or eliminated. The relationship of the symbolic universe to particular institutions and roles and to societal precariousness is significant:

> the symbolic universe provides a comprehensive integration of all discrete institutional processes. The entire society now makes sense. Particular institutions and roles are legitimated by locating them in a comprehensively meaningful world... It is important, however, to understand that the institutional order... is continually threatened by the presence of realities that are meaningless in *its* terms. The legitimation of the institutional order is also faced with the ongoing necessity of keeping chaos at bay. *All* social reality is precarious. *All* societies are constructions in the face of chaos.[12]

Finally, Berger and Luckmann theorize about how a society also experiences conflict about the reality it inhabits when 'deviant versions' of the symbolic universe develop. Such a different view becomes 'the carrier of an alternative definition of reality'.[13] The emergence of alternative definitions of reality always leads to conflict of some sort as the 'official' version fights off any challenge that could undermine its integrative hegemony. And these conflicts always involve power struggles:

8.   Berger and Luckmann, *Social Construction of Reality*, p. 76.
9.   Berger and Luckmann, *Social Construction of Reality*, p. 90.
10. Berger and Luckmann, *Social Construction of Reality*, p. 93.
11. Berger and Luckmann, *Social Construction of Reality*, p. 95.
12. Berger and Luckmann, *Social Construction of Reality*, p. 103.
13. Berger and Luckmann, *Social Construction of Reality*, p. 107.

'The confrontation of alternative symbolic universes implies a problem of power—which of the conflicting definitions of reality will be "made to stick" in the society'.[14] This in turn involves real institutional interactions in which conflicts between definitions are played out in the social-structural base,[15] from the theoretical and literary battles of 'experts' to the flesh and blood battles of rulers and soldiers.

These further ideas of Berger and Luckmann also inform my basic orientation to an ideological analysis. Foremost, they provide the definition of 'ideology' (or alternatively 'worldview') which I shall use throughout. A particular definition of reality with its own symbolic universe and accompanying ideas about knowledge, institutions and roles is what I will call an 'ideology' or 'worldview'. This definition downplays the negative overtones of 'ideology' as a narrow, doctrinaire view of a marginal political group. But it maintains 'ideology' as a particularized and potentially conflictual version of 'reality' within a given society.

The ideas of Berger and Luckmann are reinforced and extended in the study of cultural anthropology by Clifford Geertz, particularly in his book *The Interpretation of Cultures*.[16] Additional insights helpful to understanding the importance of ideas or conceptual structures, particularly religion, in a society's culture will fill in this outline of my orientation. Geertz's description of 'culture' is similar to Berger and Luckmann's idea of a socially constructed reality, especially in a similar understanding of the role of language and symbolic formation. Geertz writes that culture

> denotes an historically transmitted pattern of meanings embodied in symbols, a system of inherited conceptions expressed in symbolic forms by means of which men communicate, perpetuate, and develop their knowledge about and attitudes toward life.[17]

In another essay he calls culture 'the fabric of meaning in terms of which human beings interpret their experience and guide their actions'.[18]

The expression of a culture in specific institutions and roles, in specific social structures and social relations, is also identified by Geertz. He

14. Berger and Luckmann, *Social Construction of Reality*, p. 109.
15. Berger and Luckmann, *Social Construction of Reality*, p. 120.
16. C. Geertz, *The Interpretation of Cultures* (New York: Basic Books, 1973).
17. Geertz, 'Religion as a Cultural System', in *Interpretation of Cultures*, p. 89.
18. Geertz, 'Ritual and Social Change: A Javanese Example', in *Interpretation of Cultures*, p. 145.

notes as well the relationship of conceptual structures to actual power relations in a society:

> Ideas—religious, moral, practical, aesthetic—must be carried by powerful social groups to have powerful social effects; someone must revere them, celebrate them, defend them, impose them. They have to be institutionalized in order to find not just an intellectual existence in society, but, so to speak, a material one as well.[19]

What is helpful about Geertz's conceptions as a complement to Berger and Luckmann is that 'culture' may be a more accessible idea than a 'social construction of reality'. It is easy to conceive of the context in which the ancient Israelites lived as a particular culture, complete with its own characteristic social order, institutions, ideas, power struggles, roles, art and so on. But the overtones of society as a comprehensive 'reality' given in Berger and Luckmann are also important and not inimical to the idea of culture as a 'world-defining' context. This conception would thus propose, for example, that while ancient Israelite culture defines a 'world' with elements similar to, say, the culture of ancient Egypt, the two were different 'realities' and thus had differing expressions in the lives of the people who inhabited them.

Geertz, in describing the task of the cultural anthropologist, also helps to express what I see as the goal of this chapter. Among other descriptions, he portrays an anthropologist's work as 'gaining access to the conceptual world in which our subjects live'[20] and uncovering 'the conceptual structures that inform our subjects' acts'.[21] In my study, I hope to gain access to the conceptual world of the author through an ideological analysis of the narrative.

Finally, because Geertz addresses religion as one of the specific cultural formations that shape human lives, his work is useful in understanding openly religious material such as that found in a biblical narrative. Because religion mediates realities wider or more lasting than everyday life, dealing with the realm of the 'really real'[22] through symbolic complexes, it is central to an understanding of any culture. Both the fundamental and symbolic qualities of religion are inherent in the paradigm Geertz uses to view religion in culture:

19. Geertz, 'The Politics of Meaning', in *Interpretation of Cultures*, p. 314.
20. Geertz, 'Thick Description: Toward an Interpretive Theory of Culture', in *Interpretation of Cultures*, p. 24.
21. Geertz, 'Thick Description', p. 27.
22. Geertz, 'Religion as a Cultural System', p. 112.

sacred symbols function to synthesize a people's ethos—the tone, character, and quality of their life, its moral and aesthetic style and mood—and their world view—the picture they have of the way things in sheer actuality are, their most comprehensive ideas of order. In religious belief and practice a group's ethos is rendered intellectually reasonable by being shown to represent a way of life ideally adapted to the actual state of affairs the world view describes, while the world view is rendered emotionally convincing by being presented as an image of an actual state of affairs peculiarly well-arranged to accommodate such a way of life.[23]

While sketching the theoretical bases for my analysis, it is important to recognize significant limitations of the scholars whose work I use. Geertz has been recognized as an important theoretician in the field of anthropology. However, the anthropologist Henry Munson, Jr, in a coherent critique of Geertz's work, shows how Geertz fails at times to carry through his own theoretical insights.[24] For example, Geertz theorizes about the impact of political realities on culture, yet ignores this impact in his descriptions of actual cultural forms.[25] In focusing on 'little stories' about and by the cultures he studies, Geertz misses their larger contexts of politics and power. His interpretations thus often illustrate 'the danger of trying to interpret specific events without adequate attention to the conceptual structures and historical contexts in which they are enmeshed'.[26]

Using Geertz for my analysis will necessitate several correctives to this shortcoming. First, I will emphasize those of his theoretical writings in which power and structural/contextual realities are acknowledged. Combining Berger and Luckmann's theory with Geertz's adds another balance because they clearly place individual 'stories' within larger political/ideological/power contexts. Finally, specific societal power structures that had an impact on the ideology of the Deuteronomistic History are detailed and discussed in the next chapter. In these ways, both 'conceptual structures' and 'historical contexts' will be adequately addressed in my analyses of 2 Kings 11–12.

With these correctives, the theories of Berger and Luckmann and Geertz formulate my basic orientation to the concepts of reality, world/culture, worldview/ideology, and religion. It should be clear that turning

23. Geertz, 'Religion as a Cultural System', pp. 89-90.
24. H. Munson, Jr, *Religion and Power in Morocco* (New Haven: Yale University Press, 1993).
25. Munson, *Religion and Power*, p. 183.
26. Munson, *Religion and Power*, p. 10.

to an ideological analysis once more involves a shift in perspective in approaching the text. Narrative analysis focuses on 'narrator' and 'reader'. Rhetorical analysis widens the circle to concentrate on an 'author' and an 'audience' and especially the deliberate communication of persuasive viewpoints from the former to the latter. In a sense, I now set the story in a wider yet still concentric circle in examining how it reflects the worldview of its author. An ideological analysis maintains a sense of author and audience and the text as communication. But now the perspective shifts to the ideational context, the world, in which both author and audience stand. The sharing of this world allows communication to happen—both author and audience generally 'speak the same language'. However, the author, as evidenced by rhetoric, seems to be attempting to persuade the audience about certain ideas about the world they share. What can be said about the conceptual structures on which the author evidently relies and to which the author tries to win the audience's adherence?

The ideological analysis which follows will be largely descriptive. I want to draw together the evident rhetorical indications into a more systematic description of the various ideas that seem important, always basing the description in what the story says. Again, my theoretical point is that this ideology is intrinsic to the narrative itself. However, because the story is a part of the Deuteronomistic History, it will be appropriate and necessary to set the story and its ideology within that wider context. Tracing the important ideological themes present within the Deuteronomistic History will thus fill out the ideas and concepts used by the author.

My task is not to give an overview of Deuteronomistic ideology, nor to trace every mention of 'kingship' or 'covenant' within the History. Either of those tasks, while significant, is far larger than one chapter's work. Rather, I want to show how the concepts work *in this story*, with reference to enough of the larger Deuteronomistic History to see their import here. For the identification and explication of these themes in the Deuteronomistic History, I will draw selectively on the numerous studies done by scholars on various aspects of Deuteronomistic ideology and theology. Likewise, many of the topics can be usefully set into the context of other ancient Near Eastern cultures. Some references which indicate the importance or function of the ideas in these cultures will be given, always with the focus on how such references aid in understanding the narrative studied here. Because the particular ideas I highlight span the verses and scenes of the story, I shall arrange the chapter topically.

Athaliah and the Omride Dynasty

The characteristics of Athaliah as both an evil Omride princess and illegitimate ruler are portrayed narratively and rhetorically in the opening verses of 2 Kings 11 and in the regnal formulas for Jehoram and Ahaziah (2 Kgs 8.18, 27). Thus with Athaliah one aspect of the Deuteronomistic worldview comes into play.

Athaliah's birth origin in Israel in the House of Ahab links her to a nation and dynasty that are resoundingly condemned in the wider Deuteronomistic History. The thoroughgoing negative evaluation of the kings of Israel and especially the Omride dynasty is most easily seen in the regnal formulas for the northern kings, which, regardless of original source,[27] are used in the Deuteronomistic History to condemn these kings. The Israelite kings from beginning to end all do evil in the sight of Yahweh and cause Israel to sin. Their collective shortcoming lies in their following in the paradigmatic sin of Jeroboam—cultic impurity in establishing the cult places at Bethel and Dan and installing calf images on the altars (1 Kgs 12.28-30).[28] This sin reverberates throughout the history of the northern kingdom until it finally becomes the reason for its destruction at the hands of Assyria (2 Kgs 17.21-23).

Within this conception of the evil of the northern kings, the Omride dynasty is selected for special condemnation. Both Omri, the dynasty's founder, and his infamous son, Ahab, not only each do evil but do 'more evil than all who were before him' (1 Kgs 16.25, 30). In particular, Ahab multiplies his sin and thus condemnation by taking a foreign wife, Jezebel, and serving Baal (1 Kgs 16.31). So on top of perpetuating Jeroboam's cultic impropriety, Ahab adds the sins of idolatry and worship of other gods.

The evil of Athaliah's nation and family does not go unchallenged, however, in the schema of the history. At key points in the story, a prophet is sent to certain northern kings to deliver Yahweh's word of law and judgment. This second theme, the 'demand for obedience to the

27. See the useful study, 'Patterns and Texts I', in A.F. Campbell, SJ, *Of Prophets and Kings: A Late Ninth Century Document* (CBQMS, 17; Washington, DC: Catholic Biblical Association, 1986), pp. 139-68.
28. Cross, 'The Themes of the Book of Kings', p. 279.

divine command',[29] complements the theme of evil by showing how these kings not only did evil but continuously ignored the direct 'cease and desist' order of the Lord demanding an end to the unsanctioned altars, idolatrous worship and false images.

The theme of prophetic condemnation begins with Ahijah's prophecy against Jeroboam for his cultic innovations (1 Kgs 13.33-34; 14.15-16). Jeroboam's line is destroyed in accordance with this prophecy (1 Kgs 15.29-30). The founder of the next house, Baasha, does no better and fares no better in the eyes of the prophet Jehu (1 Kgs 16.2-3). Ahab comes in for condemnation from his nemesis, Elijah (1 Kgs 18.18). This prophetic censure culminates in the word that this dynasty in Israel will likewise be destroyed (1 Kgs 21.21-22). This word is repeated through Elisha (2 Kgs 9.1, 7) and is finally accomplished in Jehu's revolution so that no one is left of Ahab's house (2 Kgs 10.10, 17).

When Athaliah enters the picture as an active character in ch. 11, she is the only surviving Omride. However, according to the shaping of the larger narrative of evil northern dynasties and their prophets, she stands under the general condemnation order against the House of Ahab. Thus even though there is no prophet as a character in ch. 11, the prophetic word given by Elijah is still current and plays itself out in Athaliah's death. She participates in the evil of her house and carries it into Judah with her marriage; but she cannot escape the prophetically foretold destruction of her family.

Further, the shaping of Athaliah's character by analogical patterning reveals a bias against foreign women, especially within the royal family—queens and queen mothers—which shows up in the larger History. The typology of the foreign queen as a negative character type has been studied with reference to such women as Jezebel and Maacah—Athaliah's analogues.[30] The description of Solomon's foreign wives and how they turned his heart to follow other gods (1 Kgs 11.1-10) expresses directly the idea of the danger of the foreign woman and gives the conceptual background of the author's aversion. While Athaliah's portrayal does not completely fit the type of 'foreign

29. W.E. Lemke, 'The Way of Obedience: I Kings 13 and the Structure of the Deuteronomistic History', in F.M. Cross, W.E. Lemke, and P.D. Miller, Jr (eds.), *Magnalia Dei* (Garden City, NY: Doubleday, 1976), p. 312.

30. A. Brenner, *The Israelite Woman: Social Role and Literary Type in Biblical Narrative* (Sheffield: JSOT Press, 1985), pp. 17-32.

woman',[31] the inferences and innuendos created by the analogical patterns shape the audience's perception and point to the larger bias. Neither by birth origin (foreign) nor gender (female) nor religious sentiment (intimation of her connection with the Baal temple in Jerusalem) is Athaliah permitted to assume the throne in Judah.

The Deuteronomistic ideology that stands behind and shapes this characterization of Athaliah provides a pre-eminent example of the androcentric perspective in biblical texts. Cheryl Exum, among many other scholars, has studied such 'gender ideology...in order to reveal strategies by which patriarchal literature excludes, marginalizes and otherwise operates to subjugate women'.[32] Regardless of the 'historical' Athaliah's actions or motives, she is cast by the worldview of the Deuteronomist to fit ideas of evil, danger and illegitimate power—all of which are inherent in her status as foreign, female and apostate. The rhetorical shaping detailed in the last chapter gives a case study in how patriarchal ideology can influence narrative strategies and thus audience opinion. Strategies such as explicit moral censure, guilt by association, and analogic patterns allow the male author of the text to deny legitimacy, authority or credibility to the female character. What is particularly striking in Athaliah's case is the use of multiple condemnations (foreign, female, apostate) which create integrated and mutually reinforcing negative judgments. It is telling that Jezebel, Athaliah's kinswoman and closest northern analogue, is subject to similar multiple condemnations.

This analysis of Athaliah has identified the conceptions about her and the Omride family which form the source for the rhetorical structuring studied in the previous chapter. I have not tried to develop any original or comprehensive reading of the Deuteronomistic portrayal of the northern kings or foreign women. Rather, I have reported the concepts that are evident in texts from the Deuteronomistic History as scholars have identified them. Athaliah as a narrative character and rhetorical vehicle is a 'window' through which to view this ideological conception.

Evident in the Deuteronomistic author's reality is a strongly held and expressed ideology which condemns all of the dynasties of the northern kingdom, with special attention to the House of Ahab and particular focus on the women of the royal house. Insights from Berger and

31. L.S. Schearing, 'Models, Monarchs and Misconceptions', p. 115.
32. J.C. Exum, *Fragmented Women: Feminist (Sub)versions of Biblical Narratives* (JSOTSup, 163; Sheffield: JSOT Press, 1993), p. 9.

Luckmann aid in understanding the function of this ideology. This characterization of the northern kingdom in the History can be understood as a weapon in the fight against the 'heresy' the north represented—the alternative definition of reality which could possibly undermine the official reality. Such a heresy must be combated by dominant institutions using various repressive procedures.[33] The particular weapon in use here is that of nihilation, by which 'the threat to the social definitions of reality is neutralized by assigning an inferior ontological status...to all definitions existing outside the symbolic universe'.[34] In the worldview of the Deuteronomist, the northern kingdom through its kings destroyed any hope it had for a Yahweh-blessed status and continuously and unfailingly embraced evil. Thus its direct incursion into Judah's monarchic line through Athaliah had to be and was delegitimated and condemned in the strongest possible terms.

Temple and Priest

The next topics which need attention from an ideological perspective are those of the temple and the priest or priests. In both cases, only a brief summary of a very large field of research can be offered, focusing on the ideology of each term and bypassing many significant questions of the history, practices and textual traditions surrounding both terms.

In both the narrative and rhetorical analyses, the temple played a central role as the setting for the action in ch. 11 and as the object of the king's attention in ch. 12. The marked repetition of the phrase 'the House of Yahweh' in both chapters signals the importance of the temple in the rhetorical arguments, and thus in the ideology behind the rhetoric. The statements made and the assumptions used about the temple clearly point to the larger worldview, the ideology, which the author attempts to communicate to the audience. A description of the idea of the temple reflecting its more general representation in Deuteronomistic thought and its ancient Near Eastern context will aid in understanding how it blends with other ideological concepts in 2 Kings 11–12.

The best place to start in understanding the ideology of the temple is a brief review of the place of the temple in the cultures of the ancient Near East, particularly Mesopotamia and Syria/Palestine. This can then be

---

33. Berger and Luckmann, *Social Construction of Reality*, p. 107.
34. Berger and Luckmann, *Social Construction of Reality*, p. 115.

related to the view of the temple in the Deuteronomistic ideology, especially as expressed in the narrative of Solomon's building and dedication of the temple in 1 Kings 5–9. Ancient temple ideology in the Mesopotamian region must be understood within a complex of related ideas central to the basic premise of human society constituted as a reflection of the divine realm, with the unpredictable involvement of the divine beings. The human realities, that is, the king's realm and his palace and the temple in the capital city, were a microcosmic expression of the divine order and thus subject to its direction through the power of the city's god. G.W. Ahlström explains these basic connections:

> The cosmological aspect of the city has its roots in the idea of the city as the abode of the god, the ruler of cosmos and nation. Because the temple, as the visible expression of his domain, was, at the same time, the king's property, the capital was the ruling center of both the god and his vice regent, the king. Therefore, temple and palace should be seen as two aspects of the same phenomenon: together they constituted the essence of the state.[35]

The temple played a central role as the dwelling place of the god who established and guarded the city and state. The temple's existence and dominance in turn expressed the security and power of the state and its king. 'Temples were the structures par excellence for communicating to a wide audience the authoritative rule of the regime responsible for erecting them.'[36] As the link between the god and the human realm, the temple's well-being was linked to the well-being of the nation. 'The house in which the god lived was maintained and provided for in due form in order to secure for the city the prosperity and happiness which the god's presence was taken to guarantee.'[37] This crucial link to the king meant that temple building and maintenance were the king's responsibility and privilege. 'The relationship between the king and the gods is well illustrated by the ceremonies connected with the erection or restoration of temples. No greater service could be rendered to a god than the building of his house.'[38]

35. Ahlström, *Royal Administration and National Religion*, p. 3.

36. C. Meyers, 'David as Temple Builder', in P.D. Miller, Jr, P.D. Hanson and S.D. McBride (eds.), *Ancient Israelite Religion: Essays in Honor of Frank Moore Cross* (Philadelphia: Fortress Press, 1987), p. 364.

37. A.L. Oppenheim, *Ancient Mesopotamia: Portrait of a Dead Civilization* (Chicago: University of Chicago Press, 1964), p. 108.

38. H. Frankfort, *Kingship and the Gods: A Study of Ancient Near Eastern*

Moshe Weinfeld lists other aspects of the ideology of the temple city in Mesopotamian thought. These included the idea that the temple stood in the most exalted place in the realm, physically some great mountain where possible, and was conceptually the center of heaven and earth.[39] The temple city as the god's dwelling is 'shrouded in splendor and brilliance',[40] richly and ornately expressive of the god's awesome presence. To this center of divine awe, the nations come in worship and bring tribute and gifts befitting the great sanctuary.[41] From this location of divine dwelling, righteousness and justice are said to emanate and to overcome the forces of oppression and evil in the land.[42]

Against this background, Hurowitz describes and details the elements of temple-building narratives in Mesopotamian and Northwest Semitic writings. By cataloging and discussing the elements of more than 20 extrabiblical temple-building accounts, he is able to show not only that building activities are a prevalent theme in the writings of Western Asia,[43] but also that they follow a predictable literary pattern.[44] He then makes a detailed comparison of this traditional literary form and Solomon's temple narrative in 1 Kgs 5.15–9.25. He finds that Solomon's account has striking similarities to the general pattern and in particular to elements of accounts from the Assyrian period.[45] Variations in the literary pieces that go into the account in Kings show, however, that literary conventions from other possible sources (trade letters, administrative receipts) influenced the biblical account. The developing narrative was also shaped by the particular history and theology of the Deuteronomistic author.[46]

The ideology of the temple in the Deuteronomistic worldview reflects

Religion as the Integration of Society and Nature (Chicago: University of Chicago Press, 1948), p. 267.

39. M. Weinfeld, 'Zion and Jerusalem as Religious and Political Capital: Ideology and Utopia', in R.E. Friedman (ed.), *The Poet and the Historian: Essays in Literary and Historical Biblical Criticism* (Chico, CA: Scholars Press, 1983), p. 106.

40. Weinfeld, 'Zion and Jerusalem', p. 114.

41. Weinfeld, 'Zion and Jerusalem', pp. 108-109.

42. Weinfeld, 'Zion and Jerusalem', p. 111.

43. V. Hurowitz, *I Have Built You an Exalted House: Temple Building in Light of Mesopotamian and Northwest Semitic Writings* (JSOTSup, 115; Sheffield: JSOT Press, 1992). p. 18.

44. Hurowitz, *Exalted House*, p. 128.

45. Hurowitz, *Exalted House*, p. 314.

46. Hurowitz, *Exalted House*, p. 316.

this general Near Eastern background. The conception of the temple as the essence of the god's rule and power, in glory and splendor in the city and state, lies behind the whole Deuteronomistic idea of the House of Yahweh. Both the physical presence of the temple itself as visual communication and the narratives about the temple as verbal communication set forth the powerful symbolism of the sanctuary.[47] This temple is the unimpeachable symbol of Yahweh's divine favor.

But the conception of the temple in the Deuteronomistic worldview is more specific as well. Near Eastern thought conceived of the temple as the dwelling of the god. The temple in Deuteronomistic ideology includes but modifies this idea. The Deuteronomistic scheme excluded the idea that Yahweh actually dwelt in the temple. Rather, the sanctuary is the place Yahweh chooses so that his name will dwell there. 'There is not one example in the deuteronomic literature of *God's dwelling* in the temple or the building of a house *for God*. The temple is always the *dwelling of his name*, and the house is always built *for his name*.'[48] This is evident throughout the narrative of temple building. Solomon, early in his dedication oratory, five times identifies the temple as the house for the name of Yahweh (1 Kgs 8.15-20). When Yahweh confirms the consecration of the temple, he appears to Solomon and states that he has put his name there forever (1 Kgs 9.3).

This is the ideological grounding of the temple as the most sacred locus of Yahwistic power and prestige, the location of Yahweh's name replete with all the expected majesty of the god's earthly manifestation. When the narrative of Athaliah's overthrow appeals to the symbolism of the temple as a sacrosanct space, it reflects these notions. When Jehoiada commands the power of the temple as a site for his conspiracy and the king's coronation, he relies on the temple's awesome and unassailable representation of Yahweh's divine will.

A second specific correlation between Near Eastern thinking about temples and the Deuteronomistic temple evokes notions of law and covenant. As temples generally are associated with the rule of righteousness and justice, so the temple-building narratives directly gather in a conception of Yahweh's covenant with the people which issues in commands, ordinances and statutes. As Solomon is building the house, God speaks to tie the building of the temple directly into the covenant:

47. Meyers, 'David as Temple Builder', p. 362.
48. M. Weinfeld, *Deuteronomy and the Deuteronomic School* (repr.; Winona Lake, IN: Eisenbrauns, 1992 [Oxford: Clarendon Press, 1972]), p. 193.

> Concerning this house that you are building, if you will walk in my
> statutes, obey my ordinances, and keep all my commandments by walking
> in them, then I will establish my promise with you which I made to your
> father David. I will dwell among the children of Israel and will not forsake
> my people Israel (1 Kgs 6.12-13 NRSV).

This very aspect of the temple's connection with covenant and law is
found in the Athaliah story. Standing in the temple after the king is
crowned and Athaliah is dead, Jehoiada makes 'the covenant between
the Lord and the king and the people, to be the people of the Lord'
(2 Kgs 11.17). Here the temple acts as a guarantor of the covenant,
lending its Yahwistic certitude through the mutual association of God's
sanctuary and God's pact with the people. (The ideology of the
covenant also lends other ideological underpinnings to the Joash
narrative which will be covered in the next section).

A third aspect of temple ideology emerges as central to the
Deuteronomistic conception and its use in 2 Kings 11–12. Temple narratives in neighboring cultures, which form the wider context of the
Israelite temple, all reflect the close connection between the god and the
king visible in the temple. The temple symbolizes the god's divine sanction for the king's rule. 'With the religious sphere existing as an integral
and critical aspect of political authority, divine sanction of a regime provided the ultimate and incontrovertible justification for its coercive
power.'[49]

In the worldview held by the Deuteronomistic school, the temple connotes this aspect of royal ideology because the establishment of the
temple is a concomitant reality to the establishment of the Davidic
dynasty in the Deuteronomistic History. It is David's rule, and
Solomon's after him, and the rule of all their legitimate successors that
the Deuteronomistic Solomonic temple guarantees. This connection is
nowhere shown more clearly than in 2 Samuel 7. Regardless of the
probably complicated literary history of this passage,[50] juxtaposition of
temple and dynastic promise is prominent. McCarthy, in an influential
article, argued for the centrality of 2 Samuel 7 in the structure of the
Deuteronomistic History.[51] The chapter carries this weight because it

---

49. C. Meyers, 'David as Temple Builder', p. 362.

50. P.K. McCarter, Jr, *II Samuel* (AB, 9; Garden City, NY: Doubleday, 1984),
pp. 190-231.

51. D.J. McCarthy, SJ, 'II Samuel 7 and the Structure of the Deuteronomistic
History', *JBL* 84 (1965), pp. 131-38.

combines the significant idea of the temple as the proper center for worship with the destiny of David's royal line. 'In the deuteronomist's eyes, the very "constitution" of the kingship makes the proper worship of Yahweh the king's great duty and great glory.'[52] McCarter, following McCarthy, sees the same Deuteronomistic connection. He also notes that the temple–dynasty association has roots in the ideologies of Israel's neighbors:

> There was...an ancient and widely understood association between a king's erection of a temple to a particular god (or gods) and the hope for divine sanction of the continuing rule of the king and his descendants. In the present case we may speak of a connection between the establishment of a royal dynasty and the provision of a temple for the dynastic god. The common factor is permanence—the perpetuity of dynastic rule and the perdurability of a monumental temple.[53]

Ishida has studied the particular terminology in 2 Samuel 7 for its ideological meaning.[54] Four key words used in the chapter especially indicate the existence of a royal dynasty: *bayit*, 'house', *zeraʿ*, 'offspring', *kisseʾ*, 'throne', and *mamlakah*, 'kingdom'. By using these four terms consistently, the Deuteronomistic redaction of the chapter reveals 'the basic structure of the royal-dynastic ideology, in which a royal dynasty is established when the royal authority is succeeded by the same lineage'.[55] The connection between the promise of dynasty and the building of the temple in 2 Samuel 7 rests largely on the double meaning of the word 'house', *bayit*, both as 'temple/palace' and 'dynasty'. While denying to David the honor of building a house for Yahweh, the passage assures him that his house will endure as kings over the people of Judah (2 Sam. 7.13). Overall, the chapter points ahead to a double founding—of David's house in Jerusalem and Yahweh's house on Mount Zion, both of which find initial fulfillment in Solomon.

> The declaration of Yahweh's choice of the Davidic dynasty was, beyond question, a piece of political theology intended to secure the royal throne in Jerusalem, and to serve as a divine authorization for its occupants. The same is true of the allied doctrine of Yahweh's election of Mount Zion... The introduction of a Yahweh sanctuary in Jerusalem was closely related, therefore, to the Davidic royal house...the doctrine of the joint

52. McCarthy, 'II Samuel 7', p. 137.
53. McCarter, *II Samuel*, p. 224.
54. Ishida, *The Royal Dynasties in Ancient Israel*, pp. 99-107.
55. Ishida, *The Royal Dynasties in Ancient Israel*, p. 107.

election of David and Mount Zion was nothing short of a divine authorization and sanction for the whole Davidic state.[56]

The confirmation of this link is given when the double fulfillment is achieved: only after the building of the temple is the dynastic promise given to Solomon (1 Kgs 9.1-5).[57]

The close association between the temple and divine sanction for the Davidic dynasty helps to explain the importance of the temple as setting and symbol in 2 Kings 11. The temple's unfailing commitment to the line of Davidic kings supports Jehoiada's actions in the temple on behalf of Joash, the legitimate successor. No clearer symbolic liaison could be found than the state sanctuary's justification for the continued dominance of the line which founded both it and the state. The setting of the conspiracy for Joash in any other locale would have negated one of the most powerful premises for Joash's legitimate claim to the throne. For the ideology reflected in the story, the temple is the crucial locus. (The ideology of dynastic succession will be further explored in the section on kingship).

This conception of the temple in the Deuteronomistic worldview, both generally and in the story of Athaliah and Joash, is thus multi-faceted. The temple represents Yahweh's divine formation of and presence with the people. It is an awesome and magnificent symbol of the divine-human link, as generally conceived in the cultures of that time and era. The temple is further associated with a distinct notion of order in society expressed in the covenant. And above all, the temple stands for the divine sanction for human kingship expressed specifically in the Davidic dynasty.

In terms of the understanding of ideology being used in this chapter, the role of the temple in Deuteronomistic thought and in the story of 2 Kings 11–12 is as the primary institution that expresses the cosmic order and legitimizes the human order. Geertz, in discussing religion as a cultural system, notes that a religion as a system of symbols formulates 'conceptions of a general order of existence' or a 'cosmic framework'.[58] But this is not an abstract exercise for the culture holding these symbols. 'For those who are committed to it, such a religious system seems to mediate genuine knowledge, knowledge of the essential conditions in

56. Clements, *God and Temple*, p. 50.
57. B. Halpern, *The Constitution of the Monarchy in Israel* (HSM, 25; Chico, CA: Scholars Press, 1981), p. 139.
58. Geertz, 'Religion as a Cultural System', p. 98.

terms of which life must, of necessity, be lived.'[59]

Seen in the terms of the social construction of reality, the conception of the temple represents a commitment to a total symbolic universe which defines the cosmically significant interactions of God with the people in the forms of particular social orders, or institutions. Berger and Luckmann emphasize the integrative power of such a symbolic universe:

> *all* the sectors of the institutional order are integrated in an all-embracing frame of reference, which now constitutes a universe in the literal sense of the word, because *all* human experience can now be conceived of as taking place *within* it.[60]

The multi-faceted symbolic power of the temple corresponds to its role as the central defining locus of the universe it represents for the Deuteronomistic worldview. The ideology of the priest or priests in the Deuteronomistic worldview and in 2 Kings 11–12 can be dealt with in a similar but more brief fashion. The narrative and rhetorical analyses revealed that the priest, Jehoiada, and to a lesser extent, the priests collectively in ch. 12 were portrayed in particular ways. The cultures of ancient Mesopotamia form the general background for any Israelite conceptions of priesthood. Oppenheim describes the personnel and workings of the temple generally as that of the 'household' of the god, in which the persons involved were responsible for the ongoing care of the god's needs.[61] Although called priests, the personnel were understood to be the servants or slaves of their master, the god. The types of roles associated with the functioning of the god's house included cultic personnel such as a chief priest and assistants, scribes and others who ran the business aspects of the temple, workers or craftspeople who cared for the building and its contents, and any exorcists and diviners considered necessary.[62] In all cases, the king was considered the principal patron and, in some Assyrian records, the high priest of the god. As such, the king's role in the upkeep of the temple was crucial.[63]

Evidence from the Ras Shamra texts seems to show parallels in the ideas of priestly roles and organization in the area of ancient Canaan, a

59. Geertz, 'Ethos, Worldview, and the Analysis of Sacred Symbols', in *Interpretation of Cultures*, p. 129.

60. Berger and Luckmann, *Social Construction of Reality*, p. 96.

61. Oppenheim, *Ancient Mesopotamia*, p. 96.

62. Oppenheim, *Ancient Mesopotamia*, p. 106.

63. Oppenheim, *Ancient Mesopotamia*, p. 108.

yet closer context for the Israelite cultus. The king was conceptualized as responsible for the 'perpetual communion with the god of the community' and thus had a sacramental status in the heroic texts.[64] In administrative texts, the king's role seems to have evolved to a less central priestly role and the priests came from twelve families with perhaps the domination of the priestly office by one royal family.[65] Various kinds of functionaries are associated with the temple, including priests, consecrated persons, traders, artisans, singers, silver casters and others.[66] One role that the priests carried out was to be the 'custodians of tradition',[67] verifying the accuracy of the important myths.

The Deuteronomistic traditions modify the notions of priesthood received from their wider cultural context. Weinfeld notes the general Deuteronomic tendency to demythologize and desacralize received tradition.[68] This affects the conception of the priests' role. Many of the priestly duties in the cultus, as evidenced in the Priestly tradition, are not even mentioned in Deuteronomy.[69] Sacrifice and the various laws detailing sacrificial procedures to be followed by the priests are largely modified so that the mediation of the priests is absent. 'Deuteronomic sacrifice consists primarily of offerings which are consumed by the offerer in the sanctuary and are designed to be shared with the poor, the Levite, the alien resident, the orphan and the widow.'[70] Even the sacrosanct status of the priests as holy through purification and sanctification is muted so that the whole people become a holy people 'by virtue of their election by God'.[71]

The Deuteronomistic conception of the priest and priests, as evidenced in the Deuteronomistic History, is largely defined in relation to the king, not as a role having independent sacral or political status.[72] The king has the power to appoint or banish the priest, as in Solomon's removing Abiathar (1 Kgs 2.26-27). Religious reforms are portrayed as initiated by

64. Gray, *The Legacy of Canaan*, p. 153.
65. Gray, *The Legacy of Canaan*, p. 158.
66. Gray, *The Legacy of Canaan*, p. 156.
67. Gray, *The Legacy of Canaan*, p. 159.
68. Weinfeld, *Deuteronomic School*, p. 188.
69. Weinfeld, *Deuteronomic School*, p. 188.
70. Weinfeld, *Deuteronomic School*, p. 211.
71. Weinfeld, *Deuteronomic School*, p. 227.
72. R. de Vaux, OP, *Ancient Israel: Its Life and Institutions* (New York: McGraw–Hill, 1961), p. 375.

kings, not priests; so it is with Asa (1 Kgs 15.12-13), Hezekiah (2 Kgs 18.3-4) and Josiah (2 Kgs 23). The priest is, however, an important part of the king's administration, ranking in the listings of David's and Solomon's officials (2 Sam. 20.25; 1 Kgs 4.2). The priest Uriah follows King Ahaz's plans for a new altar as commanded (2 Kgs 16.11). The 'elders of the priests' are part of the group King Hezekiah sends to seek Isaiah's word (2 Kgs 19.2). The priest Hilkiah is part of the group Josiah sends to seek Huldah's word (2 Kgs 22.12).[73]

This conception of the role of priest as secondary to the king in the Deuteronomistic worldview fits in well with the role of Jehoiada in 2 Kings 11–12. While there the priest does initiate a reform, it is one fully in the service of restoring the rightful king to the throne, and is not conceived of as an independent action. Jehoiada in ch. 12 is clearly the king's servant. He 'instructs' the king, and carries out the king's plan for financing the temple repair. The other priests in ch. 12 may assert themselves against the king's first plan but end in silent acquiescence to his second plan. What importance the priest Jehoiada does have in the story comes from his association with the temple and his service from that sacred precinct to the Davidic dynasty.

Such a conceptual role for the priests in the service of the institutions of the temple and kingship is explained well in the notion of a socially constructed reality. As seen above, the temple holds a central role as a legitimating institution in its symbolic universe. Such an organization whose role is the justification and integration of the 'world reality' is characterized by 'the development of specialized legitimating theories and their administration by full-time legitimators'.[74] The priests thus can be understood to function as legitimators of the central institutions in the society—exactly Jehoiada's role in the narrative.

Covenant

Another concept that carries weight narratively and rhetorically is that of covenant. The referential field is broad in scope for the use of the term, and actions and evaluations related to the 'covenant' occur in both chs. 11 and 12. The concept and use of the term 'covenant' in the Bible is a subject of great contention and long history in critical studies. This brief review cannot cover that field and takes a cautious stand on some

---

73. De Vaux, *Ancient Israel*, pp. 375-76.
74. Berger and Luckmann, *Social Construction of Reality*, p. 95.

of the issues involved, moving towards an understanding of the ideological use of the term by the posited Deuteronomistic author of 2 Kings 11–12.

Robert Oden's helpful review of the study of the covenant idea in ancient Israel begins with Wellhausen's view that it was a late, not very important concept in Israelite religion.[75] However, when critics were inspired by the intellectual ferment accompanying the 'perceived discovery at about the...turn of the century of the place of the social in the meaning and function of religion',[76] covenant began to be seen and studied as a much more central and early concept. The study of parallels between ancient Near Eastern treaty and law forms and particular covenant terminology seemed to uncover historical evidence for the covenant as a primary reality shaping the religion of Israel from early times.

For example, Baltzer, who views a Hittite treaty between a great king and a vassal as the form behind covenant formulary in the Old Testament, saw that a covenant renewal was needed in Israel at the transition points between two leaders or rulers.[77] Thus in 2 Kings 11, when Joash replaces the illegitimate Athaliah, there are two covenants made. 'In the one "covenant", the people pledge allegiance to the king, in the other, the king and people together pledge themselves to be Yahweh's people.'[78]

With a similar approach to covenant as an early, shaping form for the religion of Israel, Widengren used 2 Kings 11 as a text illustrating the relationship between the king and the covenant. One important aspect of the king's function was as a mediator of the covenant.[79] Widengren places the making of the Israelite covenant as 'a central point in Israel's relations with its God'[80] in the context of a pre-exilic New Year festival. The king had a leading role: 'it was the king who...renewed the covenant between Yahweh and the people, reading on this solemn

---

75. R.A. Oden, Jr, 'The Place of Covenant in the Religion of Israel', in Miller, Hanson and McBride (eds.), *Ancient Israelite Religion*, p. 429.

76. Oden, 'Covenant', p. 438.

77. K. Baltzer, *The Covenant Formulary* (trans. D.E. Green; Philadelphia: Fortress Press, 1971), p. 83.

78. Baltzer, *Covenant Formulary*, p. 79.

79. Widengren, 'King and Covenant', p. 1.

80. Widengren, 'King and Covenant', p. 2.

occasion from the book of the law the commandments which served as the foundation of the covenant'.[81]

After reviewing scholars like Baltzer and Widengren, Oden describes the more recent critical movement which reduces or eliminates the role of covenant as a constituting factor in Israel's religion.[82] He notes, however, that a consensus of a sort does locate the first significant development of the form or idea in Deuteronomy and its related literature. The outlines of the covenant concept as developed by scholars like Baltzer and Widengren can be used most appropriately, then, to explicate a Deuteronomistic notion of the relationship between Yahweh and the people. In this context, the typifying of that relationship as one of allegiance cast in a form of treaty or pact, issuing in commands which define the relationship and mediated by the people's leaders or kings, all point to the ideology of the covenant in the Deuteronomistic worldview.

For the task here, the use and meaning of covenant could be characterized along the lines of Dennis McCarthy's studies. On the question of the idea's history, he finds that while the major development of the concept came with the Deuteronomic school, there are some attestations to the ideas of ברית in pre-Deuteronomic texts, although it was a 'relatively unused concept'.[83] As developed in the Deuteronomistic writings, it carried over connotations from its history as a specific act but 'came to mean a solemn commitment in general'.[84] It acquires

> an association with ideas of relationship. It is tied up with a complex of recognized relationships, active relations (negotiations), terms which relate one party to another, and a common act... relation and obligation, commitment and actions, these are what we mean by covenant.[85]

In the Deuteronomistic worldview, then, covenant becomes a primary way of defining the relationship between Yahweh and the people. The people's possession of the land was dependent upon their continued right relationship with the God who brought them into the land. As briefly summarized by Gerald Eddie Gerbrandt, this relationship was

81. Widengren, 'King and Covenant', p. 19.
82. Oden, 'Covenant', p. 435.
83. D.J. McCarthy, SJ, '*Berit* in Old Testament History and Theology', in *Institution and Narrative: Collected Essays* (AnBib, 108; Rome: Biblical Institute Press, 1985), p. 50.
84. McCarthy, '*Berit* and Covenant', in *Institution and Narrative*, p. 40.
85. McCarthy, '*Berit* and Covenant', pp. 40-41.

expressed in the covenant the people entered into with Yahweh.[86] By the covenant, Israel was committed to stipulations which were found in the laws and commandments given through Moses.[87] 'Yahweh's covenant with Israel then gave Israel the necessary guidelines for a life of blessing on the land, and adherence to it was the condition for continued existence on the land as his people.'[88]

Mark O'Brien takes a similar view on the centrality of a concept of covenant or law code in the Deuteronomistic History. He states that in Deuteronomy, through the authority of Moses, the Deuteronomist 'established the deuteronomic code's status as the norm for Israel and then applied it to the remainder of the history'.[89] In applying covenant law as a norm in the telling of the history, the Deuteronomist focused on 'three areas which Dtr regarded as the essence of the code. These were fidelity to the exclusive worship of Yahweh, fidelity to centralized worship at the place chosen by Yahweh, and fidelity to the leaders appointed by Yahweh.'[90]

The expression of these three criteria of fidelity helps in understanding the interrelated concepts in the worldview being explored here. The norm of fidelity to the centralization of worship at the place of Yahweh's choosing of course ties into the conception of the temple, discussed above. The norm of fidelity to appointed leaders focuses on the king's relation to the covenant, which will be picked up in the next section. The juxtaposition of covenant and Baal-smashing in 2 Kings 11 can now be explicated by the criteria of fidelity to the exclusive worship of Yahweh as a central component of the covenant.

When the Deuteronomistic History reflects on the sins of Israel or Judah, that is, on the ways in which the covenant was broken, decisive among the sins are Baalism and the golden calves.[91] These are quintessential sins because they switch the people's allegiance to other gods and subvert the exclusive worship of Yahweh. The peroration on

86. Gerbrandt, *Kingship*, p. 94.

87. Gerbrandt, *Kingship*, p. 94.

88. Gerbrandt, *Kingship*, p. 96.

89. M.A. O'Brien, 'The "Deuteronomistic History" as a Story of Israel's Leaders', *AusBR* 37 (1989), p. 20.

90. M.A. O'Brien, *The Deuteronomistic History Hypothesis: A Reassessment* (Freiburg: Universitätsverlag, 1989), p. 30.

91. M. Weinfeld, 'The Emergence of the Deuteronomic Movement: The Historical Antecedents', in *Das Deuteronomium: Entstehung, Gestalt und Botschaft* (Leuven: Leuven University Press, 1985), p. 83.

the fall of Israel in 2 Kgs 17.1-20 serves as a focus for condemning Israel's sins. While various verses of the chapter have been assigned to different redactors by scholars, it can be taken as a Deuteronomistic text by and large.[92] In 2 Kings 17, the listing of sins by which Israel 'rejected [Yahweh's] statues and his covenant that he made with their ancestors' (v. 15) begins with the general condemnation that they worshiped other gods (v. 7). But the detailing of sins goes beyond an accounting of Israel's fall and stands as a warning to Judah:

> Israel's experience, couched in terms applicable to Judah, served the Deuteronomist in his concern for Judah's future. The use of emphatic elements, constant repetition, and the paranetic character of the chapter strongly suggest that the concern of the author is to convince his readers of the absolute necessity of exclusive worship of Yahweh.[93]

Two examples of the application of the criteria of covenant fidelity to Judah's situation are found in 2 Kings 11–12. The anti-Baalism ideology is reflected in the story of Athaliah and Joash in a positive way—the people, as a response to the making of the covenant, rid Jerusalem of the Baal temple and its priest. The call for centralized and exclusive worship of Yahweh emerges in ch. 12 in the regnal evaluation where Joash is judged for not removing the high places (more below on this).

It is now evident that the descriptions given by scholars about the meaning of 'covenant' locate the Deuteronomistic conception in an ideational world in which the relationship between God and the people is expressed in a compact or agreement. The agreement broadly defines the attitudes and actions expected of the partners in the alliance, with the primary obligations for the people of Israel expressed in stipulations or commandments. These laws in turn define their life as a people in the land and the norms for them and their leaders. Particularly since fidelity to Yahweh involves the abolishment of any rival allegiances, Baal can have no place in their life when a true king is made.

In his cultural anthropology, Geertz analyzes the power of religious concepts of law in a way helpful to seeing the importance of the covenant. A religion's vitality in the mundane, as opposed to the meta-physical, sphere is attributable to its finding the source of law in the

92. See O'Brien, *Hypothesis*, p. 209 for discussion and another reconstruction. If the passage is not taken as Deuteronomistic, the same themes of exclusive worship and anti-Baalism can be well supported by other Deuteronomistic texts.

93. P. Viviano, '2 Kings 17: A Rhetorical and Form-Critical Analysis', *CBQ* 49 (1987), p. 559.

fundamental nature of reality. 'The powerfully coercive "ought" is felt to grow out of a comprehensive, factual "is", and in such a way religion grounds the most specific requirements of human action in the most general contexts of human existence.'[94] With this perspective, the covenant's laws are not merely good human relations but expressions of how God intends things to be and of how things really are.

The evocation of the concept of covenant in 2 Kings 11 is general and seems deliberately to call to mind a broad and fundamental view of God's cosmic order for dealing with the people. In the action of king-making, the basic relationship of the people as a whole, their king and Yahweh is invoked. Ideologically, the mention of covenant-making thus functions to set the specific action of king-making within its symbolic universe. In the scheme of Berger and Luckmann, this is indeed the correlation between the symbolic universe and institutions in any society: 'the symbolic universe legitimizes the institutional order on the highest level of generality'.[95] The king can be properly installed only by remembering the larger, universal world in which all actions make sense.

King and Dynasty

The most significant ideological complex in 2 Kings 11–12 concerns the king and the Davidic dynasty. Evident from the rhetorical analysis is the story's insistence that the Yahweh-sanctioned rule of the Davidic line has been preserved by the coronation and installation of Joash. In ch. 12, a good king's relationship to the temple is portrayed in which the king has authority over the temple and acts as its patron to ensure its maintenance and well-being.

The views about kingship expressed in this story can be set into the context of the ancient Near East and the Deuteronomistic worldview in a way that displays their ideological groundings. The overall cosmic view of the relations between the gods, the human world and the state with its king and temple, explained above, forms the most basic conceptual field. Within this field, the king is both a cosmically and humanly significant figure as the 'go-between' who mediates the cosmic and human realms. 'Whatever was significant was imbedded in the life of the cosmos, and it was precisely the king's function to maintain the harmony of that

94. Geertz, 'Ethos, Worldview', p. 126.
95. Berger and Luckmann, *Social Construction of Reality*, p. 105.

integration.'[96] In the long stream of Mesopotamian thought, the king was a human figure, a member of the human community, yet as the 'point man', he was 'charged with maintaining harmonious relations between human society and the supernatural powers'.[97]

With the king in so central a role, kingship became the primary defining institution in Mesopotamian civilization, extending through the court and temple into all reaches of life and the realm. A full-blown royal ideology was characterized by several motifs in the ancient world. The reigning king, as subjugator of foreign people, deserves and receives tribute and taxes from vanquished enemies.[98] The realm of the king is often said to extend to far borders, conceptually reaching to the natural boundaries of seas, rivers and mountains.[99] The king becomes a protector of justice and righteousness, ideally protecting the poor and ensuring the end of the wicked.[100]

With such concepts prevalent in the cultures surrounding Israel, it is no surprise that the ideology seen in its writings, particularly those of the Deuteronomist, reflects this background in seeing a central role for the king. Von Rad, surveying the Deuteronomistic theology of history, holds that the word of Yahweh which directs the judgment and salvation of the nation centers on the kings: 'They are the real object of this operative word, it is they who are sustained by it and they who are destroyed by it. The people stands and falls with them.'[101] While an early influential view (held notably by Wellhausen and Noth) was that the Deuteronomist was strongly opposed to the institution of kingship, more recent studies have made a much more positive assessment of the Deuteronomistic view.[102] And while these assessments vary and cannot be covered in detail here, Weinfeld's view is helpful:

> The character of the circle involved in the deuteronomic creation emerges from the fact that the school could not conceive of a regime without a king. In contrast to the other law codes in the Tetrateuch, in which no indication of a monarchic regime can be found, Deuteronomy presents laws which reflect a typical monarchic rule. We find here not only the law of the king but a whole set of legal pericopes reflecting a monarchic state:

96. Frankfort, *Kingship*, p. 3.
97. Frankfort, *Kingship*, p. 6.
98. Weinfeld, 'Zion and Jerusalem', p. 95.
99. Weinfeld, 'Zion and Jerusalem', p. 97.
100. Weinfeld, 'Zion and Jerusalem', p. 100.
101. Von Rad, *Old Testament Theology*, I, p. 344.
102. Gerbrandt, *Kingship*, pp. 18-38.

laws about courts of justice and the supreme court, priest and prophecy, and about the military.[103]

But the Deuteronomistic worldview did not just import foreign ideas about kingship nor create a conception *ex nihilo*. Rather, as scholars who have studied this notion of kingship have shown, the school combined ideas available from its cultural background with concepts basic to its Israelite heritage.[104] Halpern details the mythos of Yahweh as divine warrior and king over the cosmos as an ancient conceptual background to the Israelite ideal of kingship.[105] Dennis McCarthy has produced a critically significant[106] interpretation of 1 Samuel 8–12 which sees a Deuteronomistic accommodation between views in Israel which were critical of kingship and those supportive of it. The careful construction of the text shows how the Deuteronomist incorporates kingship into the Israelite understanding of covenant and relationship with Yahweh.[107] Kenik, in a detailed study of Solomon's dream, 1 Kgs 3.4-15, shows how various traditions were combined into the notion of kingship through the narrative's construction. She identifies several streams of tradition combined in the Deuteronomistic idea of the king:

> The Dtr borrowed from the royal theology of the Judean court which, in turn, reflects the ideology of kings who are dependent upon a patron-god for the continuation of kingship. The Dtr integrated the tradition, presented in the Yahwist narrative, of Abraham and Moses who address Yahweh as *Adonai* thereby indicating relationship based on the Lordship of Yahweh and the servanthood of the king with the consonant possibility of the termination of the relationship. Finally, the Dtr drew upon the tradition of Moses as judge and administrator with the concern for the people of God conveyed in that tradition.[108]

The general Deuteronomistic conception of kingship indicates that the king is the central figure in the nation. This ideological role for the king is reflected in the intensity of rhetoric about kingship in the text of 2 Kings 11–12. The basic theses of both chapters concern the king; all of

---

103. Weinfeld, *Deuteronomy*, p. 55.

104. Weinfeld, 'Zion and Jerusalem', p. 93.

105. Halpern, *Constitution*, p. 147.

106. Gerbrandt, *Kingship*, p. 154.

107. D.J. McCarthy, SJ, 'The Inauguration of Monarchy in Israel', *Int* 27 (1973), p. 412.

108. H.A. Kenik, *Design for Kingship: The Deuteronomistic Narrative Technique in I Kings 3.4-15* (SBLDS, 69; Chico, CA: Scholars Press, 1983), p. 131.

the premises used in the argumentation pick up concerns related to kingship. However, several aspects of kingship bear more heavily upon 2 Kings 11–12 and must be considered in somewhat more detail. Two of these correspond to topics previously covered, the covenant and the temple's connection with the dynasty. These cross-references are significant for the integrated conceptual stance on kingship held by the Deuteronomistic worldview.

The king's relationship to the covenant and the traditions of social and sacral compacts rooted in Israel's identity is one place to start. Halpern, studying the rise of kingship in the midst of Israel's tribal and civil leadership in the pre-monarchic era, chronicles the uneasy compromise that a centralized monarchic government achieved with the civil and sacral powers of the assembly of elders.[109] While in theory the king was a partner in a contract with his people and 'his powers were circumscribed by social and sacral conventions',[110] there was always a tension between the central government and local structures, often mediated by the word of the prophet.[111] The compromise reached with the covenant ideal was that the king himself was beholden to the covenant and, in fact, was central to the nation's upholding of the covenant. McCarthy places the roots of this idea in the early social compact between the king and the people. This evolves into a notion of sacral compact in which 'the king manifests in himself the more or less explicit ideals of the community...If he lives them, he and the people are God's community, otherwise not.'[112]

In the fully developed Deuteronomistic concept of kingship, the king is obligated to keep the covenant which both assures his place in the society and limits his powers.[113] He is judged by the criteria of fidelity to the covenant ideals: exclusive worship of Yahweh, centralized worship of Yahweh, and the word of Yahweh's leaders, the prophets.[114] Both his own rule and the life of the people depend on the king's fulfillment of this obligation:

109. Halpern, *Constitution*, p. 246.
110. Halpern, *Constitution*, p. 249.
111. Halpern, *Constitution*, p. 247.
112. D. McCarthy, 'Compact and Kingship: Stimuli for Hebrew Covenant Thinking', in *Institution and Narrative*, p. 90.
113. Kenik, *Design*, p. 140.
114. O'Brien, *Hypothesis*, p. 290.

> Since Israel's continued existence as a people on the land was dependent
> on her obedience to the covenant, and since the king's ultimate responsi-
> bility was to insure this continued existence, the king's role was then to
> make sure that the covenant was observed in Israel.[115]

The relationship of king and covenant helps to explain the ideological importance of covenant concepts in 2 Kings 11–12. For the Deuteronomistic shaper of the story, proper kingship could not be restored unless the making of the covenant (11.17) was completed, and the king handed the symbols of his covenantal, Torah-based authority (11.12). The ideology did not need to be explained at length; rather the symbolic representations of the covenant and the mention that the covenant was restored evoked the necessary worldview. The new king's successful keeping of the covenant as instructed (12.3) reflects the covenant concern that the king be the primary representative of covenant fidelity.

The ideology of the temple likewise contains a focus which centers on the king's relationship to the sanctuary. As noted above for the cultures of the Mesopotamian region, the king's special connection to the state's god was marked in part by his construction of the temple. The building of the temple is thus a part of royal ideology throughout the region that serves as Israel's cultural milieu.[116] This applies no less to the upkeep and maintenance of the temple than to its construction. Any decay of the sanctuary could be interpreted as a sign of the gods' disfavor or punishment and 'a well-functioning shrine a sign of their goodwill'.[117] In Ugaritic writings, temple construction is credited with helping recover fertility and healing society's ills.[118] So the constant maintenance of the sanctuary devolved upon the king as a part of his obligations.[119]

In Deuteronomistic thought, the emphasis on the king's construction, adornment and upkeep of the temple is evident. The attention to types and acquisition of building materials and the emphasis on the opulence of its appointments in the Solomonic account of temple building reflect this concern with the king's attention to the temple. Solomon's procuring of the cedars of Lebanon (1 Kgs 5.2-10) corresponds to the literary depiction of the flow of rich or sacred materials from foreign peoples

---

115. Gerbrandt, *Kingship*, p. 99.
116. Hurowitz, *Exalted House*, p. 313.
117. Frankfort, *Kingship*, p. 269.
118. Halpern, *Constitution*, p. 59.
119. Oppenheim, *Ancient Mesopotamia*, p. 108.

that portrays the centrality of the king and his building.[120]

The ideological connection between the king and his care for the temple is intrinsic in 2 Kings 11–12. In the account of the temple financing, the temple reflects the conception of sanctuaries reviewed at length above, including, for the Deuteronomist, Solomon's pre-eminent status as temple builder. Like his predecessor Solomon, Joash takes on the temple as a focus for concern. Ideologically, his role as caretaker for Yahweh's sanctuary is paramount; he fulfills his role with insight and competence in the narrative. Even the listing of workers and materials which characterizes narratives about royal temple building as a genre has its place in 12.11-12.

However, the main ideological concern in ch. 11 is the dynasty. The discussion in the previous section established the temple's connection to the idea of the dynasty in Deuteronomistic thought. The promise of a Davidic dynasty in the Deuteronomistic History has been the subject of debate as to its conditionality or unconditionality in the Deuteronomistic worldview. At issue are texts where a conditional, covenantal view makes the perpetuation of the promise depend upon fidelity to the covenant, as well as other texts where a continuing dynastic line seems assured with no conditions attached.[121] This is not the place to settle that debate. However, for the purposes of analyzing 2 Kings 11–12, several points are relevant. The importance in the Deuteronomistic view of the covenant and of the king's obligation under the covenant has already been established. Further, the dynastic promise contained in 2 Samuel 7 is a major element in the book of Kings.[122]

A description of the full accommodation of these themes in the Deuteronomistic ideology and the History may only be achieved by recognizing the complexity of ideological references and assessments in this literature. Certainly for the chapters under consideration here both an unwavering dynastic promise and a covenantal view of kingship are applicable. A discussion of the theme of the dynastic promise will fill out its importance for this study, without undermining the relevance of fidelity to covenant stipulations on the part of the king.

When the promise of a dynasty is given to David, it comes by the word of the prophet Nathan (2 Sam. 7). When the promise is confirmed

---

120. Hurowitz, *Exalted House*, p. 209.

121. For various views see: Cross, *Canaanite Myth*, pp. 219-89; Gerbrandt, *Kingship*, pp. 158-73; and O'Brien, *Hypothesis*, pp. 163-71.

122. Cross, *Canaanite Myth*, pp. 281-85.

to Solomon after the dedication of the completed temple, it comes in Yahweh's word in a vision (1 Kgs 9.1-5). When the kingdom is divided, thus revealing a most basic threat to the continuation of the Davidic dynasty, the perpetuation of a kingdom and house for David is assured (1 Kgs 11.29-39). In this instance, the word comes by the prophet Ahijah who tells Jeroboam of his own coming kingdom and dynasty, while reaffirming the promise to David in the new format of 'one tribe' in Jerusalem (1 Kgs 11.32). The promise to David's line is expressed in the phrase 'so that David my servant may have a lamp forever before me in Jerusalem' (1 Kgs 11.36). The term *nîr* has usually been translated 'lamp' although it has a possible meaning of 'dominion'.[123] However translated, it represents the presence in Jerusalem of the Davidic dynasty and, as a whole, Ahijah's prophecy is used to reassert the theme of the Davidic promise.

Also noteworthy here is the role of Yahweh's word, usually through a prophet, which sets the promise and confirms it. This is in line with a general description of the Deuteronomistic worldview which highlights the role of the prophets in relation to kings (or other leaders) throughout the History. O'Brien, among others, shows how the word of Yahweh which calls for fidelity to the covenant comes through the prophets and is addressed to kings, so that their fidelity to the prophetic word demonstrates fidelity to Yahweh.[124]

The Davidic promise, including a reference to the 'lamp' in Jerusalem, is recalled twice more in the History, once with direct relevance to 2 Kings 11-12. In 1 Kgs 15.4-5, the reign of the otherwise evil Abijam, son of Rehoboam, is justified by appeal to David and David's fulfillment of the commandments of Yahweh:

> Nevertheless for David's sake the Lord his God gave him a lamp in Jerusalem, setting up his son after him and establishing Jerusalem, because David did what was right in the sight of the Lord, and did not turn aside from anything that he commanded him all the days of his life, except in the matter of Uriah the Hittite (NRSV).

And in 2 Kgs 8.16-19, Jehoram of Judah's reign is introduced with the attribution of evil because (Athaliah) the daughter of Ahab was his wife. Yet his evil does not destroy Judah, according to the narrator's summary here. 'Yet the Lord would not destroy Judah, for the sake of his

123. M. Cogan and H. Tadmor, *II Kings*, p. 95.
124. O'Brien, *Hypothesis*, p. 35.

servant David, since he had promised to give a lamp to him and his descendants forever' (NRSV). It is worthy of note that one possible accommodation between unconditional dynastic promise and conditional covenant allegiance is expressed in these passages—David's keeping of the commandments assures the survival of his dynasty in spite of the evil of these two kings.

Through Jehoram's regnal summary the promise for the Davidic dynasty and the 'lamp' in Jerusalem comes to have direct bearing on the story of Athaliah and Joash. Jehoram's evil could have destroyed the Davidic dynasty through the very practical effect of his evil wife's, Athaliah's, murder of all the descendants of the kingdom (11.1), the dynastic line. The threat Athaliah posed by the murder of the descendants of the kingdom was a threat to the central promise of a continuing Davidic line on the throne of Judah. No accommodation could be made with her actions.

The fact that the promise to David had been given through the significant format of the prophetic word also has bearing. The absence of any direct prophetic presence in 2 Kgs 11–12 can be explained ideologically. No direct prophetic word concerning the dynasty is needed because the clear and durable promise to David given in Nathan's and Ahijah's prophecies is still in effect. They are the prophets of 2 Kings 11–12 and their word is still active as the Davidic dynasty meets and overcomes its most deadly challenge.

The centrality of dynastic ideology also emerges in the story's insistence on Joash's legitimacy. The royal-dynastic ideology demanded that a true Davidide be seated upon the throne. Getting rid of Athaliah was not enough; a son of the former king, Ahaziah, must rule. So Joash's legitimacy is underscored in numerous ways by statement, analogy and symbol in the narrative's rhetoric.

It is evident that kingship and dynasty are critical concepts for understanding 2 Kings 11–12. Analyzed in terms of the social construction of reality, the king's role in the society is circumscribed by the worldview which sets him as a part of a larger whole and defines his relationships to other institutions such as the covenant and the temple. In this way a 'role typology'[125] is constructed that says what the king should be and do. But more importantly, the king's place in the conceived social order is as the central representative of the cosmos, the prime keeper of the law, the caretaker of the temple.

125. Berger and Luckmann, *Social Construction of Reality*, p. 74.

The king is thus the central participant in the symbolic universe which integrates and legitimates the whole social order. The true king rules by Yahweh's power and word, is of David's line, is subject to the covenant, is installed on the throne of the kingdom, and is the builder or restorer of the House of Yahweh.

> [T]he political order is legitimated by reference to a cosmic order of power and justice, and political roles are legitimated as representations of these cosmic principles. The institution of divine kingship in archaic civilizations is an excellent illustration of the manner in which this kind of ultimate legitimation operates.[126]

Further, the threat to the dynastic line represented by Athaliah and her murder of the king's descendants threatens the very integration of Judahite society. This creates a 'marginal situation'—potential chaos in the ordering of the kingship and thus in the cosmic order.

> The constant possibility of anomic terror is actualized whenever the legitimations that obscure the precariousness [of social reality] are threatened or collapse. The dread that accompanies the death of a king, especially if it occurs with sudden violence, expresses this terror.[127]

The symbolic universe expressed in the Deuteronomistic worldview must take the threat into account and reduce or eliminate it. So the narrative portrays the re-establishment of legitimate dynastic kingship in Judah, that is, the re-establishment of the necessary components of the symbolic universe the Deuteronomist inhabits: Judah under the Davidic kings as Yahweh's covenant people.

> It may readily be understood why such [chaos-producing] events have to be followed at once with the most solemn reaffirmations of the continuing reality of the sheltering symbols.[128]

Regnal Summaries and the Kings' Reigns

One final aspect of the conceptual background for kingship in Deuteronomistic thought will complete this survey. Throughout the Deuteronomistic History, when a true Davidide is seated on the throne of Judah (or when a king comes to rule in Israel), he becomes subject to evaluation based on attitudes and actions evident in his reign. Generally,

---

126. Berger and Luckmann, *Social Construction of Reality*, p. 103.
127. Berger and Luckmann, *Social Construction of Reality*, p. 103.
128. Berger and Luckmann, *Social Construction of Reality*, p. 104.

the regnal summaries report the evaluation of the Deuteronomistic narrator according to the criteria of covenant fidelity as described above. While no full accounting of the research on the formulas can be done for this study, two characteristics can be noted which relate to ideological considerations.

Virtually all of the regnal formulas use the basic judgment of the king's doing right or evil in the sight of Yahweh.[129] In addition to this overall evaluation, a number of other phrases and criteria are listed in the summaries, sometimes referring to specific actions by the kings. The similarities and variations in the patterns have been studied to search for sources for the Deuteronomistic History,[130] but that is not the focus here. Significant for this study is the primary characteristic of the regnal formulas—that they bring the ideology imbedded in the narrative into the foreground and use it to shape the impact of the whole account. (One of the ways such an ideological evaluation is made and used was seen above in Athaliah's case, but the characteristic is widespread). The report of judgment according to a particular worldview is central. 'It is not an exaggeration to see the judgment formulas as the primary communication being sought in this careful accounting of the kings of Israel and Judah.'[131]

However, a second characteristic of the regnal summaries is notable when they are viewed along with the larger narrative. No matter how the sources are determined, in the full Deuteronomistic narrative, the summaries have been combined with more or less detailed reports of incidents and actions in the reigns of the kings. The summaries and the reported incidents together create a dialectic—the summaries shaping how the incidents are viewed, the incidents supporting or commenting on the summaries. When it is recognized that the selection and reporting of incidents also contribute to the ideological depiction, then this dialectic becomes paramount in the description of Deuteronomistic ideology. The variations in the patterns of the regnal summaries combined with the varied reports of incidents and actions illustrate the capability of the ideology both to create analogic patterns and to deal with variety and complexity in the kings' reigns. Patterns are established and overall

---

129. 29 of 33 formulas from Jeroboam and Rehoboam to Josiah use the 'right or evil' judgment explicitly; it is implicit in the evil acts of Jeroboam, Jehu, Elah and Abijam. See Campbell, *Of Prophets and Kings*, pp. 139-202.

130. Campbell, *Of Prophets and Kings*, pp. 139-202.

131. Campbell, *Of Prophets and Kings*, p. 140.

judgments drawn, at the same time that phrases, incidents and reports that do not fit rigid patterns show the flexibility of the conceptual world within the general criteria for judgment.

Two examples noted by scholars will illustrate the point. Fidelity to Yahweh and fidelity to centralized worship are well established as Deuteronomistic evaluative criteria.[132] Along these lines, a number of Judahite kings are held accountable for not removing 'the high places'. But despite the criteria which condemn high places for possible non-Yahwistic and certainly non-centralized worship, six kings are still rated as 'doing right in the eyes of Yahweh'.[133] 'Maintaining the high places might detract from a king's otherwise solid reputation, but it was not enough to bring condemnation'.[134] The application of the 'he did right but...' evaluation to six kings creates a pattern but it is one which leaves room for the specifics of each reign to nuance the presentation.

A second example includes a set of reports from a number of kings' reigns which qualify their regnal evaluations. E. Theodore Mullen has noted that for the six kings who did right except for removing the high places, all receive some sort of punishment in the form of foreign oppression or political or personal misfortune.[135] One type of negative incident which acts as a punishment for these kings' cultic shortcomings is the despoliation of the state treasuries to pay tribute to a foreign invader or oppressor. This theme appears in the reigns of other kings as well, and a kind of 'history of the state treasuries' can be traced (as seen in the previous chapter) that culminates in the sacking of the treasuries by Babylon (2 Kgs 24.13). For kings who did right except for the high places as well as for kings who did evil, the loss of the state funds shows that ideological shaping is at work, according to Mullen. The pattern of cultic misconduct and foreign invasion/despoliation of the treasuries

is sufficient to suggest that the deuteronomistic concept of religious apostasy accompanied by foreign oppression operative in the Book of Judges and discernible in the accounts of Saul, David and Solomon,

132. O'Brien, *Hypothesis*, p. 288.

133. Asa: 1 Kgs 15.11, 14; Jehoshaphat: 1 Kgs 22.43; Joash: 2 Kgs 12.3-4; Amaziah: 2 Kgs 14.3-4; Azariah: 2 Kgs 15.3-4; and Jotham: 2 Kgs 15.34-35.

134. R.H. Lowery, *The Reforming Kings: Cults and Society in First Temple Judah* (JSOTSup, 120; Sheffield: JSOT Press, 1991), p. 63.

135. E.T. Mullen, Jr, 'Crime and Punishment: The Sins of the King and the Despoliation of the Treasuries', *CBQ* 54 (1992), p. 234.

remained a viable literary and ideological vehicle employed within the narrative of Kings.[136]

What this 'ideological vehicle' does is establish a pattern but it is a pattern that seems to recognize complexity within the set parameters of cultic purity. In this manner, the dialectic between the nuanced regnal evaluations and the reports on the loss of the state treasuries communicates some of the variety which the Deuteronomistic History includes. Evil kings fall prey to foreign oppression but so can 'good' kings when their otherwise right reigns are cultically misled. Even a king rated completely 'good' according to all the criteria, Hezekiah (2 Kgs 18.3-7a), can be forced to pay tribute (2 Kgs 18.15). Hezekiah's failure, later corrected according to the narrative, was in not trusting in Yahweh until after Isaiah's oracle of deliverance.[137] Ideologically shaped patterns in the regnal summaries exist but the reports comment on and nuance the application of the patterns to individual kings.

These considerations apply to 2 Kings 12 quite directly. Joash is evaluated as a king who did 'right' but did not remove the high places. This communicates that his reign cannot be classified ideologically according to only one criterion; rather a more subtle evaluation is proposed. Further, the temple financing report comments on and supports the attribution to him of being right in Yahweh's sight. Temple repair shows what a 'good' king must do and adds specification to Joash's reign. On the other hand, the report of the loss of the state treasuries, and perhaps the juxtaposing of the report about Joash's assassination, interact with Joash's not removing the high places, according to the pattern identified by Mullen. As a part of a larger pattern of cultic impropriety and foreign oppression (or personal misfortune), this negative evaluation and report reinforce the pattern and also add specification to Joash's years as king.

The use of ideological concepts for understanding events, establishing patterns among events, and allowing for detail and nuance within patterns can all be understood according to Berger and Luckmann's thesis of social reality. Every symbolic universe needs maintenance by the forces that have a stake in it, especially by those whose task it is to reinforce the power of the reality. The process of transmission of the symbolic universe must have 'specific conceptual machineries of universe maintenance'[138] that explain and justify the world as it is

136. Mullen, 'Crime and Punishment', p. 236.
137. Mullen, 'Crime and Punishment', p. 246.
138. Berger and Luckmann, *Social Construction of Reality*, p. 105.

known. These machineries also explain possible contradictions and create a 'history' that 'locates all collective events in a cohesive unity'.[139] That a king could fail to remove the high places is a problem for an evaluative ideology that says that centralized worship is a criterion for the good king. So an accommodation is made by which the ideology can include that failure even in the reigns of the kings who do right. The pattern of cultic failure and political oppression engages a concept that helps to explain past events while it allows the details of the reigns of various kings to be told without contradictions that threaten the cohesion of the symbolic universe.

Summary

The third type of analysis applied to the story of Athaliah and Joash has attempted to explicate the conceptual world which operates in the story. The study of the rhetoric of the narrative showed the kinds of premises used and arguments being made. The assumption in this third analysis was that 'behind' or 'under' these arguments was a definition of reality—how the world is and how people, especially significant people, should act—to which the arguments appealed and from which they gained their power and cohesiveness. The rhetoric argued not for its own sake but for the sake of ideas that mattered, that made a difference in the world of the author and audience.

Basic to the task of ideological analysis was the scholarly work of Berger and Luckmann on the social construction of reality and of Geertz on culture. A framework for understanding the 'world' or 'culture' of the story's author and audience as well as a definition of 'ideology' or 'worldview' based on these authors helped to focus the analysis. Particularly important was the idea of the 'symbolic universe' created by a society, which constitutes the 'world' as the society knows it. Within the society, an ideology functions to describe a particular definition of the symbolic universe complete with its own views on everything from cosmic significance to personal ethics.

Using a wide range of critics who have studied various aspects of Deuteronomistic thought, certain ideas important in 2 Kings 11–12 were explored ideologically. That is, an attempt was made to show how ideas intrinsic to the story, in light of their use and development within the Deuteronomistic History, work individually and together to reveal the

139. Berger and Luckmann, *Social Construction of Reality*, p. 103.

ideational world of the narrative. No attempt was made to be comprehensive in describing the 'world', nor in citing scholarly works. Rather, the most important concepts were studied with enough reference to the wider History and modern scholarship to propose a solid, if not definitive, version of key aspects of Deuteronomistic ideology.

A whole list of significant topics needed to be covered because the story involves roles and institutions central to the society's concept of its cosmically related order. The temple, as in other ancient Near Eastern societies, was representative of the cosmic order and legitimated the social order both religiously and politically. Its role in the story as sacred space, placing its awesome symbolic power behind Jehoiada's conspiracy, reflects the idea of the temple as the place of Yahweh's name, the guarantor of the covenant and the sanction for kingship in Deuteronomistic thought. The priest emerges in the thought-world of the story as servant of the king, a legitimating figure within the temple's legitimating ideology. The covenant shows the proper relationship between Yahweh and the people by which kings can be made and rule only under the aegis of its stipulations of fidelity. So Joash is made king with proper evocation of the covenant.

However, it is kingship which is by far the primary social institution in the story and in the Deuteronomistic universe, a concept evidently blending major ideas in Israelite history. Joash is the central figure of the story whose life and rule are at stake in ch. 11 and whose evaluation is shown in action in ch. 12. The promise to David and his heirs by the prophets Nathan and Ahijah is still active in 2 Kings 11–12 to ensure that a true Davidide inherits the throne of the kingdom. Functioning rightly only by keeping the covenant, the king can display true fidelity to Yahweh in his care for the temple. Joash does right and institutes a long-lived financial system for temple repair.

The Deuteronomistic evaluation of royal rule corresponds to the significance of the king in maintaining the social order through fidelity to the covenant. The evaluation of the Israelite kings, particularly the Omride dynasty, sets a standard for evil; this evil impinges on royal rule and worship in Judah with Athaliah as queen and a Baal temple in Jerusalem. The evaluation of Joash recognizes his doing right but holds him accountable for not removing the high places. The nuances of the evaluation play out in his reign in both his care for the temple and the loss of its treasures.

Evident at the end of this analysis is that the story is set within ideas that do define a 'symbolic universe' from a Deuteronomistic perspective. Even though no attempt was made to delineate the entire thought-world, a number of significant ideas were studied—temple, priest, covenant, kingship, dynasty, and regnal evaluation. In a number of ways the ideas overlapped—temple and kingship, kingship and covenant. Clearly a whole 'world' is posited behind the text. This universe is integrated and comprehensive, evident in an ideology shaping the story and expressed by the story. There is indeed 'reason' behind the rhetoric, a world of ideas to which the rhetoric appeals. And these ideas have to do with the most basic institutions that shape the state and its relation to its God.

As Berger and Luckmann and Geertz point out, however, a culture's ideas or an ideology do not exist in the abstract. Ideas are carried by social groups and the effectiveness of the ideas is directly related to the real power of the group holding them as a definition of reality. This insight leads directly to the questions of a sociological analysis. What type of group would use an ideology like the one explored here and express it in a story like 2 Kings 11–12? Why are the ideas of the story important? What in the story is explicated by a sociological understanding? To answer these questions, the final type of analysis must be accomplished.

Chapter 5

SOCIOLOGICAL ANALYSIS

Sociological analysis is the fourth and final perspective used to understand the story of Athaliah and Joash in 2 Kings 11–12. Once again, the
particular insights of a scholarly method can help to 'read' the narrative,
bringing an awareness to the text but staying, as always, grounded in the
text itself. The ideological analysis in the previous chapter pointed out
the need for this last type of study, raising tantalizing questions such as:
Given the symbolic universe that shapes the story, from what social
world would such an ideational universe arise? What types of people
hold such views? Why do they express these views through such a
story? What can an understanding of the social world from which the
story emerges add to the story's interpretation?

Doing a sociological analysis of a biblical text needs no general
justification because the methodology has a well-established place within
the scope of critical studies. In the past two decades, insights from sociology as a discipline have been used in various ways to interpret texts.
Even when a specific sociological method is not used, the awareness of
social roles, social stratification and the working of institutions has had
an impact. Early on, Albrecht Alt showed a sensitivity to power relations
concerning land rights in the Israelite monarchy in an essay published in
1959.[1] General analyses of the society and culture of ancient Israel
emerge in several essays in the volume about the monarchies in *The
World History of the Jewish People*.[2] Particular emphasis on social roles

1. A. Alt, 'Der Anteil des Königtums an der Socialen Entwicklung in der
Reichen Israel und Juda', in M. Noth (ed.), *Kleine Schriften zur Geschichte des
Volkes Israel* (Munich: Beck, 1959), pp. 348-72.

2. H. Reviv, 'The Structure of Society', pp. 125-46; S. Yeivin, 'Administration',
pp. 147-71; and M. Elat, 'Trade and Commerce', pp. 173-86 in A. Malamat (ed.),
*The World History of the Jewish People: The Age of the Monarchies: Culture and
Society* IV.II (Jerusalem: Massada Press, 1979).

is seen in studies such as Wilson's *Prophecy and Society in Ancient Israel*.[3] And the whole debate about early Israel has centered on the sociological formations of the people before the monarchy, highlighted by Gottwald's *The Tribes of Yahweh*.[4]

Given the varied approaches possible within a sociological methodology, the particular approach used here must be indicated. Basically, the method is to use a model of Judahite society based on a thorough cross-cultural study of societal types similar to ancient Israel. Grounded in the work of Gerhard and Jean Lenski on the typology and evolution of human societies, this approach sees societies as dynamic entities whose changes are largely fueled by technological advances.[5] Using a macro-sociological standpoint that examines a society as a systemic, evolutionary whole which responds to changes in its environment, the Lenskis classify societies into types based on their technological level of subsistence.[6] Systemic comparison shows that within any type of society, broad similarities exist which can be studied and begin to emerge as a pattern or model of that type.

The type to which ancient Israel belongs, indeed to which all of the ancient cultures of Israel's geographic area belong, is that of an agrarian society. The technological change which initiated evolution into an agrarian typology was the use of the plow, with accompanying use of animal energy. The larger agricultural yields from the new technology greatly increased the economic surplus which in turn increased the likelihood of developments in these societies such as urbanization, literacy and empire building.[7] By studying agrarian societies cross-culturally, the Lenskis can summarize the patterns these societies share:

> [E]very advanced agrarian society was much like the rest with respect to its fundamental characteristics. Class structure, social inequality, the division of labor, the distinctive role of urban populations in the larger society, the cleavage between urban and rural subcultures, the disdain of the governing class for both work and workers, the widespread belief in magic and fatalism, the use of the economic surplus for the benefit of the

3. R.R. Wilson, *Prophecy and Society in Ancient Israel* (Philadelphia: Fortress Press, 1980).

4. N.K. Gottwald, *The Tribes of Yahweh* (Maryknoll, NY: Orbis Books, 1985).

5. Lenski, Nolan and Lenski, *Human Societies*, p. 67.

6. Lenski, Nolan and Lenski, *Human Societies*, p. 81.

7. Lenski, Nolan and Lenski, *Human Societies*, p 177.

governing class and for the construction of monumental edifices, high
birth and death rates—all these and more were present in all advanced
agrarian societies.[8]

Within the broader description of characteristics intrinsic to agrarian
societies as a type are several which are important to this analysis. A
general description of these will serve as an introduction; details on these
will be given as applicable to the narrative. First, across time and across
cultures, agrarian societies are marked by a high degree of social
inequality in which the distances between social classes are large and the
upper class is economically dependent on the lower class.[9] The class of
peasants who work the land and give over most of any economic
surplus they create to the upper class constitutes the majority of the
population. A small percentage of people in an urbanized aristocratic or
elite class controls most of the land and wealth and all of the prestigious
and powerful government, military, cultural and social positions.[10] The
state and its governmental institutions serve the interests of the elites,
depending ultimately on the use of force to extract the produce, goods,
taxes, fees, labor and services the elites need from the rest of the
population.[11]

Secondly, with an aristocracy controlling the economy and the state,
agrarian societies show a propensity to organize government by monarchic rule and that rule is marked by conflict.[12] Within a single state an
'agrarian monarchy'[13] forms a social continuum with the upper class in
which land ownership, wealth, power and the throne are interchanged in
a series of intra-class conflicts.[14] When the chronic tendency to warfare
spills over and the aristocracies of neighboring regions are conquered, an
agrarian state can become an extensive empire. Empire building over-
lays the politics of the aristocracy with a concomitant extension into

8. Lenski, Nolan and Lenski, *Human Societies*, p. 219.
9. G. Lenski, *Power and Privilege: A Theory of Social Stratification* (Chapel
Hill, NC: University of North Carolina Press, 1984), p. 210.
10. Lenski, *Power*, pp. 219-20.
11. Lenski, Nolan and Lenski, *Human Societies*, p. 197.
12. Lenski, *Power*, p. 231.
13. The useful term 'agrarian monarchy' is drawn from M.L. Chaney, 'Ancient
Palestinian Peasant Movements and the Formation of Premonarchic Israel', in
D.N. Freedman and D.F. Graf (eds.), *Palestine in Transition* (Sheffield: Almond
Press, 1983), pp. 39-90.
14. J. Kautsky, *The Politics of Aristocratic Empires* (Chapel Hill, NC:
University of North Carolina Press, 1982), p. 211.

more or less organized and inefficient bureaucratic politics.[15] Overall, it
is characteristic of agrarian monarchies, as of aristocratic empires, that
government

> is government of the aristocracy, by the aristocracy, and for the aristoc-
> racy. It may perhaps be best understood as an extractive enterprise,
> created and operated by the aristocracy to maintain itself as an aristocracy,
> that is, as a class that lives off the labor of the peasantry and does not
> engage in productive labor itself.[16]

While the power of the elite to extract wealth from the peasants in a
command economy is based on the use of force, force alone is not
enough. So the third significant characteristic of agrarian societies is that
the use of force is always justified through various types of legitimation.[17] Prominent among the forms of legitimation is religion, which
provides rulers and the aristocracy with divine sanction and authority.[18]
Because the survival of elites and the state rests on exploitation, an ideology is needed which justifies the power of the few over the many, in
order to overcome any potential resistance. 'Ideology has the function of
presenting exploitation in a favorable light to the exploited, as advanta-
geous to the disadvantaged.'[19] But it also plays a role for those who
benefit from the system, for 'the ideological motivation provides them
with greater credibility and effectiveness, to others and to themselves'.[20]

The details of this basic model of agrarian society and its social orga-
nizations will be examined as they are applicable to a sociological analysis of 2 Kings 11–12. But enough has been said to typify the model
being used in the analysis. Such a sociological model highlights what is
generic to agrarian societies[21] and allows examination of the text from
that standpoint.

T.F. Carney explores how models can be useful for analysis. By

15. Lenski, *Power*, p. 230.

16. Kautsky, *Aristocratic Empires*, p. 118.

17. R. Bendix, *Kings or People: Power and the Mandate to Rule* (Berkeley:
University of California Press, 1978), p. 17.

18. Kautsky, *Aristocratic Empires*, p. 159; and Bendix, *Kings*, p. 7.

19. M. Liverani, 'The Ideology of the Assyrian Empire', in M.T. Larsen (ed.),
Power and Propaganda: A Symposium on Ancient Empires (Mesopotamia:
Copenhagen Studies in Assyriology, 7; Copenhagen: Akademisk Forlag, 1979),
p. 298.

20. Liverani, 'Ideology', p. 299.

21. M.L. Chaney, 'Systemic Study of the Israelite Monarchy', *Semeia* 37
(1986), p. 58.

providing a 'set of measures with which to conduct cross-comparisons', a model guards against anachronistic assumptions.[22] For a biblical interpretation, using a model will keep the analysis grounded in an ancient agrarian monarchical context. Further, the model indicates the complexity of the issues being considered and gives guidance for the types and levels of analysis.[23] This analysis can thus be aware of social conflicts among elites while not positing an extensive imperial bureaucracy which is not evident in monarchic Judah. Looking at the story will involve some macro-level awareness of societal structures, some middle-level concern with the power struggles of elites, and some micro-level analysis of individual social roles. And since the analysis is being applied to one story involving just a few incidents, 'a model provides some norms against which to interpret the significance of what we find to be going on. It provides a master pattern, as it were, enabling us to go about the business of pattern matching'.[24] The model will help identify elements which might otherwise go unnoticed or which might not otherwise receive the same kind of emphasis as in an agrarian monarchic context.

It is important to specify that a sociological analysis does not uncover *historical facts*. It will not tell us whether Joash really was the son of the king or exactly why the priests did not carry out his first plan for temple repair financing. Rather, an analysis of this type uncovers *sociological probabilities*—what is most likely to happen in a particular situation given the typology of the society. Typical social roles, typical individual actions and typical power struggles are portrayed, or in some cases significantly not portrayed, in the narrative. But this finding of probabilities is still an advance in analysis over any approach that is ignorant of the dynamics of societal interactions in the social world from which the Bible emerged. To know, for example, that the murder of a royal family in pursuit of the throne is an action entirely typical of aristocratic power struggles is to shield Athaliah's action from modern anachronistic morality judgments and to set it in its own context as a brutal but not unusual case.

With this fourth kind of analysis, my examination of 2 Kings 11–12 moves to what I call the largest 'concentric circle' in which the narrative

22. T.F. Carney, *The Shape of the Past: Models and Antiquity* (Lawrence, KS: Coronado Press, 1975), p. 73.

23. Carney, *Shape of the Past*, p. 74.

24. Carney, *Shape of the Past*, p. 75.

stands. The story includes the characters of a queen and a king and a priest acting with others in a series of events. To study the sociological patterns that illuminate this story is to focus on the 'circle' that encompasses the dynamics of agrarian monarchies. In this way, the broadly defined 'social world' *in* the story is analyzed. However, the same dynamics of agrarian monarchies that operate in the story world also operate in the author's and audience's world. The author who wrote the story with characters and actions and themes stood as a part of an agrarian monarchic social world just like the readers. The social world *of* the story is the same as the social world *in* the story and the 'circle' I now move to includes the world that created the story.

Turning to an analysis of the social world of the story's creation involves a shift in perspective once again. Now the author and the audience are seen in a way that makes them both actors in a societal interaction that is the writing/telling of a story. I am thus undertaking a sociological examination of characteristic patterns that might fit the creation of the story. Given the model of an agrarian monarchy, who would write such a narrative and why? But even this fourth type of analysis is based on an aspect that is intrinsic to the narrative itself because the realities of the author's social context are expressed through the social world in the story. Even as the social context is examined, the analysis stays focused on the story. So two types of analysis will be done at the same time—of sociological realities in the story (the 'story world') and in the context that created the narrative (the 'social context'). For both types, characteristic patterns will alert us to what is significant without making historical claims.

In the introductory chapter, my assumptions about the Deuteronomistic context of 2 Kings 11–12 were discussed. Generally, the 'author' of the story has been assumed to be the Deuteronomist so that, for example, when the ideological analysis was done, the Deuteronomistic worldview was taken as its wider referent. However, the theory that the Deuteronomistic History achieved primary form in the Josianic era in Judah will be used as a working assumption in this fourth analysis. This allows more specific sociological data to be brought to bear when the possible references or allegiances of the author, or the possible effects of the story, are discussed. Indeed, the numerous narrative parallels and extensive rhetorical allusions to the Josiah story in 2 Kings 22–23 already detailed in this study lend credibility to the Josianic provenance theory and make its use here comprehensible.

Finally, the analysis will be structured by topic, as was the ideological analysis. Reference to the story itself will be constant but a topical arrangement allows patterns and connections to be seen more easily.

Social Roles and Locations

An initial approach to a sociological analysis of 2 Kings 11–12 examines the general content of the story world. What social roles and social locations does the story itself portray? Such a review gives an introduction to the sociological underpinnings of the narrative, how the social realities of agrarian societies emerge in the story world. Later these same considerations will prove to be important for how the narrative functions in the social context of its author. But for now the world created *in* the story is of concern. Data to be examined are the type of characters, the social roles that they play in the story, and the geographical locations mentioned. The following review of the story is dependent on the narrative analysis, but a reprise highlights social categories. Terms that carry sociological import are italicized.

A *queen* who was *born into a foreign dynasty* and *married into the Judahite royal family* is the first character. She *murders the royal family* and *seizes the throne*. A *sister of the dead king saves one of the king's sons* and *hides him in the temple*. In the seventh year, *the priest* gathers *the royal guards* into a *conspiracy, controlling their movements in the temple to protect* the *young son of the king*. The *heir apparent* is *brought out* and is *crowned and acclaimed*, with accompanying *royal symbols* of *covenant* and *dynasty*. The *guards* and *all the people hail and celebrate the new king*. The *queen* sees and reacts to the scene with a cry of *treason*, but she *is killed* by *the army at the king's house*. A *covenant* is made which establishes a *religious and political relationship* and then *the people destroy the temple and priest of a rival sect*. The *new king takes his seat on the throne* and *the city is quiet*.

King Joash reigns 40 years in the *capital city Jerusalem*, doing what *the priest* had *taught him* all his days. However, he does *not remove the local cult places in the countryside*. He *initiates* a plan *to repair the temple*, asking *the priests* to take the *sacred donations* and use them for the repairs. But *the priests do not carry out the plan*. The king *summons the priest Jehoiada* and *the priests* and *informs them* of a new plan that *removes the priests* from the repair scheme. *The priests agree to being removed from the process. Jehoiada* installs a box *in the temple to collect the money. The priest* and *the king's secretary collect, have refined and count the money* and *hand it over* to the *overseers of the repair work*, who in turn hire *the workers* and *buy supplies.* The *overseers* are *honest* so *no accounting of the funds* is needed and the plan becomes *an ongoing procedure.* During the king's reign, *a king of a neighboring country*, Hazael of Aram, *invades the land* and *takes a city* nearby. He *turns to fight against Jerusalem*, but *Joash gives him the treasuries of the temple and palace* and *he withdraws. Joash* is *murdered by two of his servants* and is *succeeded* by his son.

What is evident from this review is that while the narrative functions as a story, has its own rhetorical impact and expresses ideological views, it is also full of important sociological data. Practically every person, action and location can be seen as significant on the basis of the sociological model described above. Some of these elements should be highlighted and discussed.

Very clearly almost all of the characters in the story are representative of the elite, aristocratic class present in any agrarian society. A king, a queen, the king's sister, the king's secretary, and the king's (murderous) servants are all people from the royal court. The guards, runners and Carians are likely the private military force of the monarchy. The priest and the priests are the highest religious officials of the land. The overseers probably hold administrative office in the religious institution. A king from a neighboring country is an enemy but also an aristocrat in his own context. The only clearly non-elite characters are the workers who actually carry out the labor of temple repair. As artisans and skilled workers they serve the elite class, according to the model, but are not aristocrats themselves.

The only major characters whose elite status is open to question are 'the people of the land' who play a role in making Joash king. The term has undergone extensive critical discussion; this is not the place for a detailed review of its meaning. However, a few scholarly readings of it will indicate the types of interpretations possible. Roland de Vaux takes the phrase in its pre-exilic use to refer to 'the whole body of citizens', an alternate phrase for the 'people of Judah'.[25] He specifically notes that 'nowhere does the expression mean a party or social class'.[26] H. Reviv takes it as a kind of 'middle class' developing from the tribe and congregation of early Israel. This middle class supported the monarchy and

25. De Vaux, *Ancient Israel*, p. 71.
26. De Vaux, *Ancient Israel*, p. 71.

worked against the powerful upper classes and 'high-placed pressure groups' which he takes as 'the high officials and the rich'.[27] Bustenay Oded provides an excellent brief summary of research on the term עם הארץ in his essay 'Judah and the Exile'.[28] He notes that the problems with the term do not permit a precise definition,[29] and that the only sure thing is that '"the people of the land" was a political-social element which was loyal to the house of David'.[30]

While the term may never be defined exactly and may be used in different ways even in the pre-exilic literature, a few characteristics of its usage can be illuminated by the sociological model. The starting point can be Oded's summarizing comment that the עם הארץ play a political-social role in support of the Davidic dynasty—exactly what they do in 2 Kings 11–12. The sociological model is clear on the lack of political participation by most of the population in agrarian societies, that is, by the peasants. It would be difficult therefore to read the term as 'a body of citizens' or 'all of the people of Judah'. Further, there rarely exists in agrarian societies anything like a 'middle class' in any modern sense, so that is not a likely meaning either.

The other aspect of the term that may be a hint as to meaning is the reference to the land. The people 'of the land' who were most likely to have the wherewithal to participate in the making of kings are the landed aristocracy. As wealthy landowners, either by inheritance or land grant from the crown, these elites would join with other upper-class members in having a keen interest in who was king. As sociologists of these agrarian systems have noted, 'the landed and aristocratic groups always participated actively in political struggle'.[31] Without attempting to solve the debates over the meaning of the term 'the people of the land', for this analysis I will understand it as members of the wealthy, landed aristocracy that do play a political role in support of the Davidic dynasty.

If the term עם הארץ is taken as an elite group as proposed, this means that all of the characters and social roles mentioned in the story world are of the elite class (or, as artisans, serve that class). Nowhere do the

27. Reviv, 'Structure of Society', p. 146.
28. B. Oded, 'Judah and the Exile', in J.H. Hayes and J.M. Miller (eds.), *Israelite and Judean History* (Philadelphia: Westminster Press, 1977), pp. 456-58.
29. Oded, 'Judah', p. 457.
30. Oded, 'Judah', p. 458.
31. S.N. Eisenstadt, *The Political Systems of Empires* (New York: Free Press, 1963), p. 177.

concerns or life of the peasant majority have an impact on the story. The narrative focuses on the court, the king, and the highest officials; these are the ones who hold power in any highly stratified agrarian society.

A review of the locations mentioned is brief but produces similar results. Prominent is Jerusalem, the capital city where all of the action in both chapters takes place. In agrarian societies, the extractive economy concentrates wealth and power in urban areas. And the highest concentration is always in the center of power, the capital city.[32] Politically, economically and culturally, the capital city in such a society is the dominant urban area, which in turn makes it the dominant geographical location in the country. Some critics read a contrast between Jerusalem and the countryside in 11.20—the people of the land rejoicing but the capital city quiet.[33] But the model shows rather the overlapping interests of elites, which do not draw a boundary between city and rural, only between the powerful and the peasantry.[34]

The other two specific locations mentioned repeatedly are the temple and the palace. The ideational concept of the House of Yahweh was examined in the previous chapter; however, its ideological reality is accompanied by a sociological reality just as significant to the story. Both the temple and the palace in agrarian societies are important in several ways. As the locations of actual religious and political administration they function on a practical level as loci of control, bringing economic wealth towards the center through taxation and directing the workings of officials and bureaucrats.[35]

But more importantly, the temple and palace serve as symbols of royal and aristocratic power in a society where power matters in every aspect of life. 'Both physically and symbolically, the central governmental and religious structures dominate the urban horizon.'[36] The building of monumental architecture, characteristic of agrarian societies, takes tremendous amounts of labor and materials which thus feeds into the central powers of the state. The very location of the story of Athaliah and Joash signals its sociological import. 'Palace and temple complexes are the most important visual symbols of royal power and

32. G. Sjoberg, *The Pre-Industrial City: Past and Present* (New York: Free Press, 1960), p. 88.

33. De Vaux, *Ancient Israel*, p. 71.

34. Oded, 'Judah', p. 458.

35. Sjoberg, *Pre-Industrial City*, p. 87.

36. Sjoberg, *Pre-Industrial City*, p. 96.

indicate more precisely the location of the center within a stratified society.'[37] Like the review of social roles in the story, the social locations mentioned both confirm the sociological model being used and are illuminated by it. The narrative is about the central elite roles and central power locations in the society.

Factional Politics in Agrarian Monarchies

Further specifics from the model of agrarian society being used will extend the analysis. The model introduced the concept of an agrarian monarchy as a most typical form of government. Rule by a king through force or conquest is the pattern largely 'as a result of the militaristic and exploitative character of societies at this level'.[38] But the king does not rule alone, as the elite class from which he comes is also the group to which he owes his power on the throne. If members of that aristocratic group have the desire and the power to place a more responsive (that is, malleable) aristocrat on the throne, conflict is inevitable. 'Most members of the governing class considered political power a prize to be sought for the rewards it offered rather than an opportunity for public service, and the office of the king or emperor was the *supreme prize*.'[39]

However, the scenario is more complex because the aristocracy is not a single 'interest group'. Made up uniformly of wealthy and powerful people, it is yet a collection of landowners, military officers, religious leaders, and administrative officials.[40] Each grouping has its own interests as well as possible overlaps with other groups, especially since wealthy landowners are the common source and reference group for all the others.[41] On the one hand, because all individuals in all the groups want the means to increase their own wealth and power, conflict among them is usual. On the other hand, the self-interests of subgroups can lead them to join forces with others in coalitions or factions that seek some sort of privilege or control of land or an office, especially the throne.[42]

---

37. K.W. Whitelam, 'The Symbols of Power: Aspects of Royal Propaganda in the United Monarchy', *BA* 49 (1986), p. 170.

38. Lenski, Nolan and Lenski, *Human Societies*, p. 205.

39. Lenski, Nolan and Lenski, *Human Societies*, p. 207.

40. Carney, *Shape of the Past*, p. 61.

41. Carney, *Shape of the Past*, p. 60.

42. Carney, *Shape of the Past*, p. 62.

> In practice, the lines of conflict dividing the aristocracy may well not be
> the ones separating the court, military, bureaucracy and clergy, even if
> these are clearly distinct institutions—and often they are not. They are
> more likely to cut across these lines or to subdivide these institutions.
> Thus, a ruler's court is frequently divided into cliques and factions...[43]

The result is an inevitable series of intra-class struggles in which the
king's position is always vulnerable to assault from his aristocratic peers
or his supposed subordinates in the royal hierarchy. The king thus
always seeks to maximize control[44] against those who would weaken or
undermine him. The ministers, officials, landowners, military officers and
so on in turn seek control of the king—his policies, access to land,
wealth and positions, or the throne itself.[45] A number of variables
reflecting differences in individual states and incidents will determine the
outcome of these struggles over policy, positions, wealth or the throne,
but the tendency towards intra-class political conflict in agrarian
monarchies is clear.

The struggles of elites for power shows itself most dramatically when
the question of the succession to the throne is posed.[46] Who the next
ruler will be when the present one has died, become incapacitated, or
been removed/assassinated is a concern to every group in the elite social
structure. While dynastic succession is one typical answer, the placing of
a particular son on the throne is never a guaranteed proposition. The
uncertainties of succession show the unending difficulty in stabilizing the
authority of the king.[47]

This well-established sociological pattern of factional power politics
can be seen both in the seizure by Athaliah of the throne and in
Jehoiada's conspiracy to win the throne back for Joash. The story world
at these points is explicated well by the sociology of agrarian monarchies. The account of Athaliah's murder of all who could legitimately
claim succession to the throne and then her own seizure of power rings
true as a characteristic maneuver by an elite wishing to gain the throne.
As one already close to the court, as the queen mother, she was able to
take advantage of her son's death to make her own move. She removed
all dynastic challenge to her position by killing the king's descendants.

43. Kautsky, *Aristocratic Empires*, p. 238.
44. Bendix, *Kings*, p. 220.
45. Carney, *Shape of the Past*, p. 55.
46. Carney, *Shape of the Past*, p. 54.
47. Bendix, *Kings*, p. 223.

Thus, understanding the dynamics of elite power struggles makes her actions in the story intelligible as a type of elite power play.

But the sociological model also reveals something unexpected about the story world. According to the way the narrative is shaped, Athaliah acts alone in seizing power. No other character is mentioned as 'on her side'. When Jehoiada sets his coup in motion, one set of possible supporters for Athaliah, the palace guard, appear to change sides easily, leaving her with no royal guard. While the story twice mentions the possibility of support by violence for the queen, it never materializes. By the account of the story world, Athaliah acts alone, rules alone, and dies alone.

The model of elite power struggles alerts the analyst that this is virtually impossible sociologically. At least at the point where a usurper seizes power, someone and usually a lot of people in a powerful faction had to support him or her. Some groups always see a benefit to themselves in such changes in the monarchy[48] and it is highly unlikely that Athaliah has no supporters or co-conspirators as she seizes power. These same groups, invisible in the story world but inevitable in the social world of a monarchy, would have probably aided in her ruling over the land. They would probably also have tried, if the model holds true, to support her when her rule and their benefit was threatened by Jehoiada and Joash. However, the model also raises the possibility that when a ruler's power is threatened, his or her supporters may be quick to 'jump ship' and find a more promising candidate to support. So the lack of a visible faction at Athaliah's death is less problematic, although still worthy of note.

This same phenomenon of the lack of an apparent faction supporting Athaliah can be viewed from another perspective. A sociological understanding can also be applied to the social context of the story's creation. The author, posited as the Deuteronomist, wrote the story so that Athaliah appears to have no support, even though the author lived under an agrarian monarchy in which such things did not usually happen. A reality typical of the author's social context has been ignored by the author in the story world; for some reason, Athaliah's support group was not included in the story. This could reflect various motivations on the author's part, none of which can be verified, but the previous analyses suggest a possibility. To the extent that this reflects a deliberate attempt to deny Athaliah any grounds for justification, it is complementary to the ideological patterning already examined in the Deuteronomistic treatment of her. This alerts the critic to the possibility

48. Eisenstadt, *Political Systems*, p. 14.

that the narrative and rhetorical structures in the story world may have been shaped by ideological considerations important to the author in their own social context. Athaliah's origin was in the evil House of Omri and she brought that evil into Judah. That her wickedness could have had any support in Judah might have been anathema to the Deuteronomist and thus impossible to mention.

However that is evaluated, the story world contains a good account of faction-building at work in the story of Jehoiada's conspiracy. The elements in the narrative are elucidated clearly sociologically. The faction involves a coalition of people cutting across aristocratic divisions—palace guards, soldiers, clergy, at least one member of the royal court (Jehosheba), and the people of the land, taken (above) as landed elites active in the political process. The faction is led by a powerful member of the religious establishment—'the priest'. This group joins together to support their candidate for the throne, Joash, and manages to pull off a successful coup d'état. All of these elements fit expected patterns in the sociology of agrarian monarchies.

Several other elements are also significant from this viewpoint. The all-important question of succession to the throne is central here. The faction in the story claims to be reinstituting the legitimate dynastic succession by placing one of the former king's sons on the throne. Whether Joash was a true Davidide or not, the claim by his supporters that he was made their case for his enthronement virtually unimpeachable. Likewise, the actions of Joash's coalition display the use of every possible symbolic support for legitimation and Davidic dynastic succession, marshalling all the evidence possible for their side against any potential dissenters. One other note is worthy of mention. The candidate that the faction places on the throne is a seven-year-old boy. Such a choice coincides with a characteristic of factional politics, the tendency to support less powerful individuals for the throne, in that minors can be more easily controlled and manipulated by their adult supporters.[49]

So the story world clearly shows the significance of how factions operate and how they can be successful in elite power struggles. The story gives explicit details of a faction's maneuverings in support of Joash. And the widespread support for him by a group that cuts across elite lines of interest is rhetorically evident. No one appears who dissents from the proceedings (except, of course, Athaliah!). The contrast with Athaliah's non-existent support group could not be clearer.

49. Carney, *Shape of the Past*, p. 54.

Again, however, the social context of the story as a form of communication by the author is significant. The shaping of the story makes the Davidic dynasty's continuation the critical problem. And it suggests that in the author's own social context unwavering support for the Davidic dynasty is a central political tenet. Ideological analysis underlined the role of the Davidic dynasty in Deuteronomistic thought. What a sociological reading of this story points to is that this tenet probably had a coinciding importance politically for the social group that sponsored the writing of the story. Placing the story's composition in the Josianic context suggests that unwavering support for Josiah, the reigning Davidide in Jerusalem, is of central importance.

Sociological sensitivity further suggests that in the Josianic context a faction or political group championed this support for the Davidic king. A connection between Joash's story world and the story world created for Josiah by the Deuteronomistic author reveals the possibility of just such a faction. Like Joash, Josiah comes to the throne as a child and his securing of the throne is aided by 'the people of the land' (2 Kgs 21.24). Taking this as a politically active group of landed elites who support a malleable candidate reveals one element of the Davidic monarchic faction in both story worlds. This could easily indicate that just such an element exists in the author's own context and is being appealed to through the story of Joash.

Another note on the workings of factional politics in the succession of kings should be discussed. Very quietly, at the end of ch. 12, it is noted that Joash was assassinated by two of his servants who conspired against him. All of the sociological explication of factional infighting over the throne that applied to Athaliah and Joash earlier also applies to Joash's demise. Significant in this regard is the meaning of 'servant'; this does not indicate some sort of domestic help but rather any of the king's highly placed advisors, ministers or officials. When Joash is murdered, in contrast to the coups earlier in the story, nothing is made of the event by the author. Little rhetorical shaping is seen and the assassination seems to carry little ideological weight. It seems to be included in the regnal closing formula as a annalistic notation only. The lack of narrative, rhetorical or ideological development in the story world may indicate that the event had minimal importance for the author's social context as well. Since the dynastic succession of one of Joash's sons, Amaziah, followed the murder, no threat undermined the author's emphasis on the Davidic dynasty.

One further major topic related to factional politics focuses on the role of the military. In the politics of agrarian societies generally, the military wields significant power, not the least of which is due to its commanding the resources of physical force. So the leaders of the army, who are almost always aristocrats themselves, hold true power. This is especially the case when a professional army, as opposed to a national militia, develops in a state.[50] The professionalization of the army can be based on a permanent standing army recruited from the ruler's own people. But just as often the army or some portion of it is a mercenary force, paid professional soldiers, often of foreign origin.[51] The mercenary army is often more loyal to the throne than a national militia because its leaders are not drawn from the state's own aristocrats who have their own political agendas. But this also means that a professional or mercenary army has a powerful position in the social structure and the army's leaders 'have considerable political influence'.[52] As a force in the governmental apparatus, the military thus holds power over the king. It can be a major player in the giving and taking of the throne.[53]

The detailed account in the narrative of 2 Kings 11 concerning the deployment of the Carians and the runners has this sociological reality as its background. As noted earlier, these forces were probably a royal guard, intelligible as a private professional and (probably for the Carians) mercenary army in the employ of the monarchy. And they play a role in the story quite in line with the typical power of royal armies. Jehoiada bases his coup on their loyalty and participation. Sociological analysis suggests that he could not do otherwise because of the power a professional army holds over the throne. The line of royal guards around Joash as he stands by the pillar is a symbolic arrangement, but it is also a very practical one in terms of power politics. With the royal guard on his side, Jehoiada can place Joash on the throne. Without the royal guard, all the dynastic symbolism he could have mustered might not have done any good.

There may also be some significance for the social context of the author and audience who knew the events as a story. The narrative not only portrays how the elite royal guards act in the story world to uphold the Davidic throne, but it makes a point applicable to the author's social

50. Lenski, Nolan and Lenski, *Human Societies*, p. 181.
51. Eisenstadt, *Political Systems*, p. 131.
52. Eisenstadt, *Political Systems*, p. 173.
53. Carney, *Shape of the Past*, p. 61.

context. This is how royal guards 'should' act in all their dealings with power. Their acceptable role is as a military support for the true Davidide who holds the reins of power. Rhetorical analysis showed that their comings and goings mirror royal prerogative and power. The story world displays an attitude of loyalty which in the social context holds that the comings and goings of the royal guard are in the service of the Davidic monarchy.

Religion and the State

The role of religion in the politics of elites in agrarian societies is central and at the same time ambiguous. Both the centrality and ambiguity of religious ideas, personnel and institutions are seen in the story world of 2 Kings 11–12. And, as with the portrayal of factional politics, the portrayal of religion can be seen as making a difference in the social context which produced the narrative.

Most basically, the sociological model used here shows that the religious ideas of an agrarian society function to support and legitimize the power of the state and its political leaders. 'Religious leaders are instrumental in providing moral justification for the social order, including the dominance of the society by a privileged few.'[54] As illustrated in the discussion of ideology in the previous chapter, a 'symbolic universe' provides an overarching reality for all of life. When the 'universe' is propagated by the religious elite in a stratified society, it comes to permeate and to try to control the values and orientations of the whole society. Religious values and symbols become prominent and religion provides 'the main centers of cultural creativity and of transmitting the cultural traditions of these societies'.[55]

Religious leaders are part of the elite class in these societies, often controlling, through their religious institutions, tremendous power and wealth. As elites, they are part of the central power struggles, normally being allied with others among the political leaders.[56] In their role as legitimators of the political regime, religious leaders provide the sanction and authentication the king needs to rule.[57] So the religious institutions play a key role in maintaining the power of the state. But the role of

54. Sjoberg, *Pre-Industrial City*, p. 119.
55. Eisenstadt, *Political Systems*, p. 61
56. Lenski, Nolan and Lenski, *Human Societies*, p. 212.
57. Bendix, *Kings*, p. 22.

religion also gives its leaders a large measure of practical political power. Particularly where a religious hierarchy has the authority to confer legitimacy on the one who holds the throne, its leaders can influence both accession to the throne and the wielding of power by the ruler.[58]

The ambiguous role of religion both to confer and deny ultimate legitimation to political structures is often rooted in its intrinsic ties to the traditional culture of the society. Even when aristocratic and national institutions have been imposed on a social structure, traditional values, codes and religion and their accompanying cultural outlook survive both in local manifestations and in possible smaller groupings of elites. These traditional values and orientations of popular culture continue to be significant to the elites:

> They were the great potential allies of the ruling elites in the latter's endeavors to remain identified with the political and cultural systems and their symbols. Further, they usually were the chief connecting links between the local traditions of the vast strata of the population and the 'Great Tradition' of the cultural and political centers.[59]

To the extent that the clergy represent connections with the older or local cultural traditions, they express the symbolic and practical power of those traditions in legitimating the political elites. So the clergy, besides having political power in their own right as members of elite institutions, also have the weight of religious tradition behind them in dealing with the various political factions. 'As a rule, these contending parties depended greatly on the religious and cultural elites to be instrumental in propagating the legitimacy of their interests and for the effective communication and transmission of their respective symbols.'[60]

Within this general framework of interaction between religion and the state, several specifics can be highlighted. First could be noted the responsibility of the king to build and care for the temple. This has extensive ideological ramifications, as noted before. But it is a very practical role which the king fulfills for the religious hierarchy. By marshalling workers and resources toward the construction or repair of a building of such monumental architecture as a temple, the ruler demonstrates service to the religion of the state and its god. The king's attention not only gains him the favorable opinion of the religious elite

58. Carney, *Shape of the Past*, p. 62.
59. Eisenstadt, *Political Systems*, p. 184.
60. Eisenstadt, *Political Systems*, p. 184.

ideologically, but also can function as a *quid pro quo* for the support for him by the religious elite.[61] It can be a situation which results in gains for both sides.

Secondly, the whole edifice of religion in the state is closely tied into the basic extractive economy that takes any economic surplus from the peasant workers to support aristocrats and their institutions. The redistribution of income from the peasants to the elites, through taxation, rents and other fees, 'is an absolutely essential aspect of aristocratic empires'.[62] The central religious institutions, particularly the temple which constitutes the 'state sanctuary', depend on a share of the taxes enforced by the monarchy to support the religious establishment. As noted before, the temple serves as an ideological center which is understood as the house of the god, and this household needs resources for its daily operations; 'temples and their staffs had to be supported by a steady flow of goods'.[63] Using the revenues provided by the state, the temple becomes a complex combining the administration of religious and practical activities with areas devoted to ritual as well as workshops, storerooms and public areas.[64] All is in the service of the god and, by that, the temple is central in the economic system and political power struggles of the state.

Thirdly, the power of religious elites often guarantees to them direct access to the centers of power, particularly the court.[65] As people having access to the royal court but not directly in the service of the king, they have a relatively independent stance from which to wield their own power. This takes the form of such roles as advisors to the monarchy or participation in the formation of policy.[66] In the contentions for power between the monarchy and religious elites, the relationship is not always harmonious, however. Even though the king needs legitimation and the temple needs the monarch's consideration through financial support, tensions are inevitable. The religious elites try to control the king; he, in turn, seeks to limit their power. One of the clergy's main objectives is to maintain its independence over against the powers of other elites.[67] But

61. Lenski, Nolan and Lenski, *Human Societies*, p. 212.
62. Kautsky, *Aristocratic Empires*, p. 150.
63. Lenski, Nolan and Lenski, *Human Societies*, p. 178.
64. Meyers, 'David as Temple Builder', p. 366.
65. Eisenstadt, *Political Systems*, p. 186.
66. Sjoberg, *Pre-Industrial City*, p. 257.
67. Eisenstadt, *Political Systems*, p. 185.

the ruler's policies often include direct control of religious activities and institutions.[68]

The above considerations fill in the religious aspects of the sociological model being used. The model can now serve as background for a discussion of religious elements of sociological importance in 2 Kings 11–12. Foremost, of course, is the general portrayal of the temple in the story as a central location that has specific political interests. This is a temple that has an active role in the power struggles of the state, being directly involved in the succession to the throne. The symbolic weight of the temple stands behind Joash; when he is presented as the new king, the temple with all its connotations of religious sanctity is the scene of the action. Visible in the story is thus the combination of symbolic and practical power that religion wields. Further, that the religious center could put its support behind just one faction in the political struggles is also clear in the story.

Moving to consider the context in which the story was propagated, this role of the temple in the story could have sociological import. By portraying the temple as an active political center, the story suggests that its author commends this view to the readers. Such was probably the case in the author's society anyway (if the model describes it accurately), but here the author directly confirms that role as an appropriate one for the state religion. More specifically, the temple's role as principal support for the Davidic monarchy in the story suggests that this too is significant in the author's context. Religious establishments could give or take legitimation to the seeker or holder of the throne. The story presents the temple's unambiguous support for the Davidic descendant who seeks to regain the throne. By this it not only reveals the possible political bent of its author but shows the appropriate *Realpolitik* role for the temple in the story's social context.

The role of the priest can be considered in a similar way. Jehoiada clearly is an elite religious functionary who has access to the centers of power. He is, in fact, a king-maker, able to wield the power of giving and taking the throne. His portrayal as one commanding authority and power over the decision about the succession is entirely intelligible in light of the model. But also evident is his service to the rightful king. He is not shown using power for his own particular ends, but in the service of the restoration of the Davidic monarchy. The ideological aspect of this was noted earlier; here, the sociological aspect of the priest being

68. Eisenstadt, *Political Systems*, p. 141.

subservient to the king is highlighted. The head of the religious establishment could be independent of the monarchy. This role of service is a marked contrast to that. Jehoiada's supportive role is continued during Joash's reign. He functions as the king's 'instructor', a term connoting education but probably overlapping with advisory capacities when understood sociologically. And in participating directly in the king's second plan for temple repair he does the king's will without apparent question.

The particular portrayal of the priest's role in the story may well have sociological importance in the author's context. The author also lived in a social structure where the priest wielded power. By showing Jehoiada as powerful but in the service of the Davidic king, the author may be elucidating a social role for a contemporary priest. An entirely independent priest beholden to no political authority may not be, in the author's view, a wise or appropriate arrangement. The author presents a view which supports the Davidic monarch's power over the temple and its priest. Using sociological categories, this can be understood as an artistic expression of a political opinion. This opinion may well be that of a political faction in the author's own time as well as a theme in the story.

But relations between political and religious establishments have further influence in the story. Joash's reign in 2 Kings 12 shows him fulfilling the role of temple caretaker. This role is illumined by all of the considerations noted above about the king's relations to the temple. The added import of the narrative comes when it switches into the iterative mode so that Joash's system appears to solve the problem of temple upkeep for years to come. Thus in the story world, Joash gains all of the favorable reviews that can come from this activity for a king. When the social context of the story's writing is considered, the author appears to carry this favorable opinion into 'current events'. In fact, if (1) the Deuteronomist is writing under Josiah as posited and (2) the account of Josiah's initial efforts in the temple when the lawbook is found (2 Kgs 22.3-10) is also from the Josianic Deuteronomist,[69] then the same author uses Joash's system again in Josiah's story. Here is unique evidence of how an idea (temple repair financing) can have a sociological import in an 'old' story and still be important in a story 'current' in the author's

---

69. I follow here N. Lohfink, 'The Cult Reform of Josiah of Judah: 2 Kings 22–23 as a Source for the History of Israelite Religion', in Miller, Hanson and McBride (eds.), *Ancient Israelite Religion*, p. 462.

time. Even if neither king actually used the finance system, the portrayal of two kings 200 years apart using it to repair the state sanctuary illustrates the sociological power of an 'old' idea in a 'new' context.

The considerations about power struggles between royal and religious elites shape the interpretation of the account of Joash's two plans for financing the temple repair. The priests' failure to carry out the first plan can be seen sociologically as the priests' resistance to the king's attempt to control that aspect of their administration. But the portrayal moves quickly on to show that in the face of the king's second plan, the priests relinquish any participation in the system. This portrayal lends itself to a sociological interpretation that the king asserted his power to control the priests and was able to move them out of the way. The new plan has the cooperation of Jehoiada and the royal presence of the king's secretary. This shared administration from temple and palace marks a cooperative effort that accomplishes the king's intentions. Joash had been put on the throne by the power of the religious elites; in order to establish his power over them he takes charge of the temple repair system.

Because the system 'survives' into the author's own time, all of the sociological import of royal control over the priests survives with it in the story's social context. Specifically, in the Josiah story world, the priest and the king's secretary still administer the finance system at the king's order (2 Kgs 22.3-4). The same power relationship of the king commanding the priest as well as, of course, his own scribe, is portrayed as the 'normal' course of events in the author's time. As noted above and confirmed here, the priest and priests are not independent power brokers but are in the service of the king in the story world of both Joash and Josiah. An impact on the author's social context is suggested: that priests do well to follow the example of Jehoiada even in Josiah's day and age.

The temple repair account also alerts the critic to another sociological dimension. The funds for the repairs come from the 'sacred donations' or 'all the money that was brought into the House of the Lord'. These are best understood as direct references to the tax system which in any agrarian society funnels economic surplus from the peasants and countryside to the elites and central institutions. In the narrative analysis, discussion of terminology revealed a reference to 'smelting' the collected monies in the temple. This is a part of the same social reality of a temple as an extensive financial system. Regardless of debates about how the particular monies are described in the story, they are not to be understood as 'freewill donations' in any modern sense, but rather as parts of a taxation system that supported the state and its cult. Funds directed to the temple supported its activities as noted. Indeed, the reaction of the priests to the king's first plan can possibly be understood as their resistance to what they considered meddling in the financial administration of the temple.

The taxation system in Judah is still an open subject.[70] However, as in other agrarian societies studied,[71] probably there is ultimately no hard-and-fast distinction between 'religious' taxation and 'secular' taxation. The following comes from a historical analysis, but expresses a reality quite in line with the sociological model used here:

> Examining First Temple Judah, it is inappropriate to draw a distinction between support for the royal cult and support for the royal house. Supporting the Davidic king was the practical expression of devotion to Yahweh, and worshipping Yahweh was the Judean's patriotic duty. Just as the Davidic monarchs exercised practical authority over Yahweh's land, so the kings had ultimate say over Yahweh's treasuries. Attempts to distinguish 'cultic' and 'secular' functions of the tithe are misleading and render the biblical evidence unintelligible. The cultic tithe was the religiously legitimated state tax.[72]

By this interpretation, Joash as king has authority over how the tax funds which are channeled to the temple should be used and the story world reflects this social reality. Once again, it is useful to remember that this finance system survives into the author's own time in the account of Josiah's reform. An arrangement which is explicated sociologically from one story world is used with sociological import in another story world, where it may have direct societal impact. The author may well be showing approval of royal control of temple finances both in the story and in the 'real world'.

Another religious aspect of the story receives a new emphasis when the sociological model is considered. The analysis done so far identified the importance of the covenant idea in the story—as a part of Joash's investiture, in the covenant ceremony after he became king, and in the criteria for regnal fidelity. The study of ideology showed the covenant as

70. R.H. Lowery, *Reforming Kings*, pp. 111-16.

71. F. Crüsemann, 'Der Zehnte in der israelitischen Königszeit', cited in Lowery, *Reforming Kings*, p. 112; and J.N. Postgate, 'The Economic Structure of the Assyrian Empire', in Larsen (ed.), *Power and Propaganda*, p. 202.

72. Lowery, *Reforming Kings*, p. 116.

a dominant force shaping the life of the people with Yahweh in the Deuteronomistic ideology. The insistence by the Deuteronomist that the king demonstrate fidelity to the covenant carries a noteworthy sociological coloring. Here traditional cultural and religious values have an impact on the functioning of the king. This very type of influence by religious traditions on the power of the elites, particularly the king, was seen in the model. Tradition or culture constitutes 'the basic framework within which the chief functions of the polity are fulfilled and to which political goals must—in theory, at least—be subordinated'.[73] Even if the 'covenant' was not an ancient tradition in actual Israelite history, the Deuteronomist presented it as if it were, taking the ideal back to Moses in Deuteronomy. In the story world, the appeal to the covenant ideal thus functions in exactly the same way as an ancient religious tradition. It places limits on the political power of the king by subordinating him to inherited tradition.

Particularly if the 'covenant ideal' is a creation or new emphasis by the Deuteronomist under Josiah, this aspect of the story world has importance in the social context of the author. The ideological force of 'the king under the covenant' can be seen to have actual political force in the author's time. This has a direct confirmation in the story world created by the Deuteronomist about the contemporary king, Josiah. He too stands under the covenant and paradigmatically fulfills the requirements of fidelity to the covenant (2 Kgs 23.1-25).[74] The explicit approval of the author for these attitudes and actions of Josiah make clear the social impact the author expected the story worlds of both Joash and Josiah to have on his social context.

Finally, two other religious aspects of the story of Joash can be explicated sociologically. Within the narrative, two types of religious establishment other than the temple are mentioned. In ch. 11, the Baal temple in Jerusalem is destroyed by the people. And in ch. 12, Joash's otherwise good evaluation is muted by his failure to remove the high places. In both cases, the model suggests that these non-Yahwistic religious centers make sociological sense. In agrarian societies both sects and minority religions can exist within the larger society.[75] Sometimes they are connected to local traditions which survive the imposition of a 'state'

73. Eisenstadt, *Political Systems*, p. 225.
74. Again following Lohfink, 'Cult Reform of Josiah', in dating this from the Deuteronomist under Josiah.
75. Sjoberg, *Pre-Industrial City*, pp. 263-64.

religion. Others come from the influences of foreign elites, either through trade and communication networks or through alliances between elites[76] (see below on marriage).

What the story world makes clear is that these non-Yahwistic centers should not be tolerated. This also is fully explicated by the model. The development of political control by elites involves the use of certain religious ideas and the cooperation of certain religious elites which all together becomes a 'state religion'. This tends to centralize control of religious activities and the monies to support them into the power of the capital city with its state sanctuary. Dissenting religious elites, local traditions and outlying cult centers can then come under attack either directly from official actions or through losing the competition with the much more powerful central religion.[77]

Both within the story world and through the story's communicative power in its social context, intolerance for non-Yahwistic religion is central. In the story, the inception of Joash's reign is marked by the destruction of the Baal temple. His failure to remove the high places is a failure to centralize the cult to the temple in Jerusalem, and thus a failure of fidelity to the covenant stipulation that requires centralization of worship. Both as a positive example and as a negative example, Joash embodies the ideological viewpoint of the Deuteronomist. In the time of the story's writing, however, the Deuteronomist has a thoroughly positive example in Josiah for the exclusive worship of Yahweh. Into the story world about Josiah, the same criteria are woven and he fulfills them without fault, as he keeps the covenant. Once again, the explicit approval for Josiah, the author's contemporary, illustrates the social impact that Joash's story could have on the author's own time and context. By becoming alert to the sociological force of various elements in the story world, the possible influence of these same elements in the social context of the story's writing is illuminated.

International Politics

Two aspects of what might be termed the international politics of agrarian monarchies occur in the story of Athaliah and Joash. The terminology here is problematic, for aristocratic societies can only loosely be described as 'nations' having 'foreign affairs' or 'international relations'.

76. Lowery, *Reforming Kings*, p. 107.
77. Lenski, *Power*, p. 209.

Rather, the control by elites over a particular geographical area overlaps and conflicts with the claims of other elites for those same areas. With the perpetually fluid boundaries of an agrarian monarchy or empire, an international war can just as readily be viewed as a civil war.

> Instead of clearly defined nations, territories under a single ruler were largely governed by him indirectly through aristocratic governors or vassals who attained various degrees of de facto and de jure independence from him...Rulers fought their vassals, tributaries or provincial governors and viceroys and the latter fought among themselves.[78]

What a victor gains when a neighboring area is conquered or maintained as a province or vassal state is the right to extract the wealth of that area for his or her own elites. What can be lost is the extractive wealth and the elites' privilege, power, positions and lives.

Just such a reality is reflected in Hazael of Aram's incursion into the territory of Judah. From Judah's perspective, Hazael's was an invading army, attempting to control their land by conquest, as he had done to Gath. From Hazael's perspective he was extending the reach of Aram into the western regions to gain land and the rights to the region's economic surplus. When Joash is reported to give Hazael the contents of the temple and palace treasuries, he is only doing what any monarch might do to buy off an aggressor.[79] (Note also the sociologically clear presumption in the text that it is Joash the king who has such control over the treasuries of both the palace and the temple). If Hazael would be content with tribute, particularly if he did not want to, or did not have the strength to, establish a permanent presence in Judah, then Jerusalem and Joash's throne could be saved from outright annexation to the territory of a rival elite.

Another form of 'international' relations is the making of various treaties which align the elites of neighboring territories without actual warfare. Chief among these alliances is a marriage contract between elites of two countries. 'If rulers *are* their empires, then family relations between rulers *are* relations between their empires, and a family union through marriage becomes an alliance or even a territorial union between empires.'[80] The marriage of Athaliah into the House of David is just such an alliance. The accompanying cooperation between Israel and

---

78. Kautsky, *Aristocratic Empires*, pp. 230-31.
79. Kautsky, *Aristocratic Empires*, p. 232.
80. Kautsky, *Aristocratic Empires*, p. 233.

Judah against Hazael during Ahaziah's and Joram's reigns is one fruit of the association (2 Kgs 8.28-29). In the eyes of the Deuteronomist, the evil influence that Athaliah brought from the House of Omri into Judah is another, much more problematic result. But all of this is completely typical of the patterns expected on the basis of the model.

Indeed the warfare and shifting alliances among Israel, Judah and Aram which are mentioned many times in the chapters surrounding 2 Kings 11–12 are all reflective of these same social realities which mark the politics of neighboring elites. And it is a reality which the author must have known well in the contemporary context, except that the scene during Josiah's reign is dominated by new forces, chiefly Assyria and Egypt and Babylon. But the endless permutations of elite struggles against neighboring elites for land, wealth and position remain typical.

Propaganda in the Politics of Elites

A final aspect of social realities in an agrarian monarchy is applicable to the story world and to the social context of 2 Kings 11–12. This is the role that propaganda plays in the communication of power which elites, especially the king, depend upon for their legitimation. Noted above in the general model was the necessity for elites to justify their place and power in the society, particularly through the use of religiously-based ideological constructs.

> The essentially coercive power represented by dynastic states derives legitimacy from the close connection of such states with divine sovereignty. The religious sphere...is an integral and critical component of political power and authority.[81]

An expanded discussion of the communication of legitimating ideologies by elites will bear results for understanding not only the story world but also the social context in which the story was created by an author as a form of communication to an audience. This discussion makes connections with the ideological analysis from the last chapter because the content of the persuasive message given in the propaganda of elites is based on the very ideological constructs considered already.

The idea of communication is a helpful basic concept to start the discussion. The editors of a significant book series on the topic, *Propaganda and Communication in World History*, provide a 'brief

---

81. Meyers, 'Jachin and Boaz', p. 175.

outline of the process of communication'.[82] Generally, an act of communication can be described by answering the following: 'Who/ says
what/ in what channel/ to whom/ with what effect?'[83] The editors expand
this brief form to catch more of the implications of communication:

Who initiates the message?
What is the content of messages?
With what intentions are messages initiated?
In what situations do communications take place?
What channels and other assets are available to
   communicators?
What strategies render the assets effective in
   accomplishing a communicator's message?
What audiences are reached?
With what effects?[84]

Using these questions, any act of communication can be described.
But the questions also allow a distinction to be drawn between open-
ended communication and propaganda, which the editors define as
'deliberately manipulated communication' or 'a deliberate effort to
influence outcomes of controversy in favor of a preference'.[85] Applied
to the topic of this section, it can thus be said that while a king in an
agrarian monarchy might communicate many types of messages to
many audiences, the deliberate structuring of certain messages to legitimize his power and position is 'propaganda'. In the case of propaganda,
the critical questions above highlight the king's intention of legitimation
or justification, the channels available to the person atop the elite power
structure, and the (intended) effect on an audience of securing other
elites' assent to the king's power.

The applicability of such definitions of communication and propaganda for ancient agrarian societies is illustrated by Leo Oppenheim in
the first volume of the *Propaganda* series. In describing the workings of
propaganda in the Neo-Assyrian and Neo-Babylonian empires, he uses
these definitions and a sociological model similar to the one developed
here. Excerpts from his introduction are worth quoting at length:

82. H.D. Lasswell, D. Lerner, and H. Speier (eds.), *Propaganda and
Communication in World History*. I. *The Symbolic Instrument in Early Times* (East-
West Center, Honolulu: University Press of Hawaii, 1979), p. 6.
83. Lasswell, Lerner and Speier (eds.), *Symbolic Instrument*, p. 7.
84. Lasswell, Lerner and Speier (eds.), *Symbolic Instrument*, p. 8.
85. Lasswell, Lerner and Speier (eds.), *Symbolic Instrument*, pp. 4-5.

> To function effectively, Mesopotamian kingship had to wield its inherent
> political power in two ways, or, as one could also phrase it, in the context
> of this volume, the king had to communicate meaningfully in two direc-
> tions: with his own subjects and with the outside world, which means his
> enemies.[86]

> Thus the state as a political unit within the interplay of similar units was
> held together and kept functioning by its central symbol, the king, who
> represented it both to the outside world and to his own subjects. For such
> purposes, the king used linguistic and non-linguistic sets of signs as well
> as physical constructs, monuments, and monumental buildings... All this
> served to establish the divine right of the king to claim respect, loyalty,
> obedience, services, taxes and tribute—whatever the specific situation
> required.[87]

Oppenheim goes on to apply this understanding to two Neo-Assyrian
royal texts, letters to the god Assur by Sargon II and Esarhaddon. He
shows how they function as political propaganda, attempting to defend
the king's actions against possible dissent and opposition.[88]

This understanding of propaganda, useful in studying Mesopotamian
empires, has also been used by Keith Whitelam and others for explicating biblical texts. Whitelam's definition of propaganda is complementary
to that in the larger study cited above. In one article, he says,
'Propaganda is defined here as the process by which a particular
worldview (ideology) is disseminated to a specific audience'.[89] The stress
on the audience is significant, for propaganda, as deliberately manipulated communication, must address the specific audience intended to
receive the message. 'The propagandist...brings to the fore certain emotions, however dormant, in order to produce the desired effect within a
particular audience.'[90] Using this understanding, Whitelam analyzes
1 Samuel 9–1 Kings 2 as a 'defense of David'. He shows that the
material can be read as 'royal propaganda' which provided an 'official
interpretation of events favorable to David'.[91]

The various channels for communicating a persuasive message in
agrarian societies reach varying audiences. All kinds of media are

---

86. A.L. Oppenheim, 'Neo-Assyrian and Neo-Babylonian Empires', in
Lasswell, Lerner and Speier (eds.), *Symbolic Instrument*, p. 111.

87. Oppenheim, 'Neo-Assyrian Empires', p. 113.

88. Oppenheim, 'Neo-Assyrian Empires', pp. 125, 131.

89. Whitelam, 'The Symbols of Power', p. 166.

90. K.W. Whitelam, 'The Defence of David', *JSOT* 29 (1984), p. 67.

91. Whitelam, 'Defence of David', p. 77.

involved, especially given the limited literacy of the population and the absence of real mass communication. 'The diffusion ("propaganda" in its etymological meaning) of the official interpretation of events takes place via the whole range of the means of communication: oral and written, objectual and situational.'[92] The only avenue of true 'mass communication' takes the form of monumental architecture. Temples, palaces and fortifications are a visible and effective portrayal of the royal power that builds them,[93] both through their presence and through the marshalling of resources to construct them.[94] Since these buildings are not dependent upon literacy for their effectiveness in communicating, their size and iconography can reach anyone in a stratified society. Likewise, religious and royal spectacles and festivals can convey the worldview of the elites to any participants.

However, in such a stratified society most of the population has no power to participate in or change policy. Thus the need for propaganda is usually limited to an audience that can make some difference in the institutions that run the society. 'If a religious ideology is to be effective in consolidating and sustaining support for the regime, it must be successfully communicated at least to that portion of the population responsible for implementing state policy.'[95] In other words, most of the efforts at communicating persuasive messages go toward the elites in the society. Whitelam expresses this point clearly, and specifically uses a sociological model:

> The struggle for power is between factions of the elite...and so the greatest concentration of propaganda is directed at this restricted audience. The elite form the most serious threat or potential threat to the king and royal family and therefore much propaganda is aimed at this elite audience in order to reiterate and reinforce the right of the king to rule and the need to deny counterclaims to the throne.[96]

That elites are the intended audience for much of the propaganda in agrarian societies is confirmed by the use of writing as a form of communication through ideologically-based royal or religious texts and inscriptions. Only a small minority in an agrarian society is literate, so

---

92. Liverani, 'Ideology', p. 302.
93. Whitelam, 'The Symbols of Power', p. 169.
94. Meyers, 'David as Temple Builder', p. 366.
95. Meyers, 'Jachin and Boaz', p. 175.
96. Whitelam, 'The Symbols of Power', p. 168.

writing is 'the exclusive property of the leisured class'.[97] Even oral
recitations from sacred or revered writings are usually done for an urban
elite class that could have access to the larger central religious sites.[98]
'The official interpretations of events through the written medium,
admittedly supplemented and reinforced by the other forms of communication available, would have been available solely to the urban elite.'[99]
All of the forms of persuasion that use writing in an agraian society are
basically propaganda by the ruling class for the ruling class.[100]

These considerations about propaganda in the politics of elites extend
the basic model of agrarian societies used in this chapter. Like the basic
model, such details can aid in understanding texts that emerged from
agrarian societies, providing patterns against which to measure the
impact and significance of what is found. Turning now to 2 Kings 11–
12, these details illumine the text and its context.

First, within the story world, the communication of persuasive messages is evident, as the rhetorical and ideological analyses have already
pointed out. As the story in ch. 11 unfolds, Jehoiada uses symbolic
instruments to communicate the legitimacy of Joash and of his own
actions in making Joash king. Among the symbols which can carry
deliberately manipulated messages to the other characters in the narrative are David's spear and shields, the crown and covenantal decree, the
line of guards around the king, and the actions of anointing, trumpet
blowing and acclamation. The procession from the temple to the palace
and the seating of the new king upon the throne also convey royal
ideology through festive and solemn actions. The temple itself clearly
plays a significant role in the story as a communicator of powerful symbolic meaning. This closely corresponds to the model which alerts the
analyst that a temple 'provides a location for ritual central to the
legitimacy of the dynasty'.[101] The 'pillar' by which Joash stands is
understood in the story itself to convey royal prerogative and presence.

Chapter 12 is not devoid of propagandistic elements in its story world
either. The king's care for the temple portrays the entire ideological construct of central sacred sites and royal legitimation. The king's actions in
successfully instituting a plan for the temple's repair shows the other

97. Sjoberg, *Pre-Industrial City*, p. 290.
98. Sjoberg, *Pre-Industrial City*, p. 288.
99. Whitelam, 'Defence of David', p. 65.
100. Liverani, 'Ideology', p. 302.
101. Whitelam, 'The Symbols of Power', p. 172.

characters both the wherewithal and power of the king. The elimination of the priests from the repair process and the presence of the priest and the king's secretary in the handling of the funds communicate the insistence of royal control over the financing. The reference to the materials used in the repair work reminds the actors in the story world of the richness and luxury of the temple.

The story world also indicates the principal origins and audience for royal propaganda. As already noted, the story's characters are the elites of the society centered in the capital city. The messages conveyed in the story originate with elites and are aimed at other elites. The use of a written media, the 'covenantal decree', within the story identifies the whole drama as an elite function. Thus in its very content, the story confirms that in an agrarian monarchy various factions of the elites are both the source and audience for the deliberately manipulated communications that convey the royal ideology.

However, the considerations about propaganda in the politics of elites illumine more tellingly the social context of the story as an act of communication. At this point the story's form as written communication becomes significant because, according to the model, literacy is associated with a social milieu of elite power dynamics. It suggests that the author was a member of the aristocratic class and may have had a real interest in the story's ability to persuade or convince. Rhetorical and ideological analyses have shown that persuasive messages are present in the story and concern a whole set of elite institutions and attitudes—temple, kingship, dynasty and so on. As seen throughout this sociological analysis, these potent ideological constructs function not only in the story world but also connect to possible 'real time' ideas and issues in the author's social context. In line explicitly with the model, the story can thus be seen as an attempt by an author to address contemporary issues through the writing of a story shaped to make persuasive points.

The model further suggests that the intended audience for such a story is the elite class. Being literate and located in urban centers, the elites are the only possible audience for a written text and the most probable audience for a text that might be read at a state sanctuary or royal function. Further, only elites have the power to concern themselves with the story's evident interests, things like royal succession and the temple's upkeep. And their interest in these matters would be keen, as the working out of the royal ideology could have a practical impact on their livelihood and power positions in the society.

Two authors already used in this study, Barré and Liverani, view the story of Athaliah and Joash in ch. 11 in just such a fashion as political rhetoric. Both suggest the kind of impact such a story might have on the politics of its time. Barré takes an earlier form of the story as a type of political persuasion in defense of Jehoiada's coup for Joash.[102] He analyzes it as a genre that 'is typically the product of royal scribes who were commissioned to use their literary skills to defend a regime that had come to power through the use of violence'.[103] Barré also describes what he finds to be the Deuteronomistic additions to the story that expand the account to include cult reform and to highlight the role of the 'people of the land'.[104] In particular the Deuteronomistic focus on the people of the land stems from this group's role with Josiah's accession[105] so that it has a 'contemporary' concern for the Deuteronomistic editor.

Mario Liverani highlights the dramatic quality of the story of Joash, its 'theatricality', as a mark of its propagandistic function.[106] He compares the story with an inscription about Idrimi, King of Alalakh, who retakes his father's throne after the dynasty had been overthrown and he had been in hiding for seven years. Noting the similarities in the events of each account, he sees that both are inspired by the political necessity to legitimate the usurpation of the throne. This kind of justification is not needed when normal dynastic succession occurs.[107] In Joash's case, the dramatic cast to the action may have been utilized by Jehoiada to shape the events themselves—creating a persuasive turn of events while the action is going on. He thus reads a historical level into the text which I have bracketed. But Liverani also notes that the presentation of the events in a literary form utilizes the dramatic to convey the purpose of the story as a defense of Joash's coronation.[108]

By highlighting the narrative's rhetoric, which addresses a situation of power politics, both of these authors complement the analysis of this study. However, in that both studies lack a systemic sociological awareness, the full import of such rhetoric in an agrarian monarchic situation

---

102. Barré, *Rhetoric*.
103. Barré, *Rhetoric*, p. 140.
104. Barré, *Rhetoric*, p. 120.
105. Barré, *Rhetoric*, p. 123.
106. M. Liverani, 'L'Histoire de Joas', *VT* 24 (1974), p. 438.
107. Liverani, 'L'Histoire de Joas', p. 442.
108. Liverani, 'L'Histoire de Joas', p. 451.

is slighted. Further, these two authors focus on an earlier form of the text as opposed to the Deuteronomistic form considered here. Particularly in Barré's case, this limits the insights of his analysis of the Deuteronomistic story. Because the concerns for cult and people of the land are seen as 'added on', the integrated rhetorical, ideological and sociological concerns of the story are never understood. By not considering 2 Kings 12 as a part of the text, Barré further limits his analysis of the Deuteronomistic portrayal of Joash's reign. Even for just ch. 11, he states that the Deuteronomistic redactor 'did not explicitly relate the restoration of the throne to Joash to his teaching concerning David's "eternal dynasty"'.[109] His method has foreclosed a full appreciation of the thorough Davidic dynastic rhetoric and ideology present in the Deuteronomistic story.

In contrast, my placing the narrative in a posited context as a part of the Deuteronomistic History written in the Josianic era has highlighted the interests of the political propaganda contained there. For this setting, the narrative conveys the types of ideological concerns of the Deuteronomistic worldview applicable to the social and political environment of Josiah's reign. This chapter has proposed what some of those concerns might be by identifying possible political realities of the author's social context that the story seems shaped to address.

As elements of a larger royal ideology, the following specific commitments appear to be urged upon the audience by the author: complete disavowal and avoidance of any contact with or influence from the vestiges of the northern kingdom's evil ways; unwavering support for the Davidic king, despite political temptations from rival factions; the importance of continuous dynastic succession on David's throne; the necessity for the 'people of the land' to support the Davidic king; the necessity for the military, particularly the royal guard, to protect the legitimate king; the priest as upholder of the Davidic dynasty, servant of the king, and primary supporter of the king's executive decisions; the king's unquestioned power over the temple, its restoration and finances; the covenant as the ideal to which the king must demonstrate fidelity; and the importance of the purity and centralization of the worship of Yahweh.

All of these messages seem to be conveyed by the story for the sake of its elite audience. All are typical of aristocratic concerns in agrarian societies. Any actual historical events or situations which the messages

109. Barré, *Rhetoric*, p. 120.

address cannot be uncovered by the analysis used here; only the generic possibilities can be identified as intended effects of the text as a communication. A study of the history of Josiah's reign could possibly identify actions or events to which these messages correspond, but that is not the focus here.

Thus, sociological sensitivity aids in viewing the narrative as a deliberate message from an elite author, such as a scribe (or scribes) in Josiah's court, to an elite audience, such as the aristocratic supporters of and dissenters from Josiah's reign and policies. Shaped as a story yet with visible political content, the narrative can be seen to function as a part of the wider royal ideology of the Josianic era. Whitelam's summary of the power of propaganda using all kinds of symbolic communication in an agrarian monarchic context fits this situation neatly:

> The greatest concentration of symbolism was aimed at the urban elite, who posed the most powerful threat, whether real or potential, to the occupant of the royal throne and his dynasty. The various forms of propaganda reinforced the right of the king and his family to rule, while the unambiguous displays of military power and wealth, linked to divine legitimacy, acted as a warning to any potential threat from within or without.[110]

Summary

This fourth analysis of 2 Kings 11–12 has utilized a sociological methodology to 'read' the text. The basic question for the analysis has been, 'What can an understanding of the social world from which a story emerges add to the story's interpretation?' To elucidate sociological elements, a model of agrarian society, based in a systemic, cross-cultural sociological method was used. This model highlights the institutions, roles, social structures and dynamics typical of an agrarian monarchy, the societal type applicable to ancient Israel. The general model identified patterns such as social inequality, monarchic government and aristocratic power structures in an extractive economy that is dependent on the productive labor of a peasant majority. The model was extended by details about the dynamics of political factions among the elites, the interactions between religion and the state, and the importance of propaganda in the politics of elites.

The model gave a basis for comparison, typical patterns against which

110. Whitelam, 'The Symbols of Power', p. 172.

to interpret the significance of what was found in the individual case of
the narrative of 2 Kings 11–12. I used the model in two ways. The first
was to examine the world within the story to see what sociologically
significant realities emerge there. Secondly, the world that created the
story was examined. Using the assumption that the story was the product of a Josianic Deuteronomistic provenance, I examined the indications
in the story that could give sociologically sensitive data about this social
context. As with the rhetorical and ideological analyses, the assumption
that the text could be viewed as a communication from an author to an
audience in a particular context was central.

The sociological model was illustrated by and at the same time illuminated a number of aspects of the story world. Prominent was the characteristic that only elite social roles and central social locations are the
concern of the story. But there were many correspondences between
the patterns suggested by the model and the elements of the story. The
interplay of political factions in elite, often violent, power struggles
illumined Jehoiada's actions. The constant struggle for the throne and
the importance of the question of succession were present in Athaliah's
portrayal and Joash's identity. That the military, especially royal merce-
naries, wielded definitive power and that aristocratic landed elites played
a determining role were both shown. One noteworthy absence in the
story was the lack of any support group for Athaliah. Such a group
would have been a political necessity for gaining the throne but had no
narrative presence.

The symbolic and practical power of religion in an agrarian monarchy
was evident through the story in the temple's persuasive power being
directly involved in politics. The priest as an actively political king-maker
was present but significantly modified to show the priest in a dependent,
supporting role, not as an independent power. The king's authority over
the temple, its priests, repair and finances, was prominent. However, a
modification of the king's power came through the idea of the Yahwistic
covenant whereby traditional cultural values limited the king's role by
fidelity to the covenant. The existence of sects and minority religions
was seen in the mention of the Baal temple and the continuation of the
high places.

Other correspondences between model and story appeared in the use
of marriage as a political alliance between elites and in Hazael's invasion
as a type of elite land-grab to extend an economic base through conquest and tribute. Finally, the role of propaganda in elite politics showed

up in the story in the use of symbols and highly symbolic actions to communicate the royal, dynastic import of Jehoiada's actions.

Sociological analysis also permitted comment on the social world of the story's creation. Because the story was written in an agrarian monarchic context, patterns from the model distinguished possible factors influencing the shape of the story and illuminated possible effects of the story within its context. A basic understanding of the limitations of literacy in such an agrarian context suggested not only that the story is *about* elites but also that it was written *by* elites and intended *for* elites. Further, the ubiquity of factional politics indicates that the story could have been fashioned to express narratively the ideological concepts of a particular elite viewpoint.

The sociological analysis uncovered possible political ideals that are championed in the story which could have had real social effects in the author's time. These include: abhorrence of all northern/Omride dynastic policies; unwavering support for the Davidide upon Judah's throne; a model of proper royal military loyalty for the king; a call for support from aristocratic landed elites for the Davidic monarch; a portrayal of the required service and duty toward the Davidic king by the temple and priests; ongoing royal care for the temple; control of the temple's finances by the king; and a picture of royal covenant fidelity.

This list of possible ideologically-based desiderata in the story does not emerge only from sociologically educated guesses about what might have been significant in the author's world. A unique kind of confirmation that these were significant views in a Josianic context comes from the direct parallels between the Joash story and the story about Josiah which reflects the author's own era. For many of the ideals just listed, a parallel or 'update' is given in the Josiah narrative. These include: legitimate Davidic succession after a conspiracy killed the king and the role of the 'people of the land' in the succession; the temple repair finance system with the priest and king's secretary as administrators; the priest as the king's servant, being commanded by the king to act; the covenant made in a public ceremony with the king standing by the pillar; and the centralization and purification of worship. What these parallels confirm is that ideological statements embedded in the 'old' story of Joash were still potent in the 'current events' surrounding Josiah's reign as narrated by the Deuteronomist.

That such correspondences between Joash's and Josiah's story worlds could have had an impact on the author's social context is possible if another of the sociological patterns is remembered. For elites, writing could be a powerful form of deliberately manipulated communication. The messages contained in Joash's story could well have served to give the 'background' to Josiah's story as well as help ground and legitimate his power, position and policies. That such a political agenda could have been accomplished through the writing of a narrative helps us to see the compelling nature of an aesthetically pleasing genre. Story-telling here emerges as an art form and a political form. So we have come full circle by finishing this sociological analysis, back to the text as a narrative which not only conveys a good story but also serves the political interests of an author in communication with an audience.

Chapter 6

CONCLUSIONS

Through the four detailed analyses just completed, I have illustrated the idea that a biblical story can be seen from several perspectives, each of which focuses on an aspect intrinsic to the telling of the story itself. The four perspectives have utilized narrative, rhetorical, ideological and sociological analyses so that the story has been seen as an artistic form, a persuasive argument, an ideological vehicle and a communication expressive of and addressed to a social context. Further, the study has supported the proposal that such a multi-disciplinary approach can reveal the inherent connectedness of the story's concerns. The aspects of the story are related to each other as concentric circles around a core; each analysis is necessary to understand both the core and its expanding interests. The center of attention has remained on the story, and at every point the analyses were used to reveal and open up intrinsic and interconnected aspects of the text.

Several attitudes and assumptions have been important. First and perhaps most significant has been the willingness to shift perspectives, to see the story from the vantage point of several scholarly disciplines. This has involved a familiarity with different methods, but more importantly, an attitude that a story is best appreciated as a complex of significations. Words can function in many ways and carry a number of interests. To be willing to let the words of a story speak with various voices requires a flexibility of interpretive stance.

A second assumption has held that a story is basically a communication between an author and an audience in a particular context. In the case of a biblical text, all three—author, audience and situation—are plural, as the text is formulated and handed on through various incarnations and engages people in a variety of times and places. But that a text in each time and place speaks from a writer to a listener or reader in that specific context is at the base of all of the analyses practiced here.

Because a story exists in a multi-faceted context, intrinsic to the story's communication are the telling of a tale, the presenting of arguments, the reflection of ideas, and the embodiment of sociological realities.

A third assumption proposed that out of the text's ongoing evolution, a particular context could be isolated for the purposes of analysis. This proposal took a 'snapshot', as it were, of the text in a posited context. Using well-established (although not uncontested) scholarly theories, a primary redaction of the story in 2 Kings 11–12 by a Deuteronomistic circle as a part of the Deuteronomistic History has been studied. The point has been to show how the particular version of the story I hold as its primary redaction could have functioned as a communication from an author to an audience as seen from a variety of perspectives. This assumption made available for the various analyses scholarship on Deuteronomistic theology and the wider interests of the Deuteronomistic History.

To accomplish each analysis, an appropriate method within the larger field has been chosen. Briefly described, the methods were narrative poetics, 'new' rhetoric, ideology as a social construct, and the sociology of agrarian monarchies. In each case, a thorough grounding in the chosen method was achieved through the study of several scholars and then the text 'read' from that perspective. These particular methods, alone and in combination, were able to focus on the interests evident in the text in an accessible manner and to maintain the sense of author-audience communication.

As separate studies, the four types of analysis each accomplished a reading of the story, sometimes in a way that consolidated previous scholarly work and sometimes in a way that presented original readings or interpretations. Narrative analysis revealed a story that moves from fast-paced intensity to moderated longevity with a turning point as the rightful Davidic king, Joash, takes his seat on the throne of his ancestors. Central oppositions are formed and resolved as Athaliah the queen threatens the monarchy but is deposed by Jehoiada the priest. Re-established dynastic kingship portrays both a good king's solicitous and long-lived care for the House of Yahweh and the uncertainties of international politics. Rhetorical study used a verse-by-verse reading to show how the words, actions, characters and scenes make persuasive points. Both associational and dissociational arguments, often using analogic and symbolic liaisons, have been found which seek the audience's adherence to theses about the reign of Joash. In particular, a case that Joash represents the re-establishment of legitimate, dynastic Davidic monarchy is made and illustrations of how he at least partially fulfills the criteria for the good Davidic king under the covenant are presented.

The ideological perspective set the story's ideas within the larger Deuteronomistic worldview. Using an analysis that sees a society's 'reality' as a social construction which defines the cosmic, religious, political, ethical and practical aspects of life, this study focused on ideas important in the story. Evil northern monarchs, temple, priest, covenant, kingship, Davidic dynasty and regnal evaluation all function as ideas that reflect the 'symbolic universe' of the story and that shape that same universe. The sociological analysis took a view of the story as expressive of and a product of the dynamics of an agrarian monarchic society. The working hypothesis of a Josianic provenance for the primary edition of the Deuteronomistic History allowed the use of more extended and specific sociological data. Using a dynamic sociological model, the story's social roles and locations betrayed its elite interests and its links to the story world of the expressly good king Josiah. The possible 'real world' impact of such sociologically significant elements as dynastic succession supported by the people of the land, Davidic monarchy, and royal control of the temple and the priests were revealed.

While the analyses work independently, the real strength of a multidisciplinary approach is seen in the interactions between the perspectives. When the four analyses work together, building on, commenting on or contrasting with each other, a necessary comprehensive understanding of the story in its posited context can be found. Without all four analyses, significant aspects of the story, its conceptual structures and its context might have been overlooked. The comprehensive understanding that has emerged has both theoretical and practical impacts.

Theoretically, the interactions of the analyses suggest a paradigm of a story as a functional complexity which was described with the metaphor of 'concentric circles'. As the analyses were applied, the movement from one circle to the next required a shift in perspective but each was a logical step. Narrative analysis revealed repetitive structures, evocative terminology, dramatic oppositions and pointed characterizations that emphasized certain elements in the story. The question such results posed was whether the narrative emphases pointed to a persuasive shaping in the story. Rhetorical analysis then revealed the use of argumentation that shaped the portrayal to secure an audience's adherence to certain theses. The question such results posed was whether the rhetoric had a basis in a wider worldview, in an ideology behind the concerns of the story. Ideological analysis then revealed the ideational concepts of the Deuteronomistic worldview, a symbolic universe that delineates the place and roles of significant people, locations and institutions. The question such results posed was whether the ideology could have ties to a certain social group, and what type of people would hold such views. Sociological analysis then revealed the dynamics of agrarian monarchies which illuminated the elite interests and shaping of the story and possible political impacts the story could have in its own context.

However, the results of this final analysis pointed back to the origin in narrative; the expanding circles cohered in the story. Each step in the movement from one concentric circle to the next can be seen in reverse, starting with the sociological perspective. In an agrarian society, the social location of elites shapes a symbolic universe, an ideology that reflects their view of the world as elites. Writing in such an elite social context can function as a vehicle for the ideology of the elites, as a narrative expresses the interests of its elite author and sponsors. The ideology in turn shapes the rhetoric in the narrative, giving direction to what is important to argue through the story. The rhetoric in turn shapes the narrative structures of the story, directing how the narrative can convey the persuasive elements in scenes, characters, plot and so on. The sociological, ideological and rhetorical interests thus depend on the narrative to find expression. Only if the narrative can convey these interests in a compelling way, as a *good story*, will the other aspects be communicated as well.

Seeing a story from several perspectives leads thus to a theoretical conclusion about the complex functioning of a good story. Not only is each aspect—narrative art, rhetorical persuasion, ideological grounding, sociological reflection—inherent in the story independently, but also, all the aspects work together in and through the story to communicate an intricately related set of meanings to an audience. The story 'means' not just *one* thing *or* another in its context, but several interrelated meanings conveyed by the same words of the text.

The interactions of the four analyses have practical impacts as well on how particular elements in the story are interpreted. In a variety of ways, the analyses comment on or complement each other. Sometimes this correlation confirms obvious emphases in the story; sometimes it emphasizes one perspective; at other times, it points out an unexpected insight.

One example of the four perspectives agreeing on a central emphasis in the story is the topic of Davidic kingship. Narrative analysis showed the resolution of the drama of ch. 11 to be Joash's sitting upon the throne of the kings—his first action as a character coincides with the re-establishment of a Davidic king. On the same topic, rhetorical analysis showed how much of the rhetoric in ch. 11 concerns kingship, complete with symbolic and analogic patterns that evoke the reigns of great kings—David, Solomon and Josiah. Ideologically, kingship is a central institution, if not *the* central institution, in the Deuteronomistic symbolic universe. Sociologically, the monarch is the central power in an agrarian society and support for the Davidic king a likely political ideal of the author's context. Davidic kingship is so intrinsic to the story that it is represented clearly in every aspect of the narrative and all the aspects work together to promote the primacy of the idea and the reality of the Davidic king.

Another congruence of perspective is seen on the topic of the temple. In both chs. 11 and 12, the temple is a locus for events and characterization narratively. Even the number of times the phrase 'the House of Yahweh' is repeated in the narrative betrays its importance. The rhetoric about the temple portrays it as a powerful sacred locus, a staunch supporter of the Davidic king, and an object worthy of awe, respect and care. The power of the temple in the Deuteronomistic worldview functions to sanction the dynasty, as well as represent cosmic order and Yahwistic blessing. The temple as a social location delineates a primary elite power structure, complete with royal, religious and financial power which can support a king and require his service. The intrinsic connections of sociology, ideology, rhetoric and narrative are revealed—elites who were party to an institution held in such high regard ideologically necessarily make arguments in writing a narrative that reflect the awesome social and cosmic integrative power of the temple.

However, viewing the story from various perspectives can also present a contrast which can provoke a nuance in interpretation. In the narrative analysis, Jehoiada is the central character in ch. 11, authoritatively 'running the show' from the temple. Narratively, then, the priest plays a central role. The twist comes in the rhetorical analysis; most of the rhetoric of the chapter is *not* about the priest but about the king and the restoration of legitimate kingship. The priest plays a rhetorical role but one that is in the service of the king. In ch. 12, the role of priestly service, not primary authority, continues as Jehoiada teaches the king and does his will. The ideological and sociological patterns behind this twist are evident when all four analyses are completed. This role of service to the king emerges from the particular Deuteronomistic conception of the priest. And the presentation of the priest as subservient to the king bears sociological weight as a possible recommended relationship between the royal and religious establishments. Jehoiada's centrality as a narrative character can be seen in the context of his rhetorical and ideological subservience to the king and the practical societal impact that portrayal carries.

Another correlation among the perspectives occurs when one perspective seems to dominate. Covenant terminology and ideas related to covenant-keeping are present in the narrative at several points. Jehoiada makes a ברית with the guards, puts the עדות on Joash, and makes a *covenant* between Yahweh, the king and the people. Joash *fulfills covenant criteria* in that he *does right* in the eyes of Yahweh because he is *taught* by Jehoiada, but he *fails to remove the high places*. In that the terms are often used without specification or detail, their rhetorical force comes not from accumulated detail but rather from evocative and symbolic persuasion. The covenant terminology serves to evoke the ideology of the covenant ideal which carries significant shaping force in the Deuteronomistic symbolic universe. Sociologically, the representation of the king evaluated by the covenant requires the allegiance of Joash in the story world and that of every king in the social context of the narrative. The ideology associated with the covenant is so powerful and omnipresent for the Deuteronomistic worldview that when all the other aspects of the story come to express covenant ideas only the most brief mention or invocation is needed. At the same time, the constant reminders of covenant ideas shape the outlines of both chapters— Joash's re-establishment is a covenantal process and his reign is evaluated by covenantal standards.

The multi-disciplinary approach also clarifies the importance and interpretation of some elements in the story. The note about Joash giving up the state treasuries to Hazael is narratively brief and undeveloped. Sociologically, it can be understood as a typical case of neighboring elites vying for land and economic rights. Only the use of rhetorical and ideological perspectives shows the significance of the incident. Rhetorical force through analogic patterning becomes evident when Joash's placation of Hazael is seen as one in a series of incidents about the loss of state treasuries. Ideological overtones emerge when the pattern of cultic misdeeds leading to foreign oppression tied to regnal evaluation is seen in the Deuteronomistic History. Through both the rhetorical and ideological perspectives, the ability of the author to deal with and convey complexity in the rhetorical situation by nuancing reports, interpretations and evaluations is evident.

In some cases, being able to analyze the text from four perspectives highlighted elements in the story that might otherwise go unnoticed. Certainly the lack of a supportive faction for Athaliah might have seemed unremarkable from only a narrative perspective. But when a sociological perspective identified that as an improbable social reality, the lack of support takes on new meaning. The clear rhetorical cast to Athaliah as evil and the ideological pattern of evil northern and Omride dynasties then suggest that here is another case of the narrative's being shaped by ideological considerations.

A multi-disciplinary approach can throw new light on narrative incidents. When the priests fail to carry out Joash's first temple repair financing plan, a narrative gap is created. Why the priests failed is never revealed and the narrative moves quickly on to the king's next plan. Rhetorical analysis showed that the gap was left undeveloped as an issue—rather the real weight went to the king's regaining authority and momentum in a second plan. Ideologically, the Deuteronomistic world-view posits the priests as the king's servants and hence a situation of institutional harmony in which the king has power over the temple and the priests. It is sociological analysis which reveals the real possibilities of power struggles between royal and religious establishments, particularly where finances are involved. Both as an example to the author's 'real-time' Josianic contemporaries and as an ideal in the story world, the priests' failure was best ignored while the king's power was underlined. The point emphasized was the king's ultimate success in controlling the religious institution, a control established so well that it lasted for centuries right into the story world of the author's context.

Finally, the multi-disciplinary approach has suggested a confirmation of one of the study's assumptions. The idea that the Deuteronomistic History received its primary shaping within the Josianic context was used as a working hypothesis, particularly relevant to the sociological analysis. However, the study itself functioned to confirm the likelihood of the hypothesis. The Joash narrative contains consistent reference, by symbol, analogy and direct parallel, to the Josianic era and Josiah's reign and actions in 2 Kings 22–23. These referents exist independently of the hypothesis about a Josianic edition; the text itself repeatedly refers the reader to the Josiah story world. The multi-disciplinary approach has been sensitive to the rhetorical, ideological and sociological elements of writing as propaganda in an agrarian monarchic context. Such sensitivity has shown how the Joash story 'makes sense' as a part of a posited Josianic worldview. Joash's narrative both tells its own story and helps to tell Josiah's story, with indications of real political import. The coherence of the story worlds suggests that both were shaped as part of a Josianic edition of the Deuteronomistic History.

After four different types of analysis, the story in 2 Kings 11–12 remains a well-told tale full of intense drama and measured regnal action. For all the words that have been said about the story, it is the words of the story which convey the depth and richness we have found. What is clear is that this story functions as a complex communication between an author and an audience in the posited context of its primary composition. The multi-faceted aspects identified are all intrinsic to the story and convey multiple meanings. The same words serve various purposes at the same time. But it is well not to lose sight of the tale itself, which engages the reader and critic in several ways—entertaining, persuading, instructing, admonishing, idealizing and inspiring. Biblical criticism can match the fascinating complexity of stories by bringing a multi-disciplinary approach to bear in interpretation.

BIBLIOGRAPHY

Ahlström, G.W., *Royal Administration and National Religion in Ancient Palestine* (Leiden: Brill, 1982).

Alt, A., 'Der Anteil des Königtums an der Socialen Entwicklung in der Reichen Israel und Juda', in M. Noth (ed.), *Kleine Schriften zur Geschichte des Volkes Israel* (Munich: Beck, 1959), pp. 348-72.

Alter, R., *The Art of Biblical Narrative* (New York: Basic Books, 1981).

—*The World of Biblical Literature* (New York: HarperCollins, 1991).

Andreasen, N.-E.A., 'The Role of the Queen Mother in Israelite Society', *CBQ* 45 (1983), pp. 179-94.

Bal, M., *Murder and Difference: Gender, Genre, and Scholarship on Sisera's Death* (trans. M. Gumpert; Bloomington, IN: Indiana University Press, 1992).

Baltzer, K., *The Covenant Formulary* (trans. D.E. Green; Philadelphia: Fortress Press, 1971).

Bar-Efrat, S., *Narrative Art in the Bible* (trans. D. Shefer-Vanson; Sheffield: Almond Press, 1989).

Barré, L.M., *The Rhetoric of Political Persuasion: The Narrative Artistry and Political Intentions of 2 Kings 9–11* (CBQMS, 20; Washington, DC: Catholic Biblical Association, 1988).

Bendix, R., *Kings or People: Power and the Mandate to Rule* (Berkeley: University of California Press, 1978).

Berger, P.L., and T. Luckmann, *The Social Construction of Reality* (repr.; Garden City, NY: Doubleday, 1989 [1966]).

Berlin, A., *Poetics and Interpretation of Biblical Narrative* (Sheffield: Almond Press, 1983).

Brenner, A., *The Israelite Woman: Social Role and Literary Type in Biblical Narrative* (Sheffield: JSOT Press, 1985).

Brueggemann, W., 'The Kerygma of the Deuteronomistic Historian', *Int* 22 (1968), pp. 387-402.

—*2 Kings* (Knox Preaching Guides; Atlanta: John Knox, 1982).

Burney, C., *Notes on the Hebrew Text of the Book of Kings* (New York: Ktav, 1970).

Campbell, A.F., S.J., *Of Prophets and Kings: A Late Ninth Century Document* (CBQMS, 17; Washington, DC: Catholic Biblical Association, 1986).

Carney, T.F., *The Shape of the Past: Models and Antiquity* (Lawrence, KS: Coronado Press, 1975).

Chaney, M., 'Ancient Palestinian Peasant Movements and the Formation of Premonarchic Israel', in D.N. Freedman and D.F. Graf (eds.), *Palestine in Transition* (Social World of Biblical Antiquity Series, 2; Sheffield: Almond Press, 1983), pp. 39-90.

—'Systemic Study of the Israelite Monarchy', *Semeia* 37 (1986), pp. 53-76.

Clements, R.E., 'Deuteronomy and the Jerusalem Cult Tradition', *VT* 15 (1965), pp. 300-12.

—*God and Temple* (Philadelphia: Fortress Press, 1965).

Cogan, M., and H. Tadmor, *II Kings* (AB, 11; Garden City, NY: Doubleday, 1988).

Cross, F.M., 'The Themes of the Book of Kings and the Structure of the Deuteronomistic History', in *Canaanite Myth and Hebrew Epic* (Cambridge, MA: Harvard University Press, 1973), pp. 274-89.

Damrosch, D., *The Narrative Covenant: Transformations of Genre in the Growth of Biblical Literature* (San Francisco: Harper & Row, 1987).

Eisenstadt, S.N., *The Political Systems of Empires* (New York: Free Press, 1963).

Elat, M., 'Trade and Commerce', in A. Malamat (ed.), *The World History of the Jewish People. IV.II. The Age of the Monarchies: Culture and Society* (Jerusalem: Massada Press, 1979), pp. 173-86.

Exum, J.C., *Fragmented Women: Feminist (Sub)versions of Biblical Narratives* (JSOTSup, 163; Sheffield: JSOT Press, 1993).

Frankfort, H., *Kingship and the Gods: A Study of Ancient Near Eastern Religion as the Integration of Society and Nature* (Chicago: University of Chicago Press, 1948).

Geertz, C., *The Interpretation of Cultures* (New York: Basic Books, 1973).

Gerbrandt, G.E., *Kingship according to the Deuteronomistic History* (SBLDS, 87; Atlanta: Scholars Press, 1986).

Gottwald, N.K., *The Tribes of Yahweh* (Maryknoll, NY: Orbis Books, 1985).

Gray, J., *The Legacy of Canaan: The Ras Shamra Texts and their Relevance to the Old Testament* (Leiden: Brill, 1957).

—*I and II Kings* (OTL; Philadelphia: Westminster Press, 1970).

Greenfield, J.C. 'Lexicographical Notes I', *HUCA* 29 (1958), pp. 217-22.

Haak, R.D., 'The "Shoulder" of the Temple', *VT* 33 (1983), pp. 271-78.

Halpern, B., *The Constitution of the Monarchy in Israel* (HSM, 25; Chico, CA: Scholars Press, 1981).

—*The First Historians: The Hebrew Bible and History* (San Francisco: Harper & Row, 1988).

Handy, L.K., 'Speaking of Babies in the Temple', Eastern Great Lakes and Midwest Biblical Societies, *Proceedings* 8 (1988), pp. 155-65.

Haran, M., *Temples and Temple Service in Ancient Israel* (Oxford: Clarendon Press, 1978).

Hauser, G.A., *Introduction to Rhetorical Theory* (Prospect Heights, IL: Waveland Press, 1991).

Hoffmann, H.-D., *Reform und Reformen: Untersuchungen zu einem Grundthema der deuteronomistischen Geschichtsschreibung* (Zürich: Theologischer Verlag, 1980).

Hurowitz, V., 'Another Fiscal Practice in the Ancient Near East: 2 Kgs 12.5-17 and a Letter to Esarhaddon', *JNES* 45 (1986), pp. 289-94.

—*I Have Built You an Exalted House: Temple Building in Light of Mesopotamian and Northwest Semitic Writings* (JSOTSup, 115; Sheffield: JSOT Press, 1992).

Ishida, T., *The Royal Dynasties in Ancient Israel* (Berlin: de Gruyter, 1977).

Jobling, D., and T. Pippin (eds.), *Ideological Criticism of Biblical Texts* (*Semeia* 59 [1992]).

Jones, G.H., *1 and 2 Kings* (NCB; 2 vols.; Grand Rapids, MI: Eerdmans, 1984).

Kapelrud, A.S., 'Temple Building, a Task for Gods and Kings', *Or* 32 (1963), pp. 56-62.

Katz, R.C., *The Structure of Ancient Arguments: Rhetoric and its Near Eastern Origin* (New York: Shapolsky/Steimatzky Publishers, 1986).

Katzenstein, H.J., 'Who Were the Parents of Athaliah?', *IEJ* 5 (1955), pp. 194-97.

Kautsky, J.H., *The Politics of Aristocratic Empires* (Chapel Hill: University of North Carolina Press, 1982).

Kenik, H.A., *Design for Kingship: Deuteronomistic Narrative Technique in I Kings 3.4-15* (SBLDS, 69; Chico, CA: Scholars Press, 1983).

Lasswell, H.D., D. Lerner, and H. Speier (eds.), *Propaganda and Communication in World History*. I. *The Symbolic Instrument in Early Times* (East-West Center, Honolulu: University Press of Hawaii, 1979).

Lemke, W.E., 'The Way of Obedience: I Kings 13 and the Structure of the Deuteronomistic History', in F.M. Cross, W. Lemke and P.D. Miller (eds.), *Magnalia Dei* (Garden City, NY: Doubleday, 1976), pp. 301-26.

Lenski, G.E., *Power and Privilege: A Theory of Social Stratification* (Chapel Hill: University of North Carolina Press, 1984).

Lenski, G., P. Nolan and J. Lenski, *Human Societies: An Introduction to Macrosociology* (New York: McGraw–Hill, 7th edn, 1995).

Levin, C., *Der Sturz der Königin Atalja: Ein Kapitel zur Geschichte Judas im 9.Jn. v. Chr* (SBS, 105; Stuttgart: Katholisches Bibelwerk, 1982).

Liverani, M., 'L'Histoire de Joas', *VT* 24 (1974), pp. 438-53.

—'The Ideology of the Assyrian Empire', in M.T. Larsen (ed.), *Power and Propaganda: A Symposium on Ancient Empires* (Mesopotamia: Copenhagen Studies in Assyriology, 7; Copenhagen: Akademisk Forlag, 1979), pp. 297-317.

Lohfink, N., 'The Cult Reform of Josiah of Judah: 2 Kings 22–23 as a Source for the History of Israelite Religion', in P.D. Miller, Jr, P.D. Hanson, and S.D. McBride (eds.), *Ancient Israelite Religion* (Philadelphia: Fortress Press, 1987), pp. 459-75.

Long, B.O., *1 Kings* (FOTL, 9; Grand Rapids, MI: Eerdmans, 1984).

—'Framing Repetitions in Biblical Historiography', *JBL* 106 (1987), pp. 385-99.

—*2 Kings* (FOTL, 10; Grand Rapids, MI: Eerdmans, 1991).

Lowery, R.H., *The Reforming Kings: Cults and Society in First Temple Judah* (JSOTSup, 120; Sheffield: JSOT Press, 1991).

Malamat, A., 'The Organs of Statecraft in the Israelite Monarchy', *BA* 28 (1965), pp. 34-65.

Martin, W., *Recent Theories of Narrative* (Ithaca, NY: Cornell University Press, 1986).

Mayes, A.D.H., *The Story of Israel between Settlement and Exile* (London: SCM Press, 1983).

McCarter, K.P., Jr, *II Samuel* (AB, 9; Garden City, NY: Doubleday, 1984).

McCarthy, D.J., S.J., 'II Samuel 7 and the Structure of the Deuteronomic History', *JBL* 84 (1965), pp. 131-38.

—'The Inauguration of Monarchy in Israel', *Int* 27 (1973), pp. 401-12.

—*Treaty and Covenant: A Study in Form in the Ancient Oriental Documents and in the Old Testament* (AnBib, 21A; Rome: Biblical Institute Press, 1978).

—*Institution and Narrative: Collected Essays.* (AnBib, 108; Rome: Biblical Institute Press, 1985).

Mettinger, T.N.D., *King and Messiah: The Civil and Sacral Legitimation of the Israelite Kings* (Lund: Gleerup, 1976).

Meyers, C., 'Jachin and Boaz in Religious and Political Perspective', *CBQ* 45 (1983), pp. 167-78.

—'David as Temple Builder', in P.D. Miller, Jr, P.D. Hanson, and S.D. McBride (eds.), *Ancient Israelite Religion* (Philadelphia: Fortress Press, 1987), pp. 357-76.

Miller, J.M., and J.H. Hayes, *A History of Ancient Israel and Judah* (Philadelphia: Westminster Press, 1986).

Montgomery, J.A., *A Critical and Exegetical Commentary on the Books of Kings* (ICC; New York: Charles Scribner's Sons, 1951).

Mullen, T.E., Jr, 'The Royal Dynastic Grant to Jehu and the Structure of the Book of Kings', *JBL* 107 (1988), pp. 193-206.

—'Crime and Punishment: The Sins of the King and the Despoliation of the Treasuries', *CBQ* 54 (1992), pp. 231-48.

Munson, H., Jr, *Religion and Power in Morocco* (New Haven: Yale University Press, 1993).

Nelson, R.D., *The Double Redaction of the Deuteronomistic History* (JSOTSup, 18; Sheffield: JSOT Press, 1981).

—'Josiah in the Book of Joshua', *JBL* 100 (1981), pp. 531-40.

—*First and Second Kings* (Interpretation; Louisville, KY: John Knox, 1987).

—'The Anatomy of the Book of Kings', *JSOT* 40 (1988), pp. 39-48.

Nicholson, E.W., *Deuteronomy and Tradition* (Philadelphia: Fortress Press, 1967).

Niehoff, M., 'Do Biblical Characters Talk to Themselves? Narrative Modes of Representing Inner Speech in Early Biblical Fiction', *JBL* 111 (1992), pp. 577-95.

Noth, M., *Überlieferungsgeschichtliche Studien* (Tübingen: Max Niemeyer Verlag, 2nd edn, 1957); ET *The Deuteronomistic History* (JSOTSup, 15; Sheffield: JSOT Press, 1981).

O'Brien, M.A., 'The "Deuteronomistic History" as a Story of Israel's Leaders', *AusBR* 37 (1989), pp. 14-34.

—*The Deuteronomistic History Hypothesis: A Reassessment* (Freiburg: Universitätsverlag, 1989).

Oded, B., 'Judah and the Exile', in J.H. Hayes and J.M. Miller (eds.), *Israelite and Judean History* (Philadelphia: Westminster Press, 1977), pp. 435-88.

Oden, R.A., Jr, 'The Place of Covenant in the Religion of Israel', in P.D. Miller, Jr, P.D. Hanson, and S.D. McBride (eds.), *Ancient Israelite Religion* (Philadelphia: Fortress Press, 1987), pp. 429-47.

Oppenheim, A.L., 'A Fiscal Practice of the Ancient Near East', *JNES* 6 (1947), pp. 116-20.

—*Ancient Mesopotamia: Portrait of a Dead Civilization* (Chicago: University of Chicago Press, 1964).

—'Neo-Assyrian and Neo-Babylonian Empires', in H.D. Lasswell, D. Lerner, and H. Speier (eds.), *Propaganda and Communication in World History. I. The Symbolic Instrument in Early Times* (East-West Center, Honolulu: University Press of Hawaii, 1979), pp. 111-44.

Patrick, D., and A. Scult, *Rhetoric and Biblical Interpretation* (Sheffield: Almond Press, 1990).

Perelman, C., *The Realm of Rhetoric* (trans. W. Kluback; Notre Dame, IN: University of Notre Dame Press, 1982).

Petersen, P.R., *Rediscovering Paul: Philemon and the Sociology of Paul's Narrative World* (Philadelphia: Fortress Press, 1985).

Polzin, R.M., *Moses and the Deuteronomist* (New York: Seabury Press, 1980).

—'I Samuel: Biblical Studies and the Humanities', *RelSRev* 15 (1989), pp. 297-306.

Postgate, J.N., 'The Economic Structure of the Assyrian Empire', in M.T. Larsen (ed.), *Power and Propaganda: A Symposium on Ancient Empires* (Mesopotamia: Copenhagen Studies in Assyriology, 7; Copenhagen: Akademisk Forlag, 1979), pp. 193-222.

Preuss, H.D., 'אצי', *TDOT*, VI, pp. 225-50.

Prignaud, J., 'Caftorim et Kerétim', *RB* 71 (1962), pp. 215-29.

Rabinowitz, I., ''AZ Followed by the Imperfect Verb-Form in Preterite Contexts: A Redactional Device in Biblical Hebrew', *VT* 34 (1984), pp. 53-62

Rad, G. von, *Studies in Deuteronomy* (trans. D. Stalker; London: SCM Press, 1953).

—*Old Testament Theology* (trans. D. Stalker; 2 vols.; New York: Harper & Row, 1962).

Reviv, H., 'The Structure of Society', in A. Malamat (ed.), *The World History of the Jewish People. IV.II. The Age of the Monarchies: Culture and Society* (Jerusalem: Massada Press, 1979), pp. 125-46.

Robbins, V.K., *Jesus the Teacher: A Socio-Rhetorical Interpretation of Mark* (Minneapolis: Fortress Press, 1992).

Robinson, G., 'Is 2 Kings XI 6 a Gloss?', *VT* 27 (1977), pp. 56-61.

Robinson, J., *The Second Book of Kings* (Cambridge Bible Commentary; Cambridge: Cambridge University Press, 1976).

Rosenbaum, J., 'Hezekiah's Reform and the Deuteronomic Tradition', *HTR* 72 (1979), pp. 23-43.

Schearing, L., 'Models, Monarchs and Misconceptions: Athaliah and Joash of Judah' (PhD dissertation, Emory University, 1992).

Scholes, R.E., and R. Kellogg, *The Nature of Narrative* (London: Oxford University Press, 1968).

Sjoberg, G., *The Pre-Industrial City: Past and Present* (New York: Free Press, 1965).

Smith, M., *Palestinian Parties and Politics that Shaped the Old Testament* (London: SCM Press, 2nd edn, 1987).

Sternberg, M., *The Poetics of Biblical Narrative: Ideological Literature and the Drama of Reading* (Bloomington: Indiana University Press, 1987).

Torrey, C.C., 'The Foundry of the Second Temple at Jerusalem', *JBL* 55 (1936), pp. 247-60.

—'The Evolution of a Financier in the Ancient Near East', *JNES* 2 (1943), pp. 295-301.

Van Seters, J., *In Search of History: Historiography in the Ancient World and the Origins of Biblical History* (New Haven: Yale University Press, 1983).

Vaux, R. de, OP, *Ancient Israel: Its Life and Institutions* (trans. J. McHugh; New York: McGraw-Hill, 1961).

Viviano, P., '2 Kings 17: A Rhetorical and Form-Critical Analysis', *CBQ* 49 (1987), pp. 548-59.

Walsh, J.T., 'Methods and Meanings: Multiple Studies of I Kings 21', *JBL* 111.2 (1992), pp. 193-211.

Weinfeld, M., *Deuteronomy and the Deuteronomic School* (repr.; Winona Lake, IN: Eisenbrauns, 1992 [Oxford: Clarendon Press, 1972]).

—'Zion and Jerusalem as Religious and Political Capital: Ideology and Utopia', in R.E. Friedman (ed.), *The Poet and the Historian: Essays in Literary and Historical Biblical Criticism* (Chico, CA: Scholars Press, 1983), pp. 75-115.

—'The Emergence of the Deuteronomic Movement: Its Historical Antecedents', in *Das Deuteronomium: Entstehung, Gestalt und Botschaft* (Leuven: Leuven University Press, 1985), pp. 76-98.

—*Deuteronomy 1–11* (AB, 5; Garden City, NY: Doubleday, 1991).

White, H., *The Content of the Form: Narrative Discourse and Historical Representation* (Baltimore: Johns Hopkins University Press, 1987).

Whitelam, K.W., 'The Defence of David', *JSOT* 29 (1984), pp. 61-87.

—'The Symbols of Power: Aspects of Royal Propaganda in the United Monarchy', *BA* 49 (1986), pp. 166-73.

Widengren, G., 'King and Covenant', *JSS* 2 (1957), pp. 1-32.

Wilson, R.R., *Prophecy and Society in Ancient Israel* (Philadelphia: Fortress Press, 1980).

Wire, A.C., *The Corinthian Women Prophets: A Reconstruction through Paul's Rhetoric* (Minneapolis: Fortress Press, 1990).

Wolff, H.W., 'The Kerygma of the Deuteronomic Historical Work', in W. Brueggemann and H.W. Wolff (eds.), *The Vitality of Old Testament Traditions* (Atlanta: John Knox, 1982), pp. 83-100.

Wright, L.S., 'MKR in 2 Kings XII 5–17 and in Deuteronomy XVIII 8', *VT* 39 (1989), pp. 438-48.

Yeivin, S., '*ʿEduth*', *IEJ* 24.1 (1974), pp. 17-20.

—'Administration', in A. Malamat.(ed.), *The World History of the Jewish People*. IV.II. *The Age of the Monarchies: Culture and Society* (Jerusalem: Massada Press, 1979), pp. 147-71.

Zevit, Z., 'Deuteronomistic Historiography in I Kings 12–II Kings 17 and the Re-investiture of the Israelian Cult', *JSOT* 32 (1985), pp. 57-73.

INDEXES

INDEX OF BIBLICAL REFERENCES

Leviticus		20.7	75	11.1-10	111
27.2	51	20.23	34, 75	11.29-39	133
		20.25	122	11.32	133
Deuteronomy				11.36	133
4.45	40	*1 Kings*		12.28-30	110
6.17	40	1.5	34	13.33-34	111
6.20	40	1.32-40	82	14.15-16	111
8.36	87	1.32	77	14.26	96
17.14-20	71	1.34	79	14.27-28	34
17.15	71	1.38	77, 85	15.4-5	133
17.18	88	1.39-40	81	15.9-15	71
		1.39	79	15.11	137
Joshua		1.46	85	15.12-13	122
8.2	44	2.3	40, 78	15.13	71
		2.26-27	121	15.14	137
Judges		3.4-15	129	15.15	96
9.25	44	3.7	76	15.18	96
		4.2	122	15.29-30	111
1 Samuel		5–9	114	16–2 Kgs 9	71
8–12	129	5.2-10	131	16.2-3	111
9–1 Kgs 2	170	5.15–9.25	115	16.25	110
11.11	42	5.29-32	93	16.30	110
12.23	87	5.29	93	16.31	110
18.13	76	5.30	93	18.18	111
30.14	75	5.31	93	20.15	42
		5.32	93	20.27	42
2 Samuel		6.9	37	21.21-22	111
1.10	78	6.12-13	117	22.43	137
5.9	60	7.15-22	81	23	122
7	117, 118,	7.51	96		
	132	8.1-13	85	*2 Kings*	
7.13	118	8.15-20	116	6.15	85
8.18	34, 75	8.36	87	8.16-19	133
15.1	34	9.1-5	119, 133	8.18	27, 69, 110
15.18	34, 75	9.3	116	8.26	27
18.1-5	42	9.15	60	8.27	69, 110

Reference	Pages
8.28-29	168
8.28	28
9–11	24
9–10	27, 29, 30, 47
9	29
9.1	111
9.7	111
10	29
10.10	111
10.11	29
10.14	29
10.17	29, 111
10.18-28	29
10.18-27	84
10.25	35, 75
10.28	47
11–12	13, 14, 17, 19, 22, 23, 25, 26, 61, 64, 66, 69, 99, 100, 102, 108, 113, 117, 119, 120, 122, 123, 126, 127, 129-34, 139-42, 145-48, 150, 158, 161, 168, 172, 176, 177, 181, 187
11	22-24, 26, 29, 31, 32, 47, 49-51, 53, 61-63, 69-72, 83, 84, 86, 97, 110, 111, 113, 119, 122, 123, 125, 127, 132, 140, 157, 165, 172, 174, 175-84
11.1-11	62
11.1-3	27, 69
11.1	27-29, 32, 48, 97, 134
11.2	27, 30, 60, 72, 80
11.3	27, 39, 70, 72
11.4-12	23
11.4-8	32, 73
11.4	32, 33, 35, 46, 49, 74, 82, 97
11.5-8	75
11.5	32, 35
11.6	32, 35, 36
11.7	33, 36
11.8	33, 36, 39, 57, 74, 76, 80
11.9-18	83
11.9-14	82
11.9-12	37, 77
11.9	37, 74
11.10	37, 77
11.11	38, 39, 78
11.12–12.19	62
11.12	38, 39, 78, 79, 131
11.13-18	23
11.13-16	41, 80
11.13	41, 42
11.14	41, 42, 80, 97
11.15	41, 43, 47, 80
11.16	26, 41, 44, 48, 60, 82
11.17-20	45, 82
11.17	45, 46, 82, 97, 117, 131
11.18-20	23
11.18	45-47, 84
11.19	45, 47, 61, 84
11.20	26, 45, 48, 60, 85, 151
12	22, 24-26, 49, 61-63, 86, 97, 113, 120, 122, 126, 127, 138, 140, 156, 162, 165, 172, 175, 184, 185
12.1-4	49, 50, 62, 86
12.1	49, 86
12.2	49, 86
12.3-4	86, 87, 137
12.3	49, 50, 95, 131
12.4	49, 88
12.5-17	50, 95
12.5-16	92
12.5-10	62
12.5-6	50, 54, 89, 93
12.5	50, 92
12.6	50, 52, 53, 89, 92
12.7-9	52, 90
12.7-8	90
12.7	52, 53, 91, 92
12.8	52-54, 91, 92
12.9	52, 54, 91, 92
12.10-17	55, 63, 91
12.10-13	58, 93
12.10-11	94
12.10	54-56, 92
12.11-12	132
12.11	55, 56, 92
12.12-13	93, 94
12.12	55, 57, 92, 93
12.13	55, 57, 92, 93
12.14-16	58
12.14-15	57
12.14	55, 92

12.15	55, 92, 93	18.3-7	138	*1 Chronicles*	
12.16	55, 57, 58,	18.3-4	122	29.19	40
	93, 94	18.15	96, 138		
12.17	55, 58	19.2	122	*2 Chronicles*	
12.18-19	50, 58, 62,	21.23-24	87	22.11	31
	95	21.24	156		
12.18	58	22–23	147, 187	*Nehemiah*	
12.19	58, 95, 96	22.1	87	9.34	40
12.20-22	60, 62, 97	22.3-10	94, 162		
12.20	60, 98	22.3-4	94, 163	*Psalms*	
12.21	60	22.4	56	19.8	40
12.22	60, 98	22.5-6	94	25.10	40
14.3-4	137	22.7	94	78.5	40
14.5	97	22.8	56, 88	81.6	40
14.14	96	22.9	57	99.7	40
15.3-4	137	22.12	122	119.2	40
15.32-38	88	23	83	132.12	40
15.34-35	137	23.1-25	165		
16.8	96	23.1-3	84	*Jeremiah*	
16.11	122	23.3	81	44.23	40
17	126	23.4-20	84		
17.1-20	126	23.4	56	*Mark*	
17.7	126	23.35	51	5.24-34	11
17.15	40, 126	24.13	96, 137		
17.21-23	110				

INDEX OF AUTHORS

Ahlström, G.W. 53, 114
Alt, A. 142
Alter, R. 12, 17, 26, 28, 30, 35, 37

Bal, M. 12
Baltzer, K. 123
Bar-Efrat, S. 17, 26, 31, 49, 55
Barr, L.M. 23, 24, 29, 33, 34, 38, 80,
    84, 85, 174, 175
Bendix, R. 145, 153, 158
Berger, P.L. 19, 103-108, 112, 113,
    120, 122, 127, 134, 135, 138,
    139, 141
Berlin, A. 17, 26, 30, 42, 52
Brenner, A. 111
Brueggemann, W. 82
Burney, C.F. 23, 33, 50, 55

Campbell, A.F. 110, 136
Carney, T.F. 145, 146, 152, 153, 155,
    157, 159, 160
Chaney, M.L. 144, 145
Clements, R.E. 81, 119
Cogan, M. 24, 31, 35, 39, 40, 42, 44,
    46, 47, 51, 55, 56, 59, 133
Cross, F.M. 15, 110, 132

Crösemann, F. 164
Damrosch, D. 12

Eisenstadt, S.N. 150, 154, 157-61, 165
Elat, M. 142
Exum, J.C. 112

Frankfort, H. 114, 128, 131

Geertz, C. 106-108, 119, 120, 126,
    127, 139, 141
Gerbrandt, G.E. 15, 124, 125, 128,
    129, 131, 132
Gottwald, N.K. 143
Gray, J. 23, 24, 30, 31, 35, 36, 39, 40,
    42, 44, 46, 48, 49, 51-53, 57-59,
    70, 81, 121
Greenfield, J.C. 52

Haak, R.D. 39
Halpern, B. 119, 129-31
Handy, L.K. 25, 72
Hauser, G.A. 18, 66, 68, 69, 74, 88
Hayes, J.H. 25, 87
Hoffmann, H.-D. 25, 29, 53, 56
Hurowitz, V. 53, 115, 131, 132

Ishida, T. 71, 84, 118

Jobling, D. 103
Jones, G.H. 23, 24, 40, 47, 51, 57, 60

Katz, R.C. 70, 71, 89, 92, 94
Katzenstein, H.J. 28
Kautsky, J. 144, 145, 153, 160, 167
Kenik, H.A. 129, 130

Lasswell, H.D. 169
Lemke, W.E. 111
Lenski, G. 20, 143-45, 152, 157, 158,
    160, 166
Lenski, J. 20, 143, 144, 152, 157, 158,
    160
Lerner, D. 169
Levin, C. 24, 25
Liverani, M. 145, 171, 172, 174

Lohfink, N. 15, 162, 165
Long, B.O. 24, 29, 32, 34, 36, 39, 41,
    43, 47, 53, 56, 57, 59, 70, 76, 78,
    84-86, 93, 98
Lowery, R.H. 137, 164, 166
Luckmann, T. 19, 103-108, 112, 113,
    120, 122, 127, 134, 135, 138,
    139, 141

Martin, W. 17
McCarter, P.K. Jr 117, 118
McCarthy, D.J. 117, 118, 124, 129,
    130
Mettinger, T.N.D. 79
Meyers, C. 81, 114, 116, 117, 160,
    168, 171
Miller, J.M. 25, 87
Montgomery, J.A. 23, 30, 31, 34-36,
    39, 44, 49, 51, 55, 57
Mullen, E.T. Jr 137, 138
Munson, H. Jr 108

Nelson, R. 15, 29, 31, 39, 40, 48, 79
Nolan, P. 20, 143, 144, 152, 157, 158,
    160
Noth, M. 14

O'Brien, M.A. 15, 125, 126, 130, 132,
    133, 137
Oded, B. 150, 151
Oden, R.A. Jr 123, 124
Oppenheim, A.L. 57, 114, 120, 131,
    169, 170

Patrick, D. 65, 66, 68, 85
Perelman, C. 18, 66, 67, 69, 70, 73-75,
    77, 79, 80, 86, 88-90, 92-95, 99

Petersen, P.R. 16, 17
Pippin, T. 103
Postgate, J.N. 164
Preuss, H.D. 76
Prignaud, J. 34

Rabinowitz, I. 59
Rad, G. von 103, 128
Reviv, H. 142, 149, 150
Robbins, V. 16, 65
Robinson, J. 78

Schearing, L. 26, 112
Scult, A. 65, 66, 68, 85
Sjoberg, G. 151, 158, 160, 165, 172
Speier, H. 169
Sternberg, M. 17, 26, 28-30, 33, 38,
    41, 43, 54, 66, 69-72, 76, 80, 83,
    87, 88, 90, 92, 95, 98

Tadmor, H. 24, 31, 35, 39, 40, 42, 44,
    46, 47, 51, 55, 56, 59, 133
Torrey, C.C. 56

Vaux, R. de 121, 122, 149, 151
Viviano, P. 126

Walsh, J.T. 17
Weinfeld, M. 15, 40, 115, 116, 121,
    125, 128, 129
Whitelam, K.W. 152, 170-72, 176
Widengren, G. 75, 123, 124
Wilson, R.R. 143
Wire, A.C. 65

Yeivin, S. 40, 142